PELÉ

PELÉ
THE KING OF SOCCER

Written by
EDDY SIMON

Illustrated by
VINCENT BRASCAGLIA

:01
First Second
NEW YORK

Chapter 1
A Day in 1950

"If I close my eyes, I can still see my first soccer ball."
—Pelé, September 2013

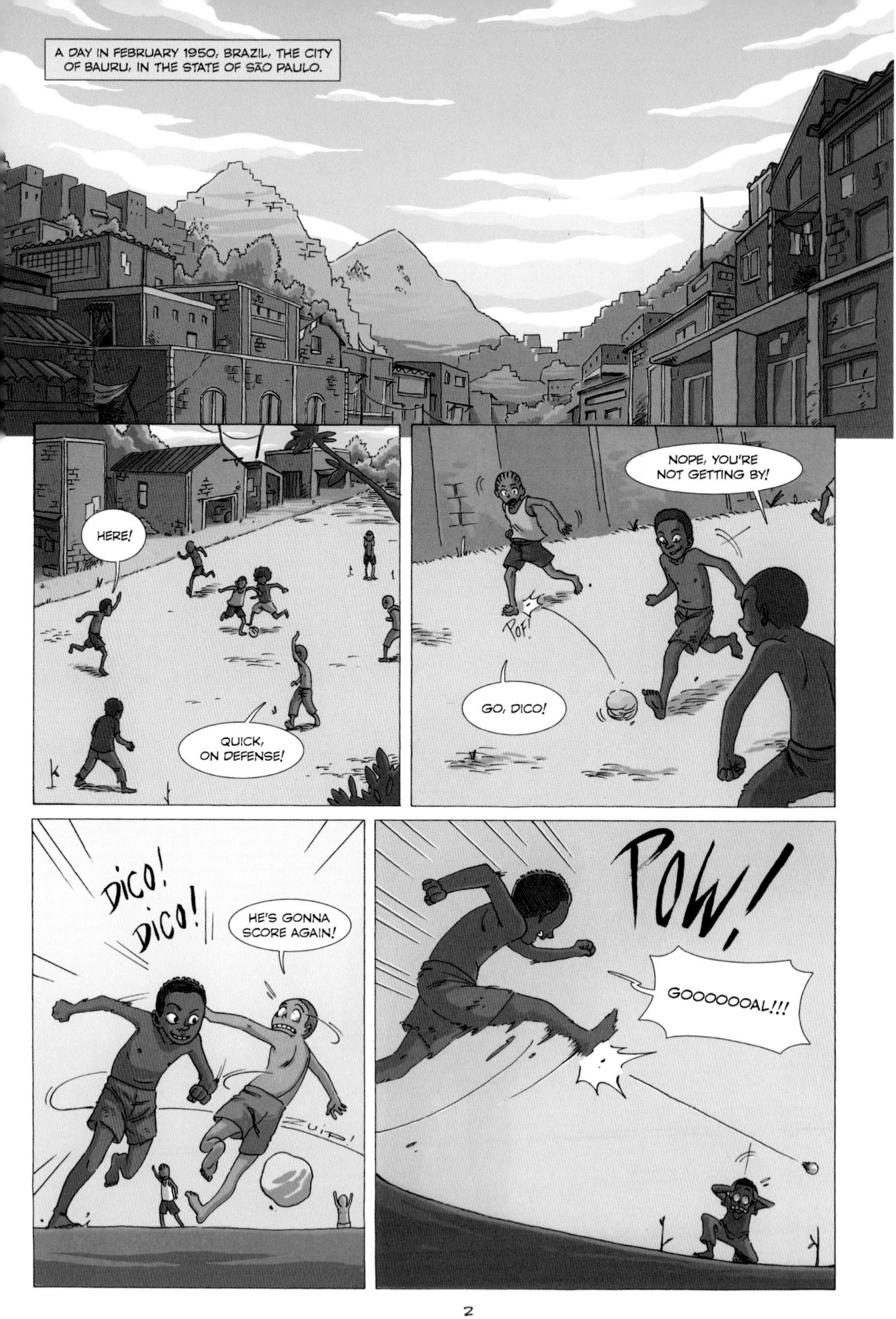
A DAY IN FEBRUARY 1950, BRAZIL, THE CITY OF BAURU, IN THE STATE OF SÃO PAULO.
HERE!
QUICK, ON DEFENSE!
NOPE, YOU'RE NOT GETTING BY!
POF!
GO, DICO!
DICO! DICO!
HE'S GONNA SCORE AGAIN!
ZUIP!
POW!
GOOOOOOAL!!!

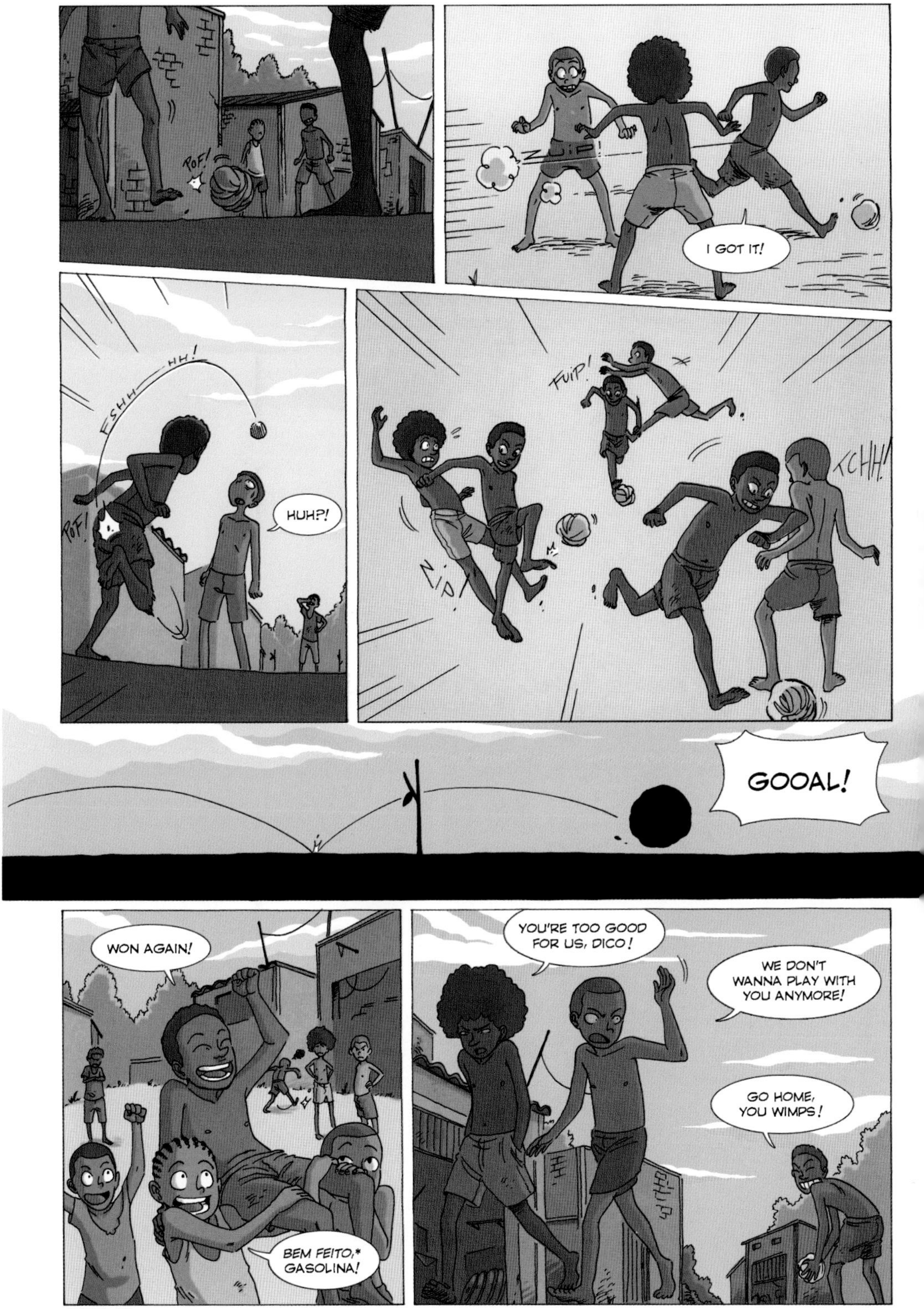
POF!
ZUIP!
I GOT IT!
FSHHHH!
POF!
HUH?!
FUIP!
ZIP!
TCHH!
GOOAL!
WON AGAIN!
BEM FEITO,* GASOLINA!
YOU'RE TOO GOOD FOR US, DICO!
WE DON'T WANNA PLAY WITH YOU ANYMORE!
GO HOME, YOU WIMPS!

*GOOD JOB.

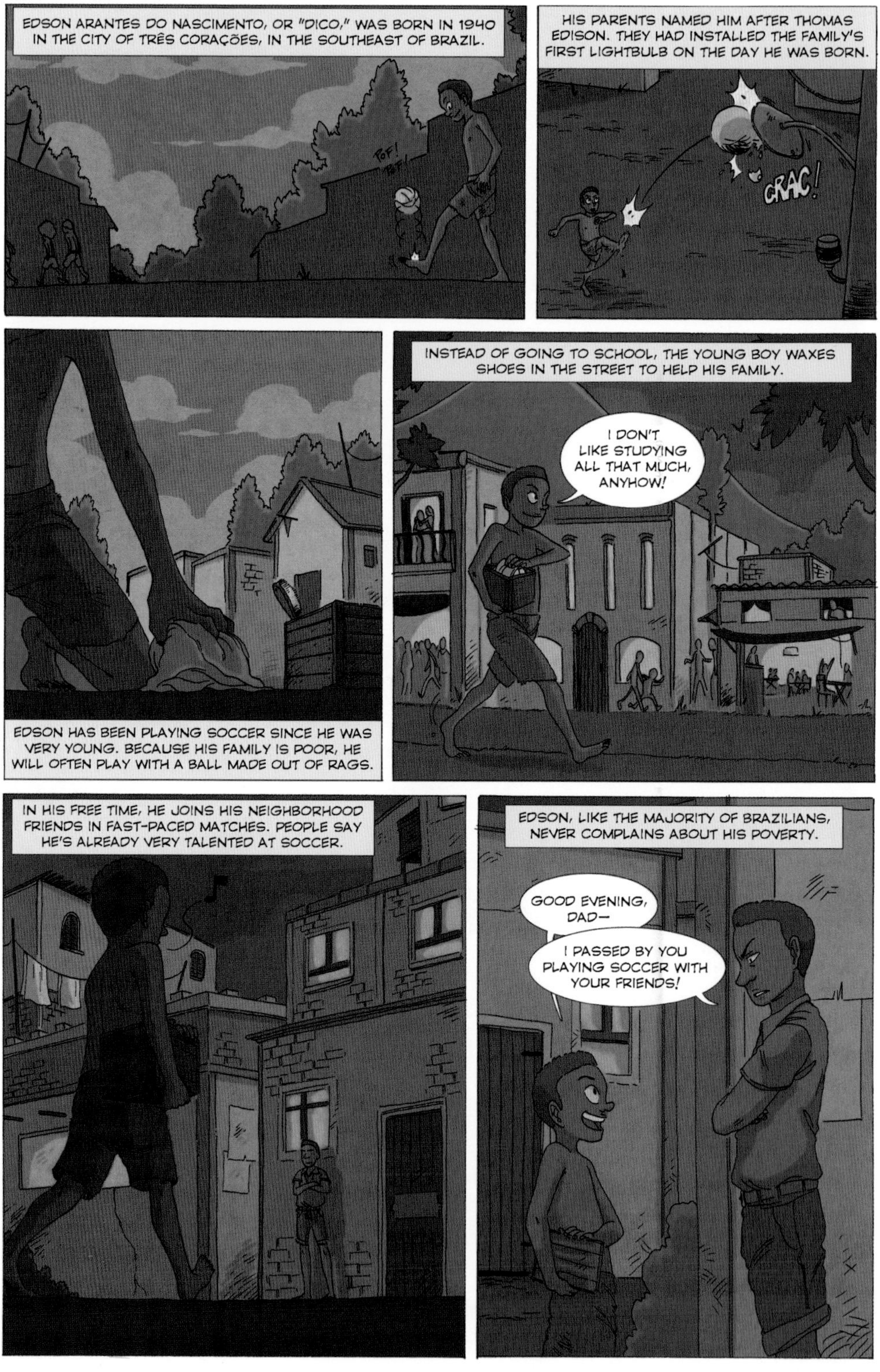
EDSON ARANTES DO NASCIMENTO, OR "DICO," WAS BORN IN 1940 IN THE CITY OF TRÊS CORAÇÕES, IN THE SOUTHEAST OF BRAZIL.
POF! POF!
HIS PARENTS NAMED HIM AFTER THOMAS EDISON. THEY HAD INSTALLED THE FAMILY'S FIRST LIGHTBULB ON THE DAY HE WAS BORN.
CRAC!
EDSON HAS BEEN PLAYING SOCCER SINCE HE WAS VERY YOUNG. BECAUSE HIS FAMILY IS POOR, HE WILL OFTEN PLAY WITH A BALL MADE OUT OF RAGS.
INSTEAD OF GOING TO SCHOOL, THE YOUNG BOY WAXES SHOES IN THE STREET TO HELP HIS FAMILY.
I DON'T LIKE STUDYING ALL THAT MUCH, ANYHOW!
IN HIS FREE TIME, HE JOINS HIS NEIGHBORHOOD FRIENDS IN FAST-PACED MATCHES. PEOPLE SAY HE'S ALREADY VERY TALENTED AT SOCCER.
EDSON, LIKE THE MAJORITY OF BRAZILIANS, NEVER COMPLAINS ABOUT HIS POVERTY.
GOOD EVENING, DAD—
I PASSED BY YOU PLAYING SOCCER WITH YOUR FRIENDS!

AND I SAW YOU MAKING FUN OF THE OTHER BOYS!

BUT—

YOU MUST RESPECT THEM! YOU DIDN'T LIFT ONE LITTLE FINGER TO GET THIS GIFT THAT YOU POSSESS!

GOD'S THE ONE WHO GAVE IT TO YOU!

YOU MUST SHOW YOURSELF WORTHY OF IT!

ONCE YOU'VE ACCOMPLISHED SOMETHING, YOU CAN REJOICE, BUT EVEN THEN, YOU SHOULD DO SO WITH HUMILITY!

DO YOU UNDERSTAND ME, DICO?

YES, DAD!

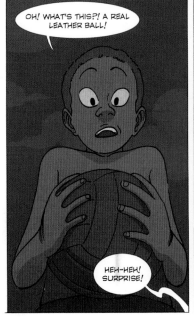

OH! WHAT'S THIS?! A REAL LEATHER BALL!

HEH-HEH! SURPRISE!

DICO'S FATHER, JOÃO RAMOS DO NASCIMENTO, OR "DONDINHO," IS ORIGINALLY FROM THE STATE OF MINAS GERAIS, A REGION WHERE PEOPLE LABOR TO EXTRACT METALS* FROM AN ARID LAND.

ALL RIGHT. COME AND PRACTICE BEHIND THE HOUSE!

*GOLD, IN PARTICULAR, DURING THE COLONIAL ERA.

5

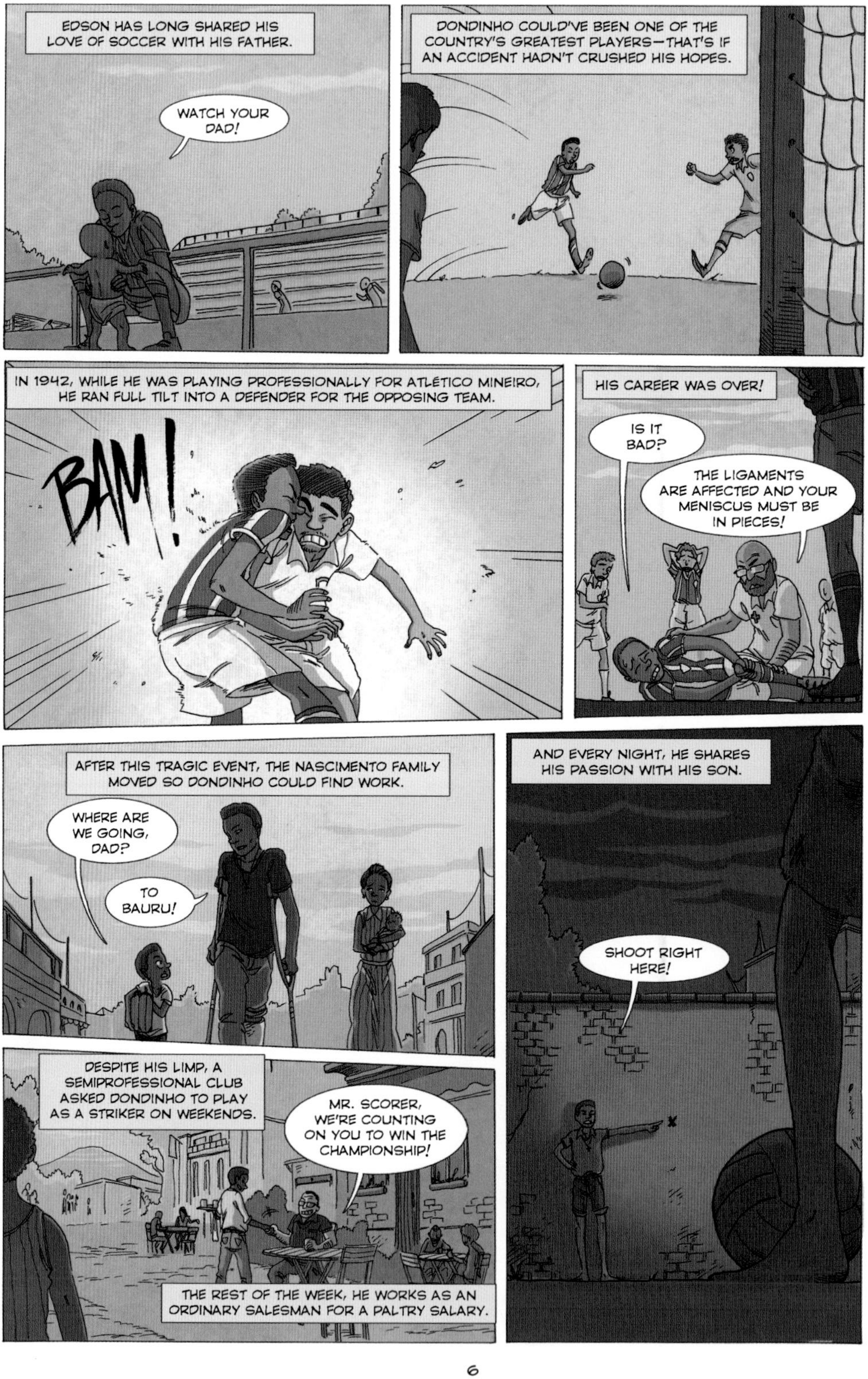
EDSON HAS LONG SHARED HIS LOVE OF SOCCER WITH HIS FATHER.
WATCH YOUR DAD!
DONDINHO COULD'VE BEEN ONE OF THE COUNTRY'S GREATEST PLAYERS—THAT'S IF AN ACCIDENT HADN'T CRUSHED HIS HOPES.
IN 1942, WHILE HE WAS PLAYING PROFESSIONALLY FOR ATLÉTICO MINEIRO, HE RAN FULL TILT INTO A DEFENDER FOR THE OPPOSING TEAM.
BAM!
HIS CAREER WAS OVER!
IS IT BAD?
THE LIGAMENTS ARE AFFECTED AND YOUR MENISCUS MUST BE IN PIECES!
AFTER THIS TRAGIC EVENT, THE NASCIMENTO FAMILY MOVED SO DONDINHO COULD FIND WORK.
WHERE ARE WE GOING, DAD?
TO BAURU!
DESPITE HIS LIMP, A SEMIPROFESSIONAL CLUB ASKED DONDINHO TO PLAY AS A STRIKER ON WEEKENDS.
MR. SCORER, WE'RE COUNTING ON YOU TO WIN THE CHAMPIONSHIP!
THE REST OF THE WEEK, HE WORKS AS AN ORDINARY SALESMAN FOR A PALTRY SALARY.
AND EVERY NIGHT, HE SHARES HIS PASSION WITH HIS SON.
SHOOT RIGHT HERE!

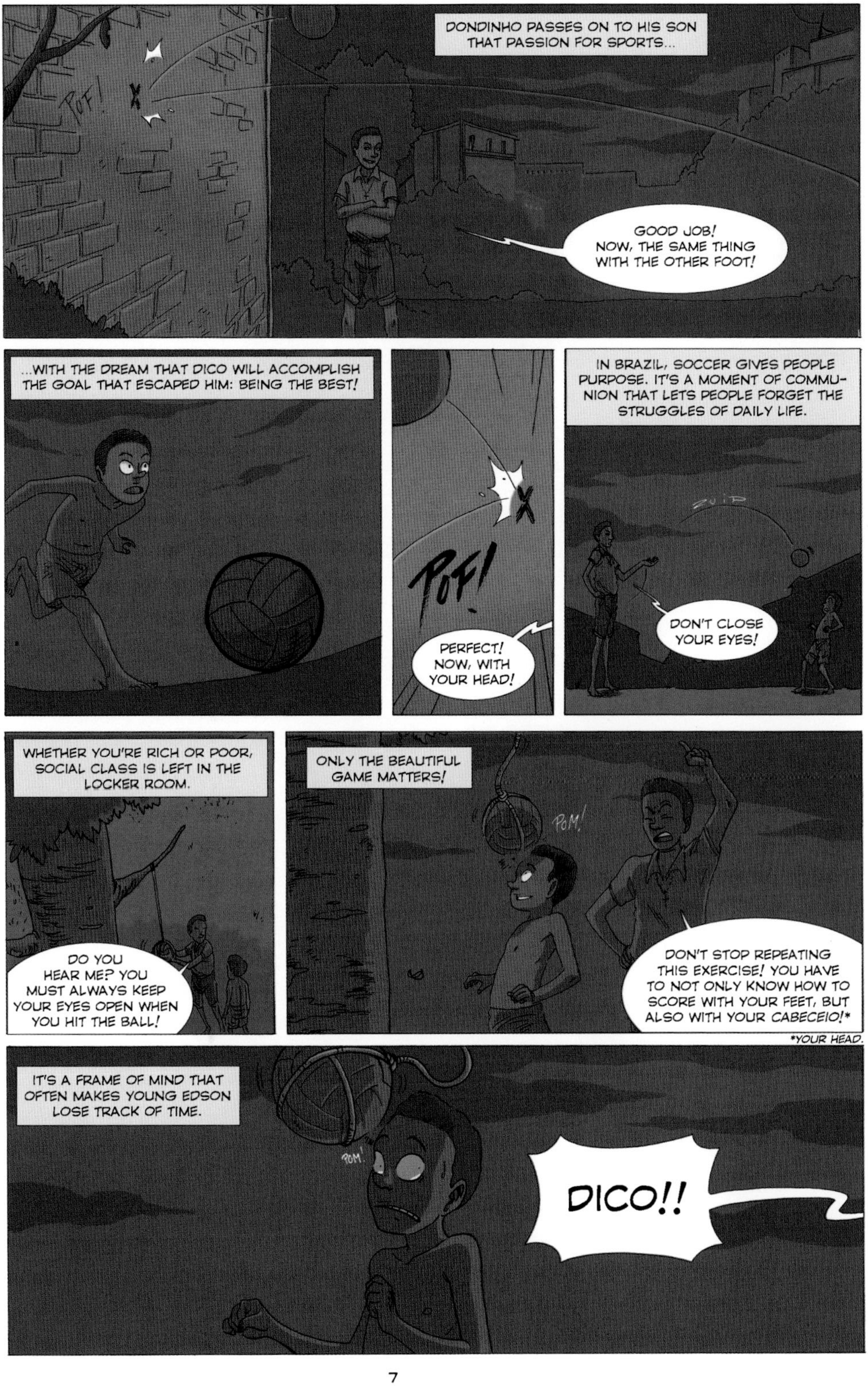
DONDINHO PASSES ON TO HIS SON THAT PASSION FOR SPORTS...
POF!
GOOD JOB! NOW, THE SAME THING WITH THE OTHER FOOT!
...WITH THE DREAM THAT DICO WILL ACCOMPLISH THE GOAL THAT ESCAPED HIM: BEING THE BEST!
POF!
PERFECT! NOW, WITH YOUR HEAD!
IN BRAZIL, SOCCER GIVES PEOPLE PURPOSE. IT'S A MOMENT OF COMMUNION THAT LETS PEOPLE FORGET THE STRUGGLES OF DAILY LIFE.
DON'T CLOSE YOUR EYES!
WHETHER YOU'RE RICH OR POOR, SOCIAL CLASS IS LEFT IN THE LOCKER ROOM.
DO YOU HEAR ME? YOU MUST ALWAYS KEEP YOUR EYES OPEN WHEN YOU HIT THE BALL!
ONLY THE BEAUTIFUL GAME MATTERS!
POM!
DON'T STOP REPEATING THIS EXERCISE! YOU HAVE TO NOT ONLY KNOW HOW TO SCORE WITH YOUR FEET, BUT ALSO WITH YOUR CABECEIO!*
*YOUR HEAD.
IT'S A FRAME OF MIND THAT OFTEN MAKES YOUNG EDSON LOSE TRACK OF TIME.
POM!
DICO!!

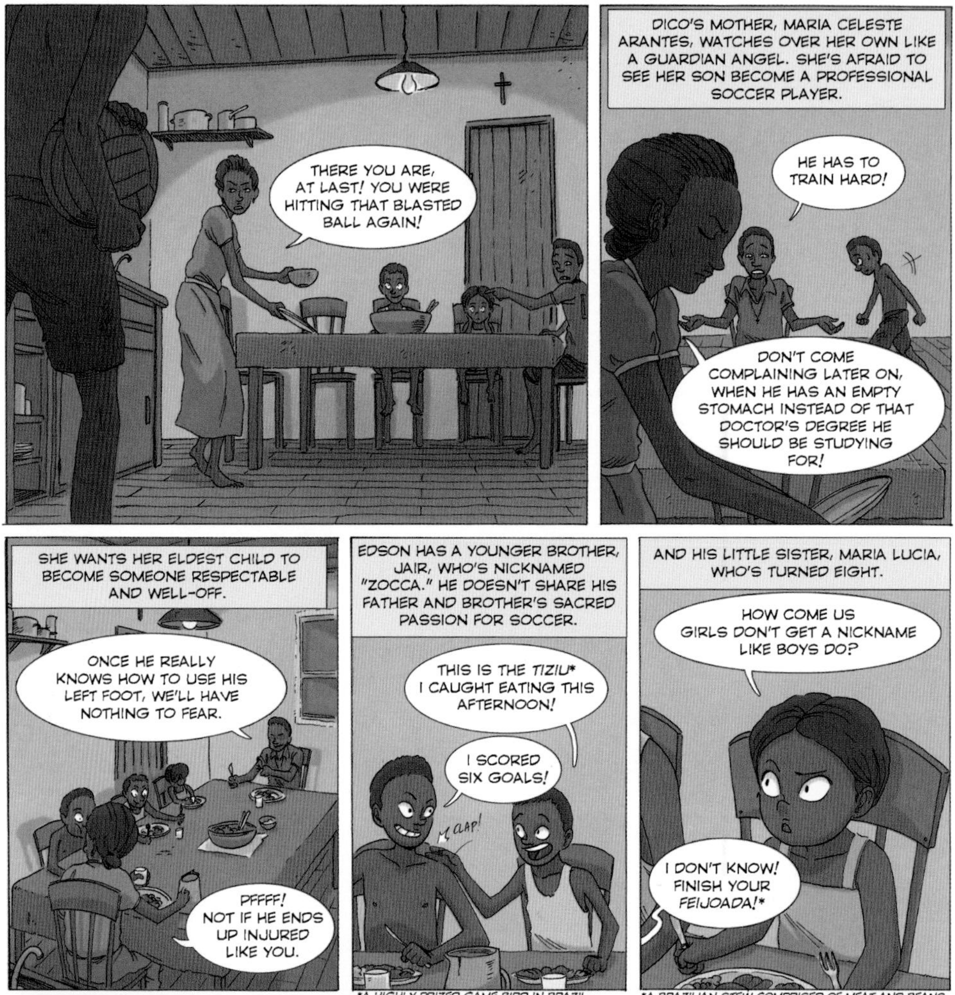
DICO'S MOTHER, MARIA CELESTE ARANTES, WATCHES OVER HER OWN LIKE A GUARDIAN ANGEL. SHE'S AFRAID TO SEE HER SON BECOME A PROFESSIONAL SOCCER PLAYER.
THERE YOU ARE, AT LAST! YOU WERE HITTING THAT BLASTED BALL AGAIN!
HE HAS TO TRAIN HARD!
DON'T COME COMPLAINING LATER ON, WHEN HE HAS AN EMPTY STOMACH INSTEAD OF THAT DOCTOR'S DEGREE HE SHOULD BE STUDYING FOR!
SHE WANTS HER ELDEST CHILD TO BECOME SOMEONE RESPECTABLE AND WELL-OFF.
ONCE HE REALLY KNOWS HOW TO USE HIS LEFT FOOT, WE'LL HAVE NOTHING TO FEAR.
PFFFF! NOT IF HE ENDS UP INJURED LIKE YOU.
EDSON HAS A YOUNGER BROTHER, JAIR, WHO'S NICKNAMED "ZOCCA." HE DOESN'T SHARE HIS FATHER AND BROTHER'S SACRED PASSION FOR SOCCER.
THIS IS THE *TIZIU** I CAUGHT EATING THIS AFTERNOON!
I SCORED SIX GOALS!
CLAP!
AND HIS LITTLE SISTER, MARIA LUCIA, WHO'S TURNED EIGHT.
HOW COME US GIRLS DON'T GET A NICKNAME LIKE BOYS DO?
I DON'T KNOW! FINISH YOUR *FEIJOADA!**

*A HIGHLY PRIZED GAME BIRD IN BRAZIL.

*A BRAZILIAN STEW COMPRISED OF MEAT AND BEANS.

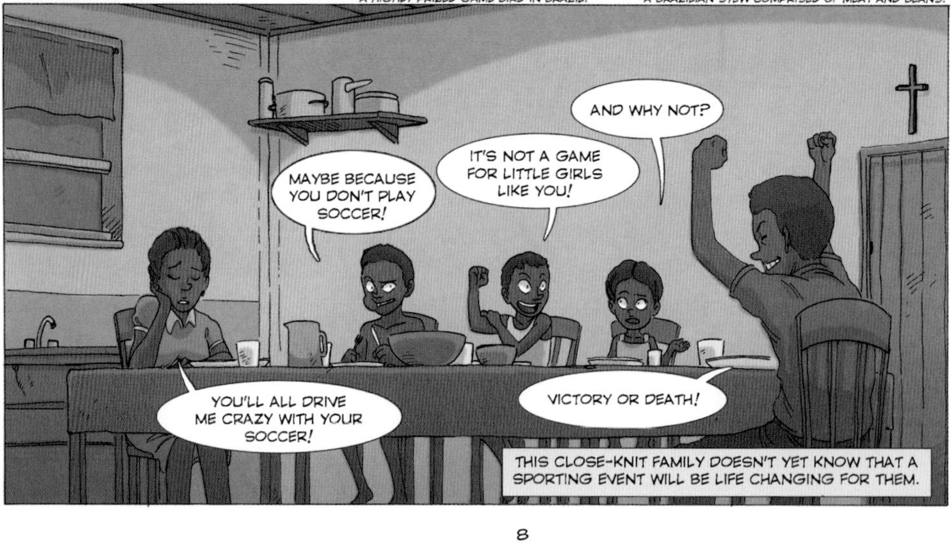
AND WHY NOT?
MAYBE BECAUSE YOU DON'T PLAY SOCCER!
IT'S NOT A GAME FOR LITTLE GIRLS LIKE YOU!
YOU'LL ALL DRIVE ME CRAZY WITH YOUR SOCCER!
VICTORY OR DEATH!
THIS CLOSE-KNIT FAMILY DOESN'T YET KNOW THAT A SPORTING EVENT WILL BE LIFE CHANGING FOR THEM.

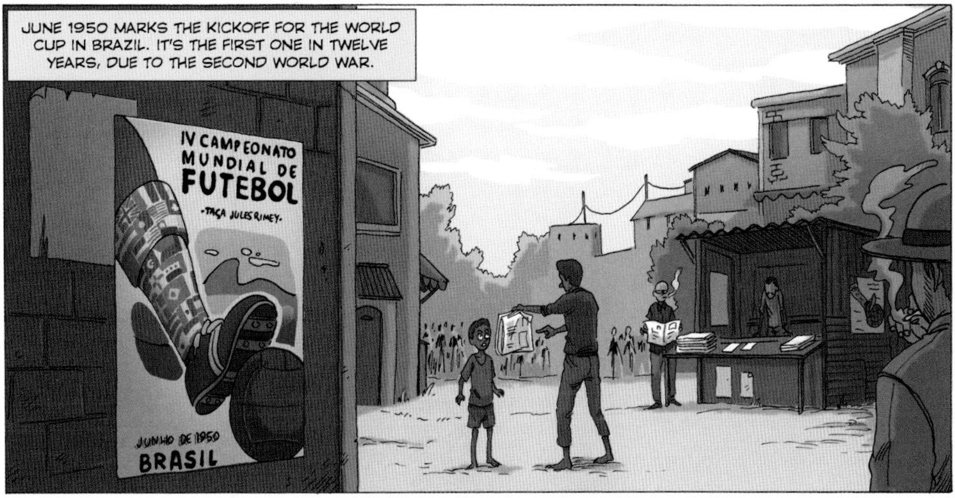
JUNE 1950 MARKS THE KICKOFF FOR THE WORLD CUP IN BRAZIL. IT'S THE FIRST ONE IN TWELVE YEARS, DUE TO THE SECOND WORLD WAR.
IV CAMPEONATO MUNDIAL DE FUTEBOL
-TAÇA JULES RIMEY-
JUNHO DE 1950
BRASIL

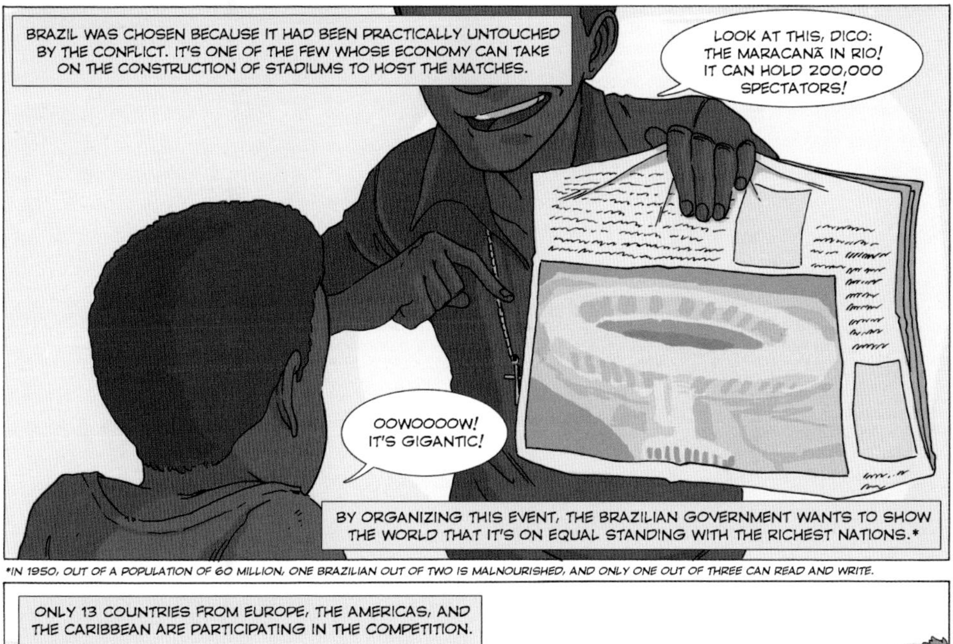
BRAZIL WAS CHOSEN BECAUSE IT HAD BEEN PRACTICALLY UNTOUCHED BY THE CONFLICT. IT'S ONE OF THE FEW WHOSE ECONOMY CAN TAKE ON THE CONSTRUCTION OF STADIUMS TO HOST THE MATCHES.
LOOK AT THIS, DICO: THE MARACANÃ IN RIO! IT CAN HOLD 200,000 SPECTATORS!
OOWOOOOW! IT'S GIGANTIC!
BY ORGANIZING THIS EVENT, THE BRAZILIAN GOVERNMENT WANTS TO SHOW THE WORLD THAT IT'S ON EQUAL STANDING WITH THE RICHEST NATIONS.*

*IN 1950, OUT OF A POPULATION OF 60 MILLION, ONE BRAZILIAN OUT OF TWO IS MALNOURISHED, AND ONLY ONE OUT OF THREE CAN READ AND WRITE.

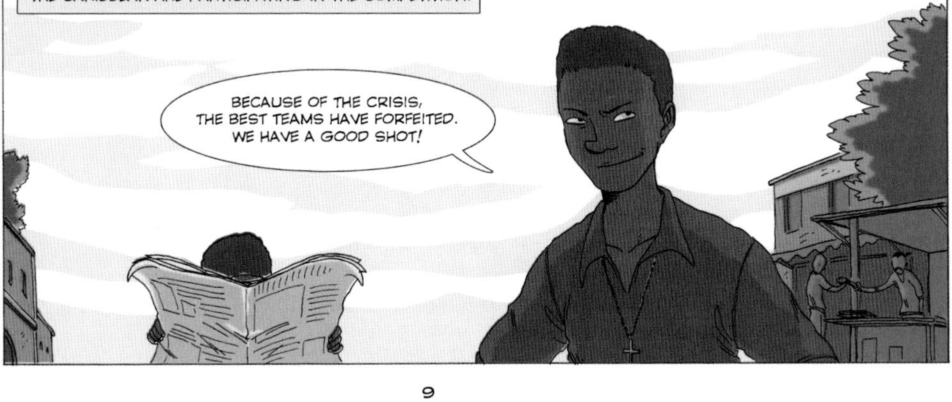
ONLY 13 COUNTRIES FROM EUROPE, THE AMERICAS, AND THE CARIBBEAN ARE PARTICIPATING IN THE COMPETITION.
BECAUSE OF THE CRISIS, THE BEST TEAMS HAVE FORFEITED. WE HAVE A GOOD SHOT!

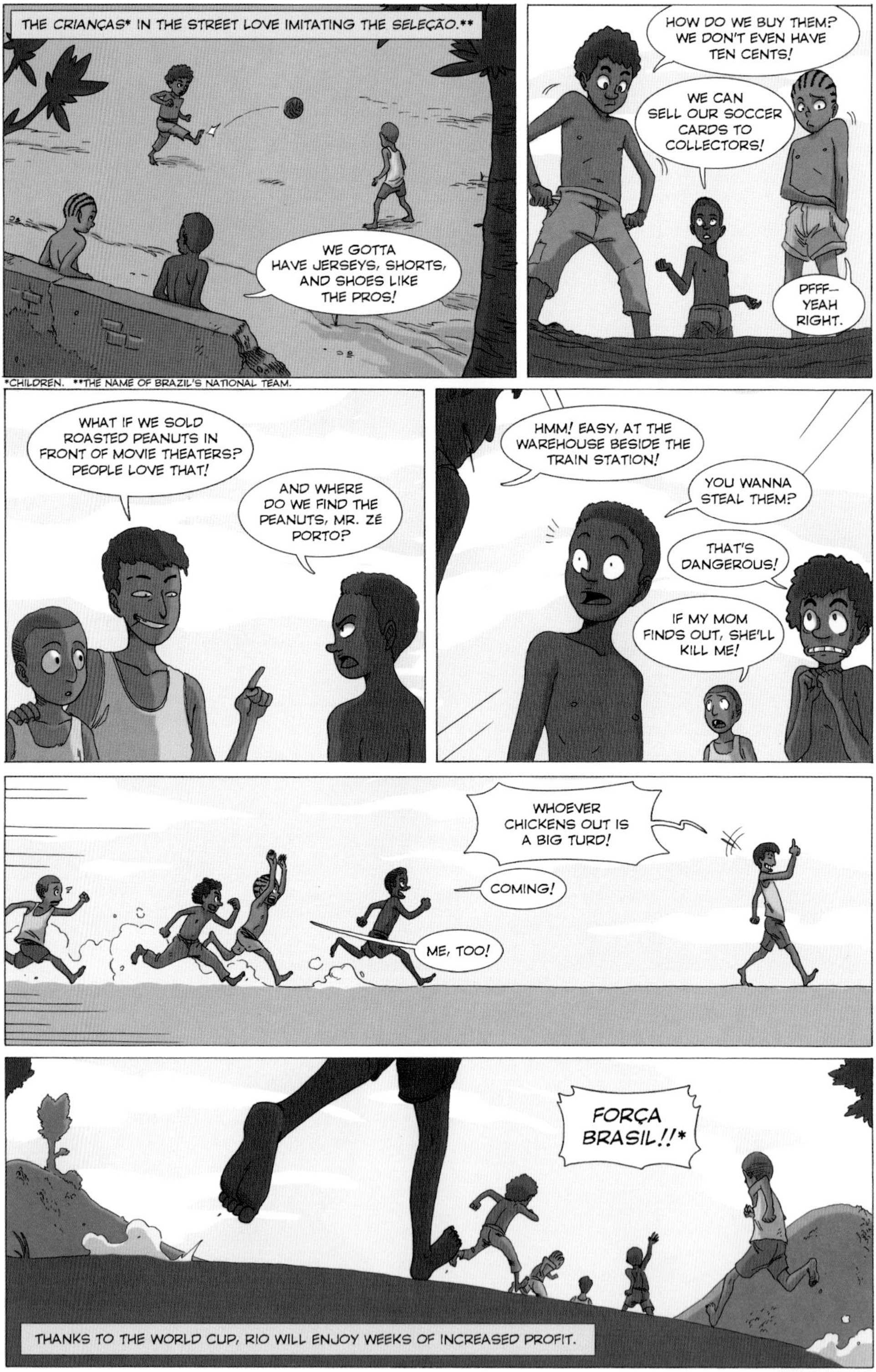
THE CRIANÇAS* IN THE STREET LOVE IMITATING THE SELEÇÃO.**
WE GOTTA HAVE JERSEYS, SHORTS, AND SHOES LIKE THE PROS!
HOW DO WE BUY THEM? WE DON'T EVEN HAVE TEN CENTS!
WE CAN SELL OUR SOCCER CARDS TO COLLECTORS!
PFFF– YEAH RIGHT.
*CHILDREN. **THE NAME OF BRAZIL'S NATIONAL TEAM.
WHAT IF WE SOLD ROASTED PEANUTS IN FRONT OF MOVIE THEATERS? PEOPLE LOVE THAT!
AND WHERE DO WE FIND THE PEANUTS, MR. ZÉ PORTO?
HMM! EASY, AT THE WAREHOUSE BESIDE THE TRAIN STATION!
YOU WANNA STEAL THEM?
THAT'S DANGEROUS!
IF MY MOM FINDS OUT, SHE'LL KILL ME!
WHOEVER CHICKENS OUT IS A BIG TURD!
COMING!
ME, TOO!
FORÇA BRASIL!!*
THANKS TO THE WORLD CUP, RIO WILL ENJOY WEEKS OF INCREASED PROFIT.
*BRAZIL STRONG.

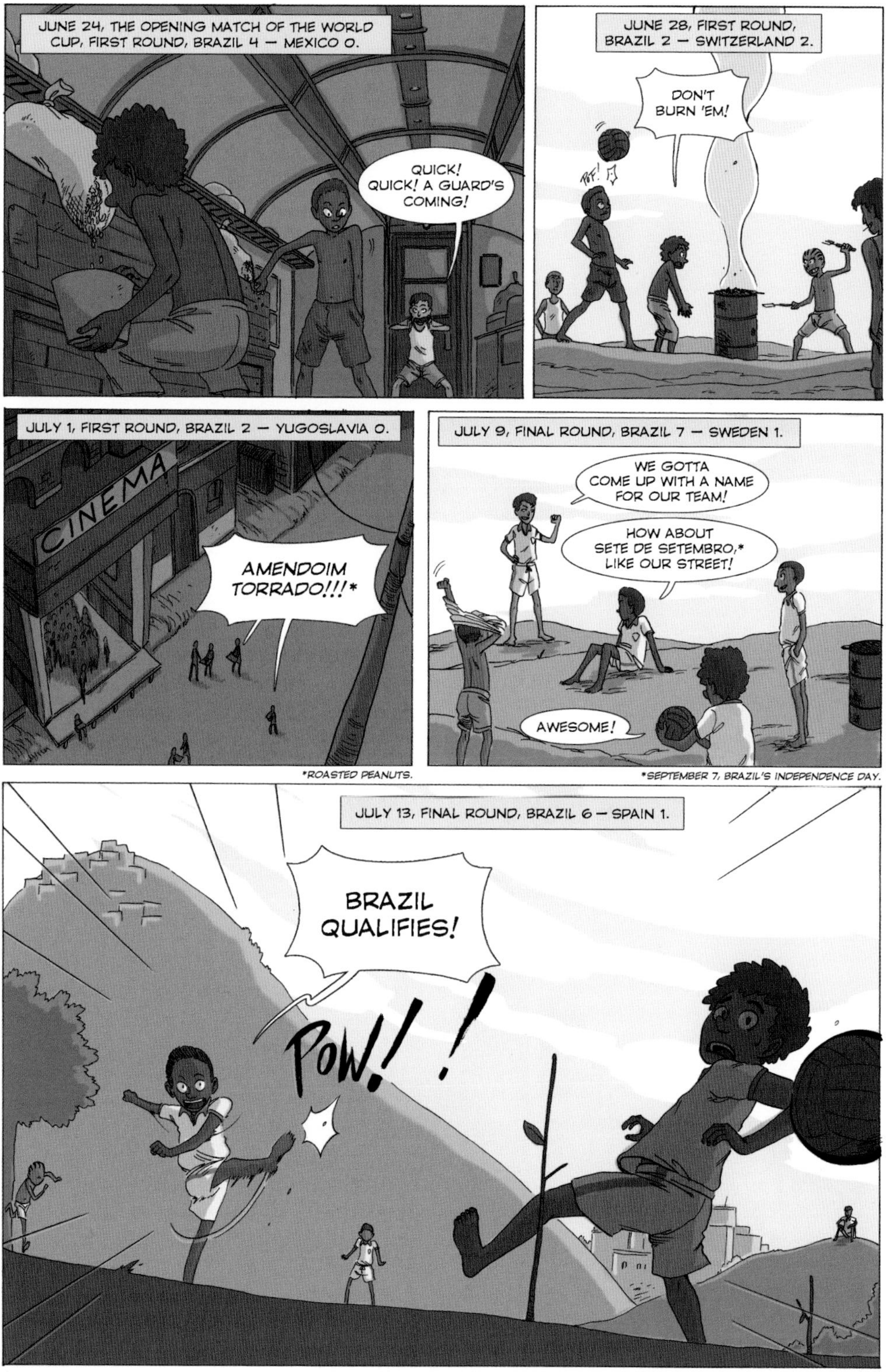
JUNE 24, THE OPENING MATCH OF THE WORLD CUP, FIRST ROUND, BRAZIL 4 — MEXICO 0.
QUICK! QUICK! A GUARD'S COMING!
JUNE 28, FIRST ROUND, BRAZIL 2 — SWITZERLAND 2.
DON'T BURN 'EM!
JULY 1, FIRST ROUND, BRAZIL 2 — YUGOSLAVIA 0.
CINEMA
AMENDOIM TORRADO!!!*
JULY 9, FINAL ROUND, BRAZIL 7 — SWEDEN 1.
WE GOTTA COME UP WITH A NAME FOR OUR TEAM!
HOW ABOUT SETE DE SETEMBRO,* LIKE OUR STREET!
AWESOME!
JULY 13, FINAL ROUND, BRAZIL 6 — SPAIN 1.
BRAZIL QUALIFIES!
POW!!

*ROASTED PEANUTS.

*SEPTEMBER 7, BRAZIL'S INDEPENDENCE DAY.

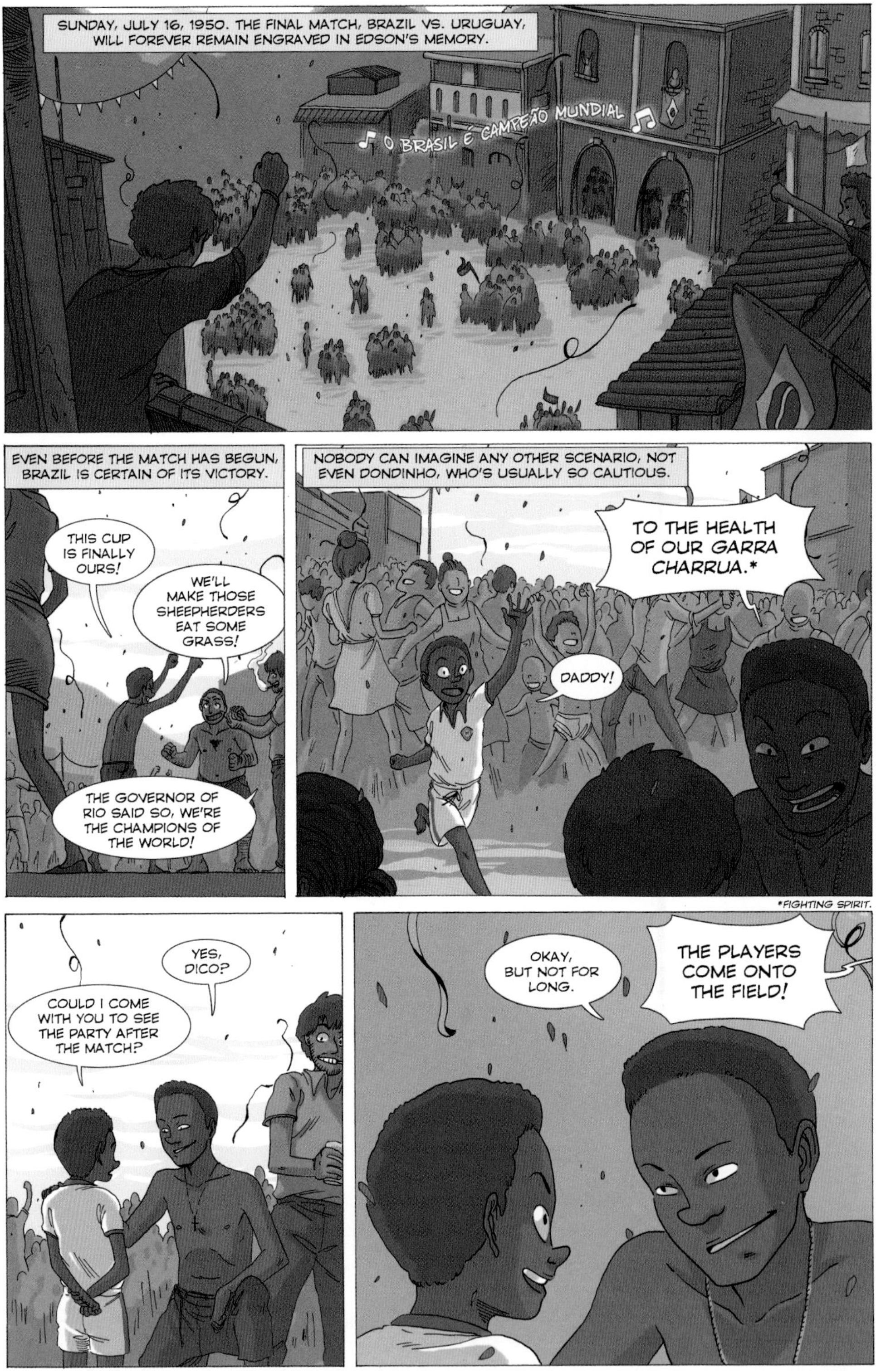

SUNDAY, JULY 16, 1950. THE FINAL MATCH, BRAZIL VS. URUGUAY, WILL FOREVER REMAIN ENGRAVED IN EDSON'S MEMORY.
O BRASIL É CAMPEÃO MUNDIAL
EVEN BEFORE THE MATCH HAS BEGUN, BRAZIL IS CERTAIN OF ITS VICTORY.
THIS CUP IS FINALLY OURS!
WE'LL MAKE THOSE SHEEPHERDERS EAT SOME GRASS!
THE GOVERNOR OF RIO SAID SO, WE'RE THE CHAMPIONS OF THE WORLD!
NOBODY CAN IMAGINE ANY OTHER SCENARIO, NOT EVEN DONDINHO, WHO'S USUALLY SO CAUTIOUS.
TO THE HEALTH OF OUR GARRA CHARRUA.*
DADDY!
*FIGHTING SPIRIT.
YES, DICO?
COULD I COME WITH YOU TO SEE THE PARTY AFTER THE MATCH?
OKAY, BUT NOT FOR LONG.
THE PLAYERS COME ONTO THE FIELD!

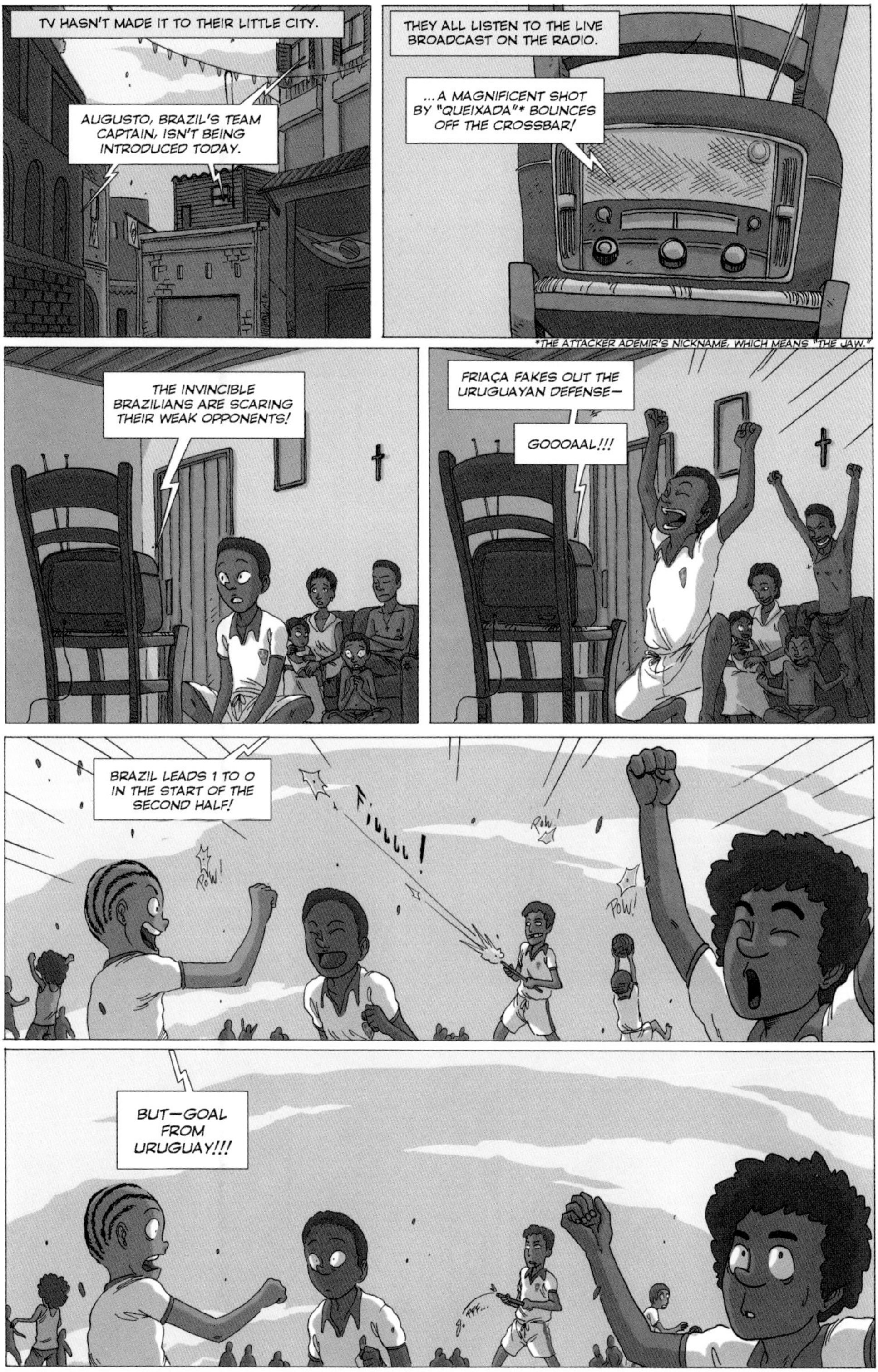
TV HASN'T MADE IT TO THEIR LITTLE CITY.
AUGUSTO, BRAZIL'S TEAM CAPTAIN, ISN'T BEING INTRODUCED TODAY.
THEY ALL LISTEN TO THE LIVE BROADCAST ON THE RADIO.
...A MAGNIFICENT SHOT BY "QUEIXADA"* BOUNCES OFF THE CROSSBAR!
*THE ATTACKER ADEMIR'S NICKNAME, WHICH MEANS "THE JAW."
THE INVINCIBLE BRAZILIANS ARE SCARING THEIR WEAK OPPONENTS!
FRIAÇA FAKES OUT THE URUGUAYAN DEFENSE—
GOOOAAL!!!
BRAZIL LEADS 1 TO 0 IN THE START OF THE SECOND HALF!
BUT—GOAL FROM URUGUAY!!!

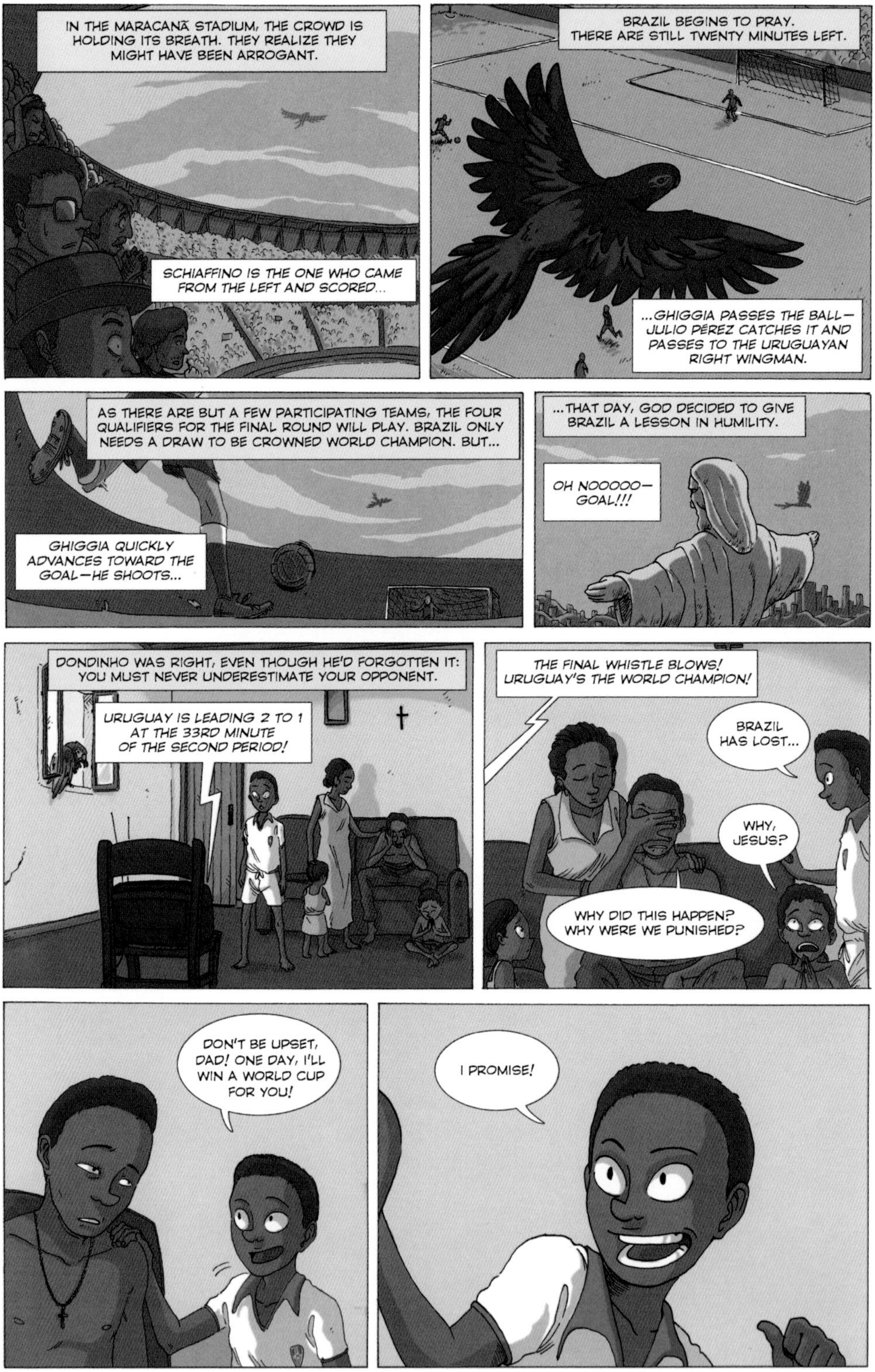
IN THE MARACANÃ STADIUM, THE CROWD IS HOLDING ITS BREATH. THEY REALIZE THEY MIGHT HAVE BEEN ARROGANT.
SCHIAFFINO IS THE ONE WHO CAME FROM THE LEFT AND SCORED...
BRAZIL BEGINS TO PRAY. THERE ARE STILL TWENTY MINUTES LEFT.
...GHIGGIA PASSES THE BALL—JULIO PÉREZ CATCHES IT AND PASSES TO THE URUGUAYAN RIGHT WINGMAN.
AS THERE ARE BUT A FEW PARTICIPATING TEAMS, THE FOUR QUALIFIERS FOR THE FINAL ROUND WILL PLAY. BRAZIL ONLY NEEDS A DRAW TO BE CROWNED WORLD CHAMPION. BUT...
GHIGGIA QUICKLY ADVANCES TOWARD THE GOAL—HE SHOOTS...
...THAT DAY, GOD DECIDED TO GIVE BRAZIL A LESSON IN HUMILITY.
OH NOOOOO—GOAL!!!
DONDINHO WAS RIGHT, EVEN THOUGH HE'D FORGOTTEN IT: YOU MUST NEVER UNDERESTIMATE YOUR OPPONENT.
URUGUAY IS LEADING 2 TO 1 AT THE 33RD MINUTE OF THE SECOND PERIOD!
THE FINAL WHISTLE BLOWS! URUGUAY'S THE WORLD CHAMPION!
BRAZIL HAS LOST...
WHY, JESUS?
WHY DID THIS HAPPEN? WHY WERE WE PUNISHED?
DON'T BE UPSET, DAD! ONE DAY, I'LL WIN A WORLD CUP FOR YOU!
I PROMISE!

Chapter 2
When Dico Becomes Pelé

"I don't want to be famous. I don't want to be a great player. I just want to be like my father." —Pelé, 1952

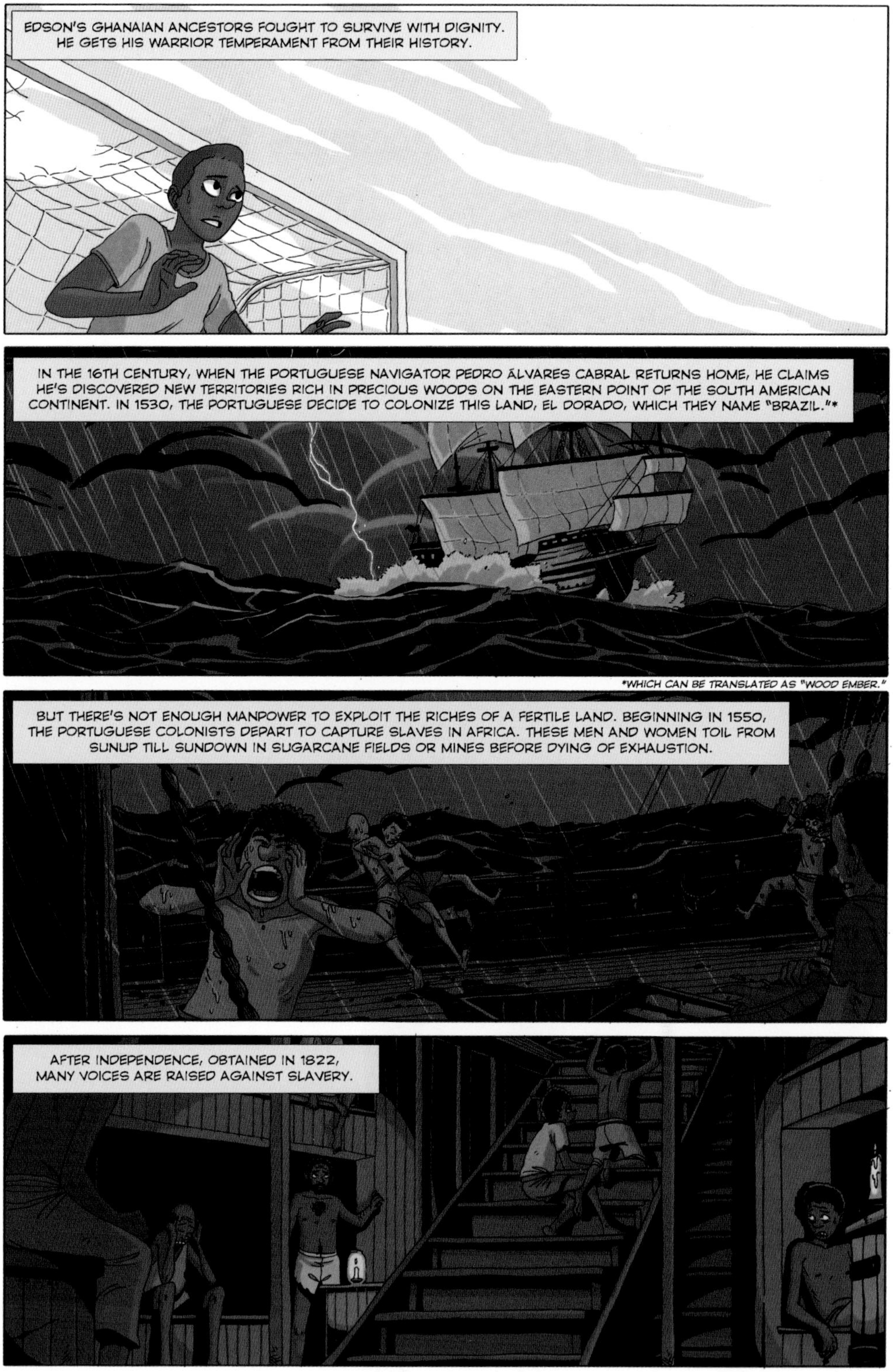
EDSON'S GHANAIAN ANCESTORS FOUGHT TO SURVIVE WITH DIGNITY. HE GETS HIS WARRIOR TEMPERAMENT FROM THEIR HISTORY.
IN THE 16TH CENTURY, WHEN THE PORTUGUESE NAVIGATOR PEDRO ÁLVARES CABRAL RETURNS HOME, HE CLAIMS HE'S DISCOVERED NEW TERRITORIES RICH IN PRECIOUS WOODS ON THE EASTERN POINT OF THE SOUTH AMERICAN CONTINENT. IN 1530, THE PORTUGUESE DECIDE TO COLONIZE THIS LAND, EL DORADO, WHICH THEY NAME "BRAZIL."*
BUT THERE'S NOT ENOUGH MANPOWER TO EXPLOIT THE RICHES OF A FERTILE LAND. BEGINNING IN 1550, THE PORTUGUESE COLONISTS DEPART TO CAPTURE SLAVES IN AFRICA. THESE MEN AND WOMEN TOIL FROM SUNUP TILL SUNDOWN IN SUGARCANE FIELDS OR MINES BEFORE DYING OF EXHAUSTION.
AFTER INDEPENDENCE, OBTAINED IN 1822, MANY VOICES ARE RAISED AGAINST SLAVERY.

*WHICH CAN BE TRANSLATED AS "WOOD EMBER."

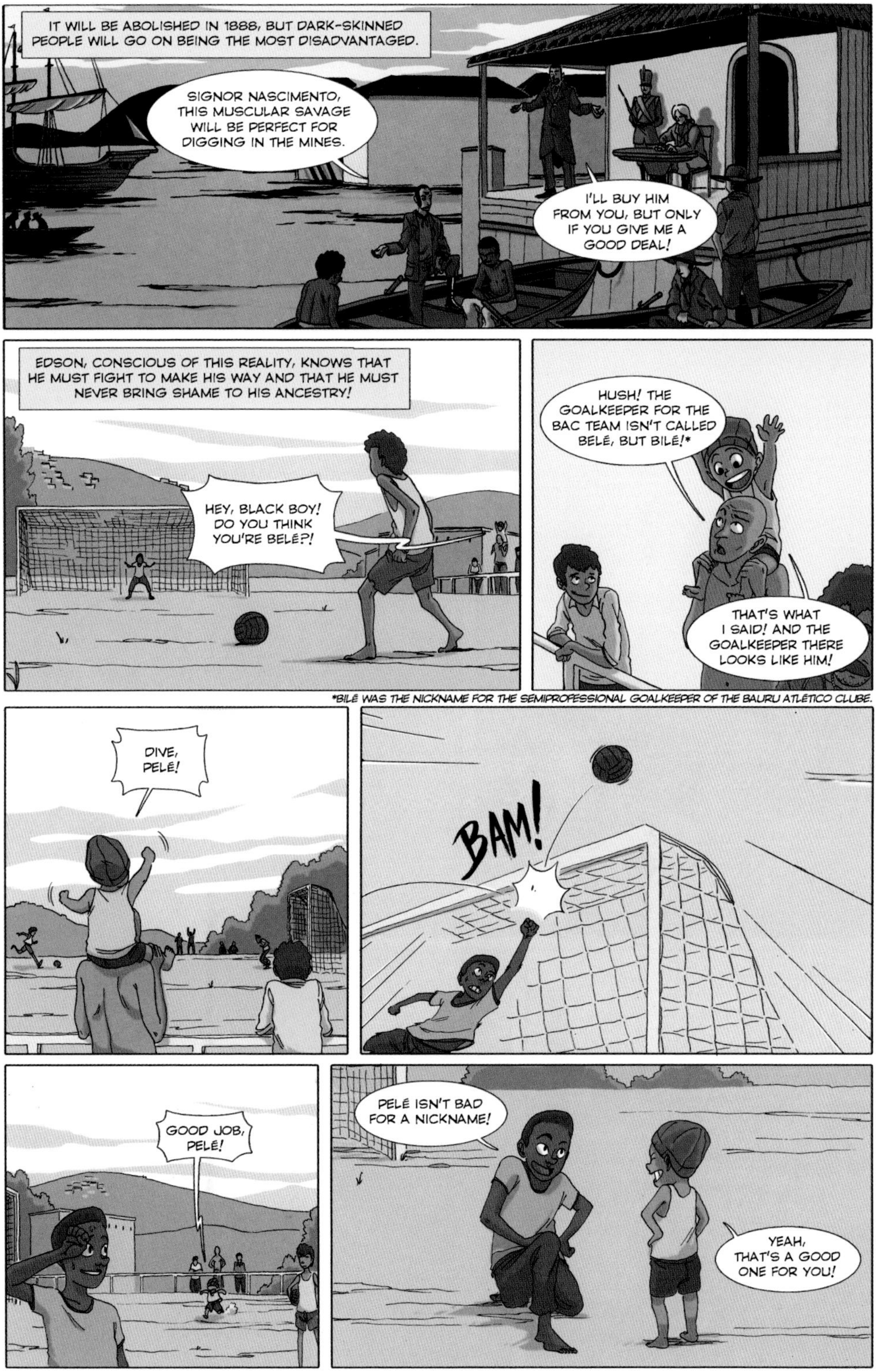
IT WILL BE ABOLISHED IN 1888, BUT DARK-SKINNED PEOPLE WILL GO ON BEING THE MOST DISADVANTAGED.
SIGNOR NASCIMENTO, THIS MUSCULAR SAVAGE WILL BE PERFECT FOR DIGGING IN THE MINES.
I'LL BUY HIM FROM YOU, BUT ONLY IF YOU GIVE ME A GOOD DEAL!
EDSON, CONSCIOUS OF THIS REALITY, KNOWS THAT HE MUST FIGHT TO MAKE HIS WAY AND THAT HE MUST NEVER BRING SHAME TO HIS ANCESTRY!
HEY, BLACK BOY! DO YOU THINK YOU'RE BELÉ?!
HUSH! THE GOALKEEPER FOR THE BAC TEAM ISN'T CALLED BELÉ, BUT BILÉ!*
THAT'S WHAT I SAID! AND THE GOALKEEPER THERE LOOKS LIKE HIM!
DIVE, PELÉ!
BAM!
GOOD JOB, PELÉ!
PELÉ ISN'T BAD FOR A NICKNAME!
YEAH, THAT'S A GOOD ONE FOR YOU!

*BILÉ WAS THE NICKNAME FOR THE SEMIPROFESSIONAL GOALKEEPER OF THE BAURU ATLÉTICO CLUBE.

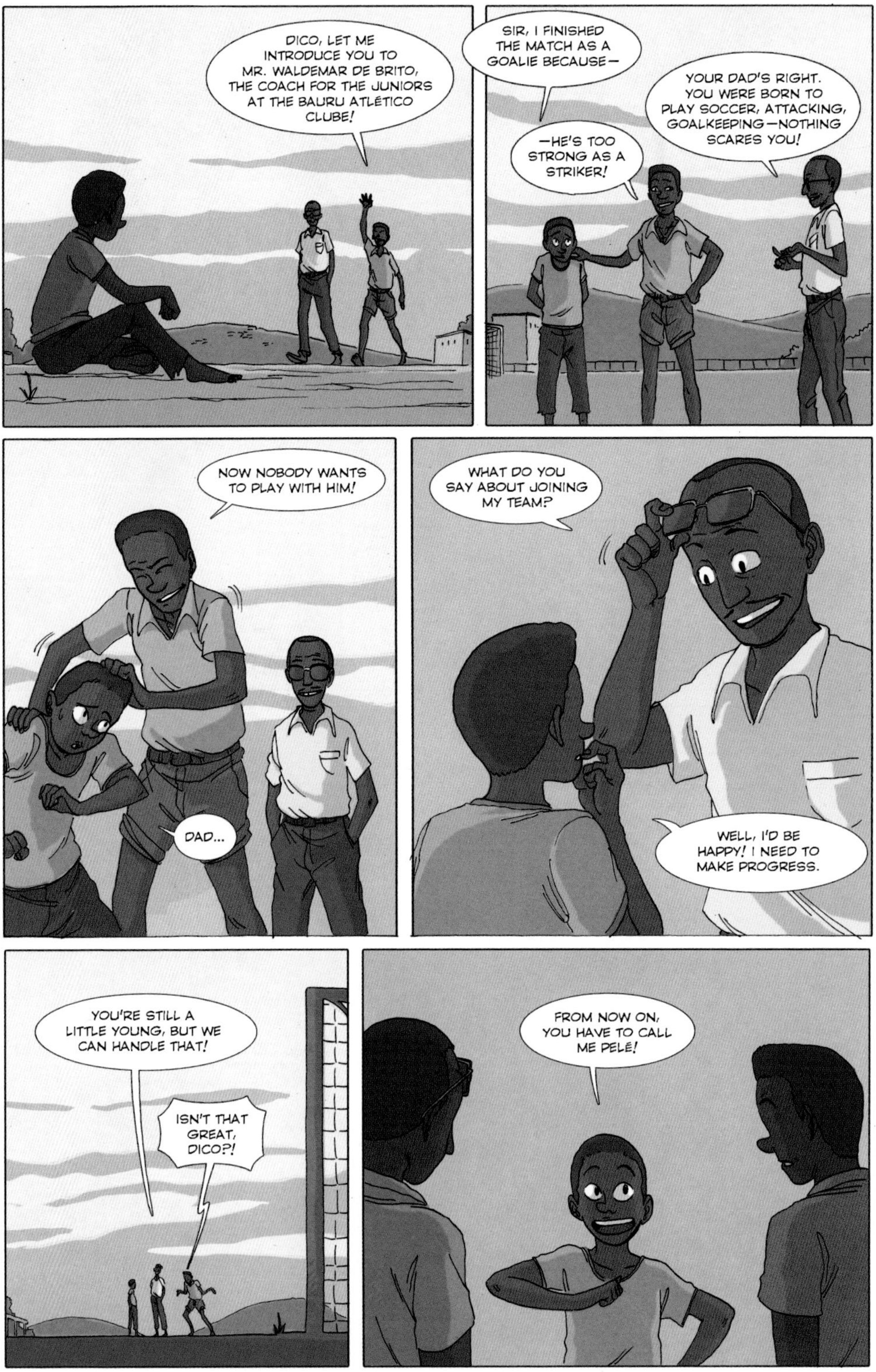
DICO, LET ME INTRODUCE YOU TO MR. WALDEMAR DE BRITO, THE COACH FOR THE JUNIORS AT THE BAURU ATLÉTICO CLUBE!
SIR, I FINISHED THE MATCH AS A GOALIE BECAUSE—
—HE'S TOO STRONG AS A STRIKER!
YOUR DAD'S RIGHT. YOU WERE BORN TO PLAY SOCCER, ATTACKING, GOALKEEPING—NOTHING SCARES YOU!
NOW NOBODY WANTS TO PLAY WITH HIM!
DAD...
WHAT DO YOU SAY ABOUT JOINING MY TEAM?
WELL, I'D BE HAPPY! I NEED TO MAKE PROGRESS.
YOU'RE STILL A LITTLE YOUNG, BUT WE CAN HANDLE THAT!
ISN'T THAT GREAT, DICO?!
FROM NOW ON, YOU HAVE TO CALL ME PELÉ!

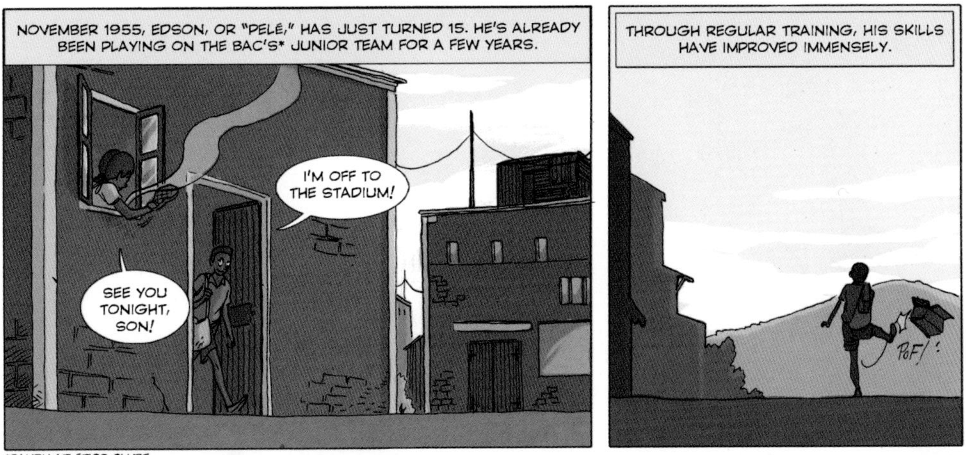
NOVEMBER 1955, EDSON, OR "PELÉ," HAS JUST TURNED 15. HE'S ALREADY BEEN PLAYING ON THE BAC'S* JUNIOR TEAM FOR A FEW YEARS.
I'M OFF TO THE STADIUM!
SEE YOU TONIGHT, SON!
THROUGH REGULAR TRAINING, HIS SKILLS HAVE IMPROVED IMMENSELY.
POF!

*BAURU ATLÉTICO CLUBE.

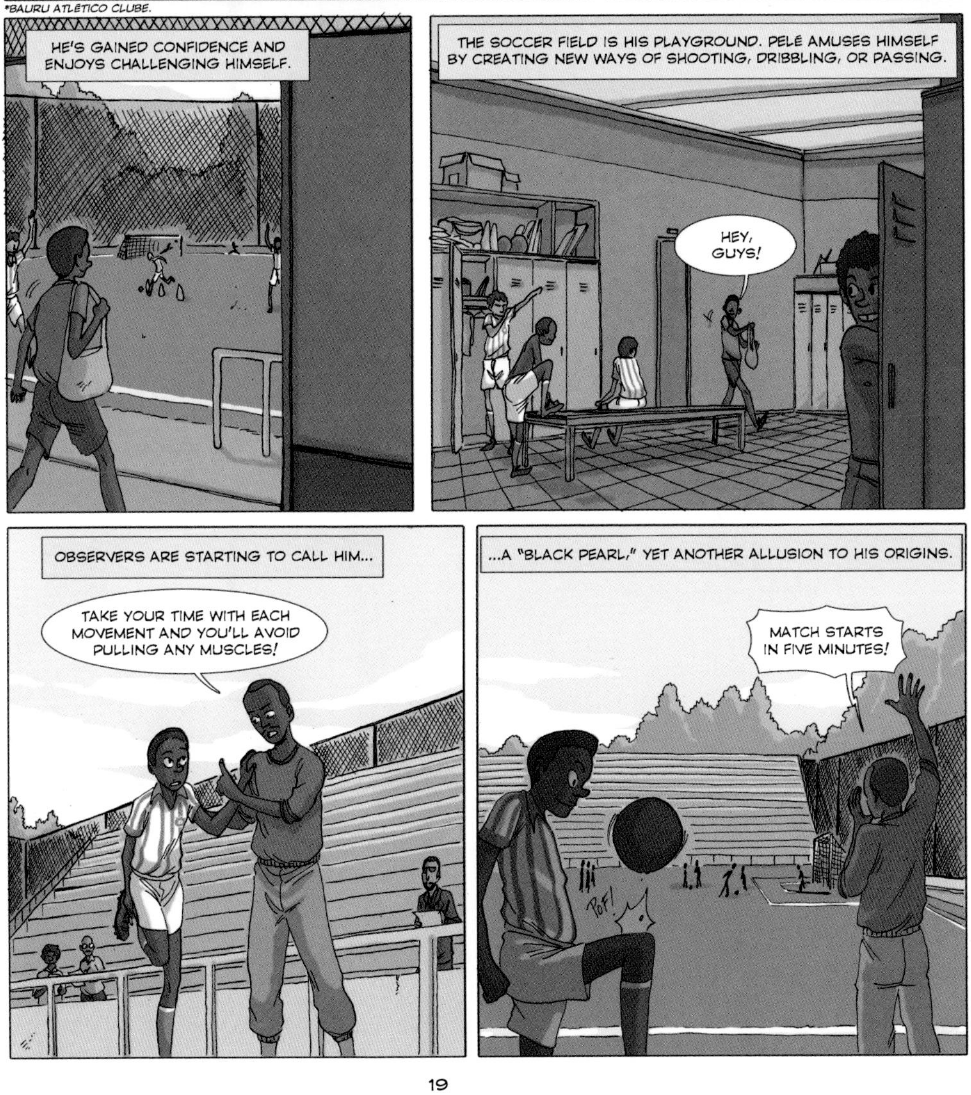
HE'S GAINED CONFIDENCE AND ENJOYS CHALLENGING HIMSELF.
THE SOCCER FIELD IS HIS PLAYGROUND. PELÉ AMUSES HIMSELF BY CREATING NEW WAYS OF SHOOTING, DRIBBLING, OR PASSING.
HEY, GUYS!
OBSERVERS ARE STARTING TO CALL HIM...
TAKE YOUR TIME WITH EACH MOVEMENT AND YOU'LL AVOID PULLING ANY MUSCLES!
...A "BLACK PEARL," YET ANOTHER ALLUSION TO HIS ORIGINS.
MATCH STARTS IN FIVE MINUTES!
POF!

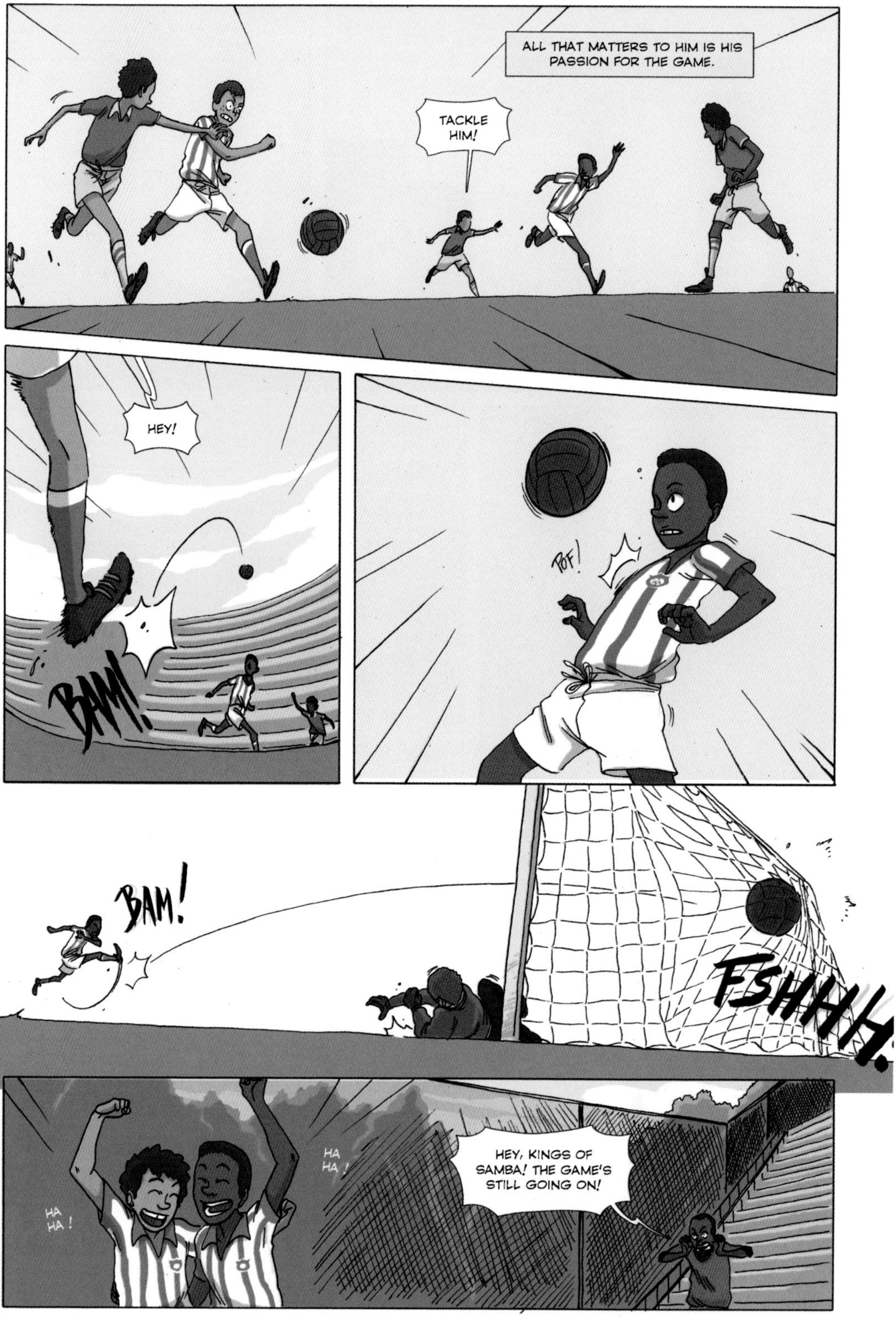

ALL THAT MATTERS TO HIM IS HIS PASSION FOR THE GAME.
TACKLE HIM!
HEY!
BAM!
POF!
BAM!
FSHHH!
HA HA!
HA HA!
HEY, KINGS OF SAMBA! THE GAME'S STILL GOING ON!

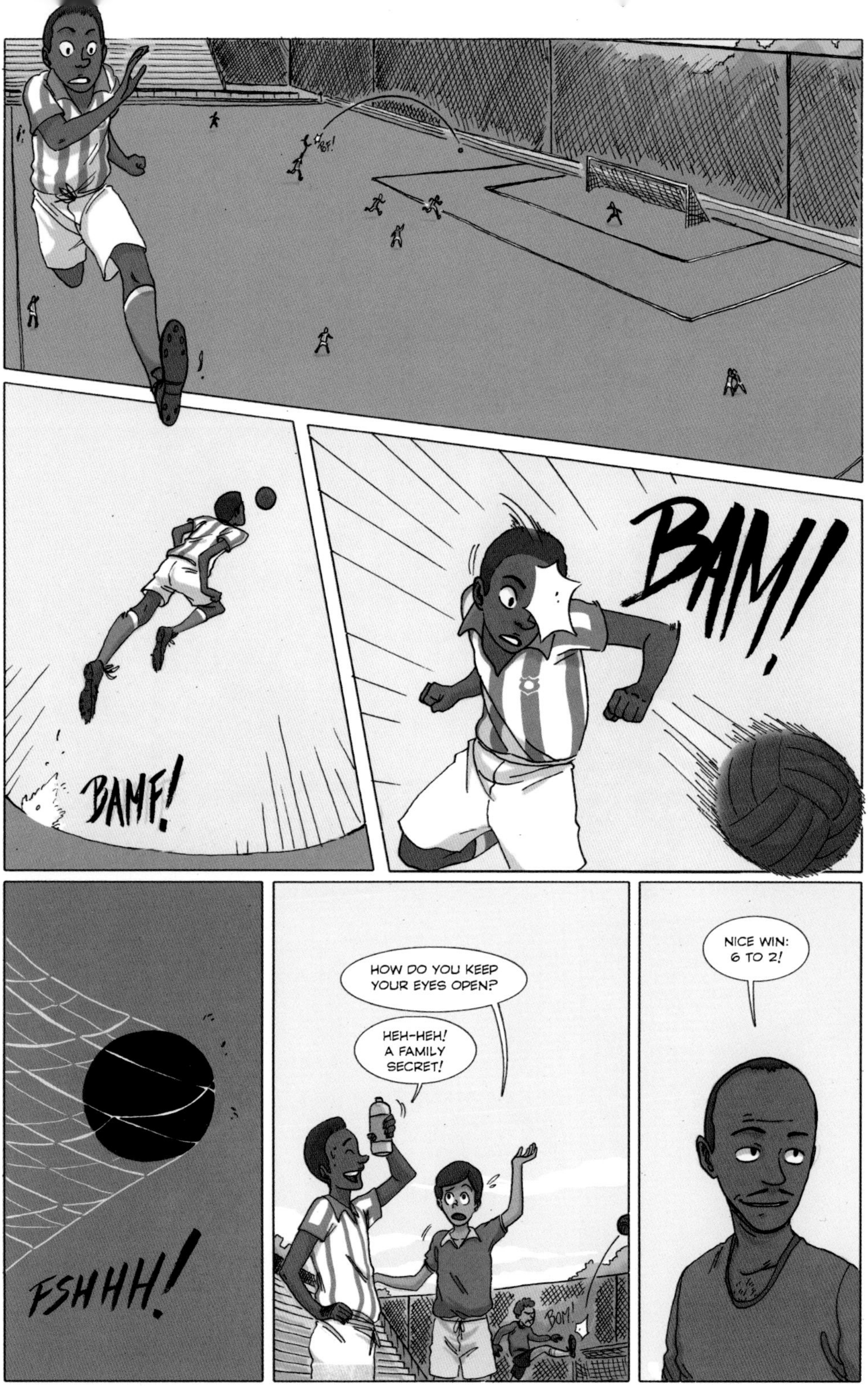

BAMF!
BAM!
FSHHH!
HOW DO YOU KEEP YOUR EYES OPEN?
HEH-HEH! A FAMILY SECRET!
BOM!
NICE WIN: 6 TO 2!

YOU TOOK FOUR GOALS ALL ON YOUR OWN, *GENIO!**

IT'S THANKS TO YOU, COACH!

NOT FOR MUCH LONGER. IT'S TIME FOR ME TO MOVE YOU ALONG.

*GENIUS.

KOF! KOF! WHAT'S THAT?

WHAT'LL BECOME OF ME WITHOUT YOU?

A PROFESSIONAL PLAYER!

HUH?

I TALKED TO THE MANAGERS OF SANTOS FC. THEY'D LIKE FOR YOU TO TRY OUT FOR THEIR CLUB!

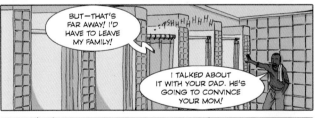

BUT—THAT'S FAR AWAY! I'D HAVE TO LEAVE MY FAMILY!

I TALKED ABOUT IT WITH YOUR DAD. HE'S GOING TO CONVINCE YOUR MOM!

OHHHH! I DON'T KNOW WHAT TO SAY—

JUST DO YOUR BEST OUT THERE. YOU HAVE A MONTH TO SHINE!

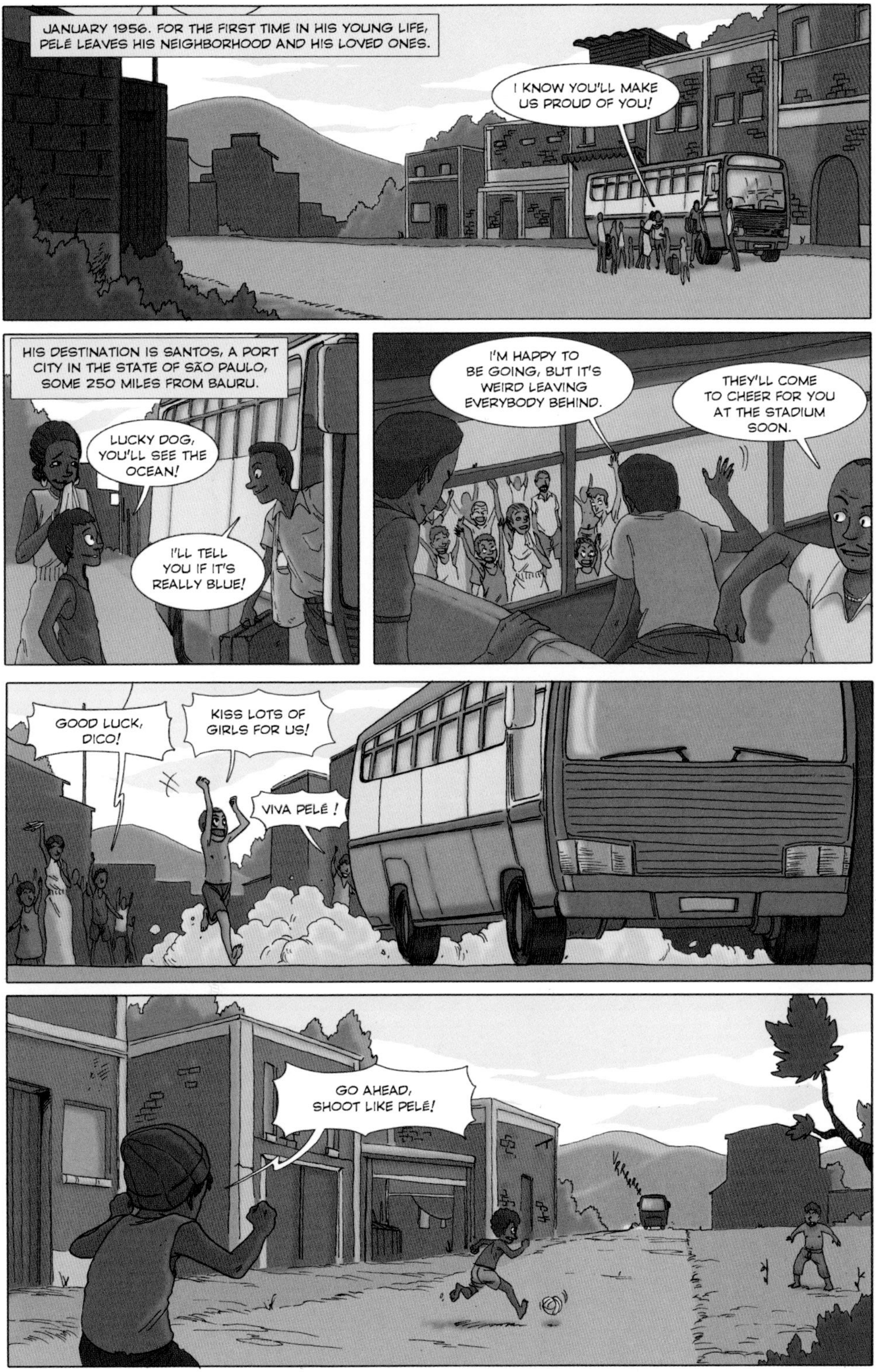
JANUARY 1956. FOR THE FIRST TIME IN HIS YOUNG LIFE, PELÉ LEAVES HIS NEIGHBORHOOD AND HIS LOVED ONES.
I KNOW YOU'LL MAKE US PROUD OF YOU!
HIS DESTINATION IS SANTOS, A PORT CITY IN THE STATE OF SÃO PAULO, SOME 250 MILES FROM BAURU.
LUCKY DOG, YOU'LL SEE THE OCEAN!
I'LL TELL YOU IF IT'S REALLY BLUE!
I'M HAPPY TO BE GOING, BUT IT'S WEIRD LEAVING EVERYBODY BEHIND.
THEY'LL COME TO CHEER FOR YOU AT THE STADIUM SOON.
GOOD LUCK, DICO!
KISS LOTS OF GIRLS FOR US!
VIVA PELÉ !
GO AHEAD, SHOOT LIKE PELÉ!
VRRRRRRR

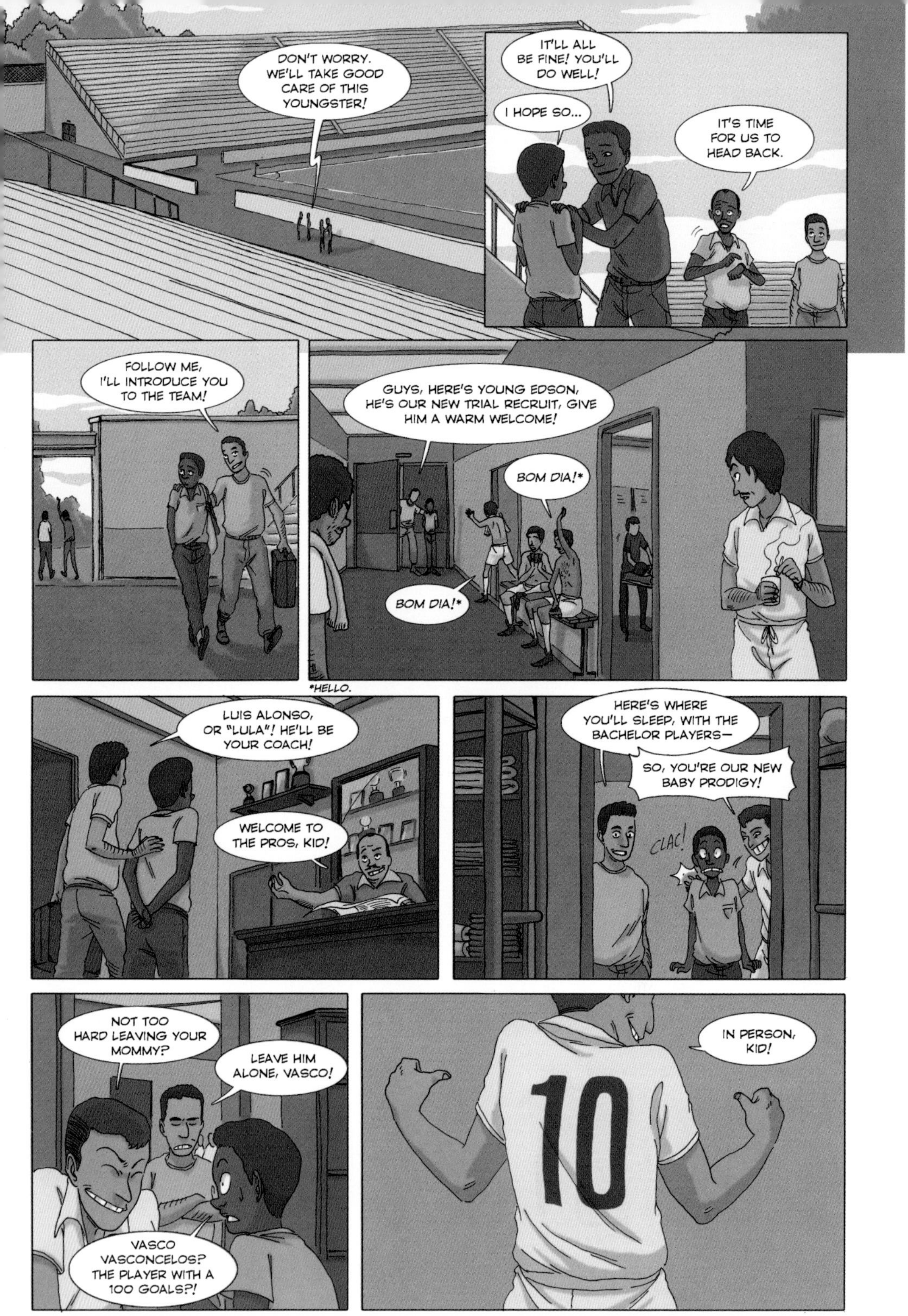
DON'T WORRY. WE'LL TAKE GOOD CARE OF THIS YOUNGSTER!
IT'LL ALL BE FINE! YOU'LL DO WELL!
I HOPE SO...
IT'S TIME FOR US TO HEAD BACK.
FOLLOW ME, I'LL INTRODUCE YOU TO THE TEAM!
GUYS, HERE'S YOUNG EDSON, HE'S OUR NEW TRIAL RECRUIT, GIVE HIM A WARM WELCOME!
BOM DIA!*
BOM DIA!*
LUIS ALONSO, OR "LULA"! HE'LL BE YOUR COACH!
WELCOME TO THE PROS, KID!
HERE'S WHERE YOU'LL SLEEP, WITH THE BACHELOR PLAYERS—
SO, YOU'RE OUR NEW BABY PRODIGY!
CLAC!
NOT TOO HARD LEAVING YOUR MOMMY?
LEAVE HIM ALONE, VASCO!
VASCO VASCONCELOS? THE PLAYER WITH A 100 GOALS?!
10
IN PERSON, KID!

*HELLO.

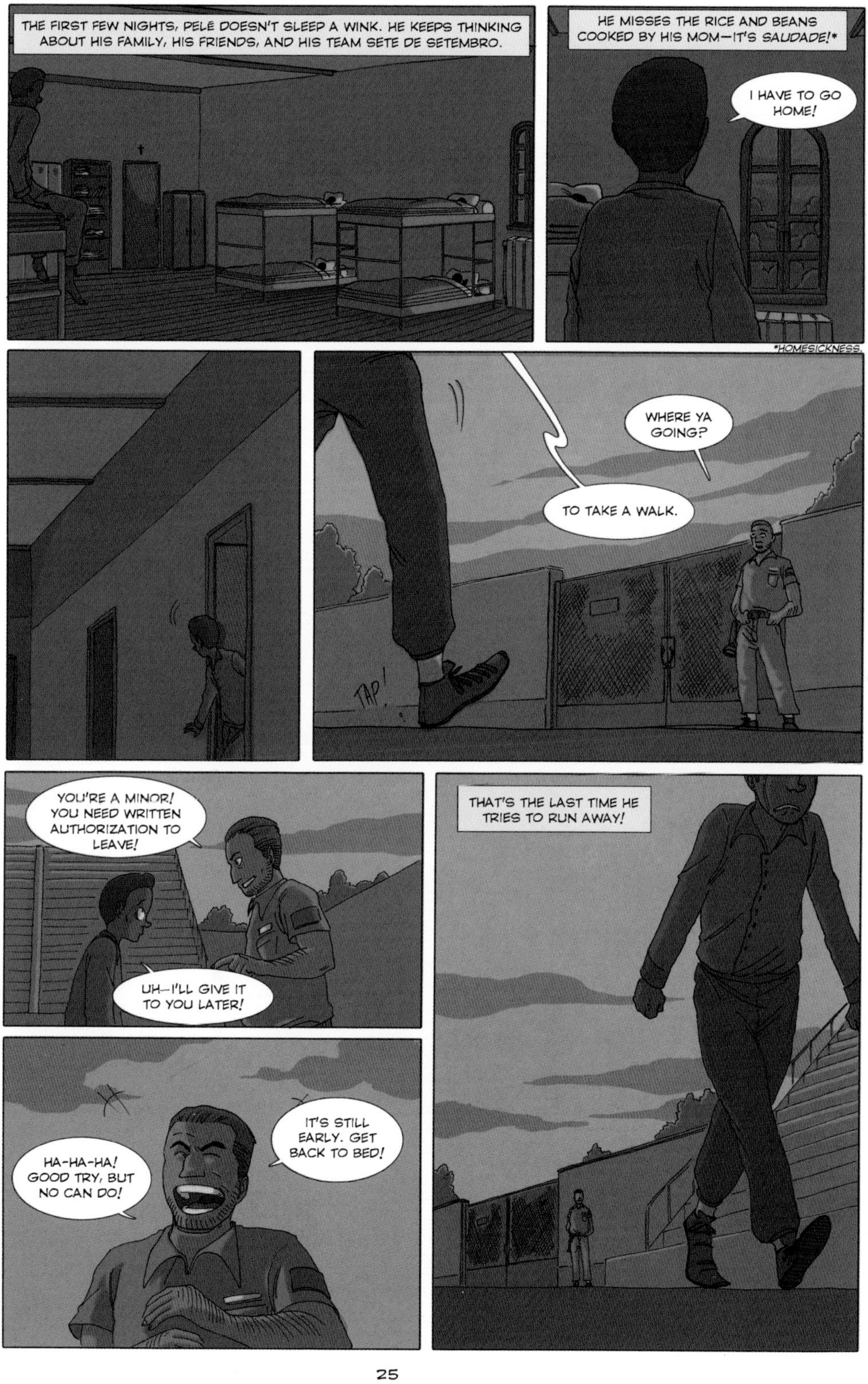
THE FIRST FEW NIGHTS, PELÉ DOESN'T SLEEP A WINK. HE KEEPS THINKING ABOUT HIS FAMILY, HIS FRIENDS, AND HIS TEAM SETE DE SETEMBRO.
HE MISSES THE RICE AND BEANS COOKED BY HIS MOM—IT'S SAUDADE!*
I HAVE TO GO HOME!
*HOMESICKNESS.
WHERE YA GOING?
TO TAKE A WALK.
TAP!
YOU'RE A MINOR! YOU NEED WRITTEN AUTHORIZATION TO LEAVE!
UH—I'LL GIVE IT TO YOU LATER!
HA-HA-HA! GOOD TRY, BUT NO CAN DO!
IT'S STILL EARLY. GET BACK TO BED!
THAT'S THE LAST TIME HE TRIES TO RUN AWAY!

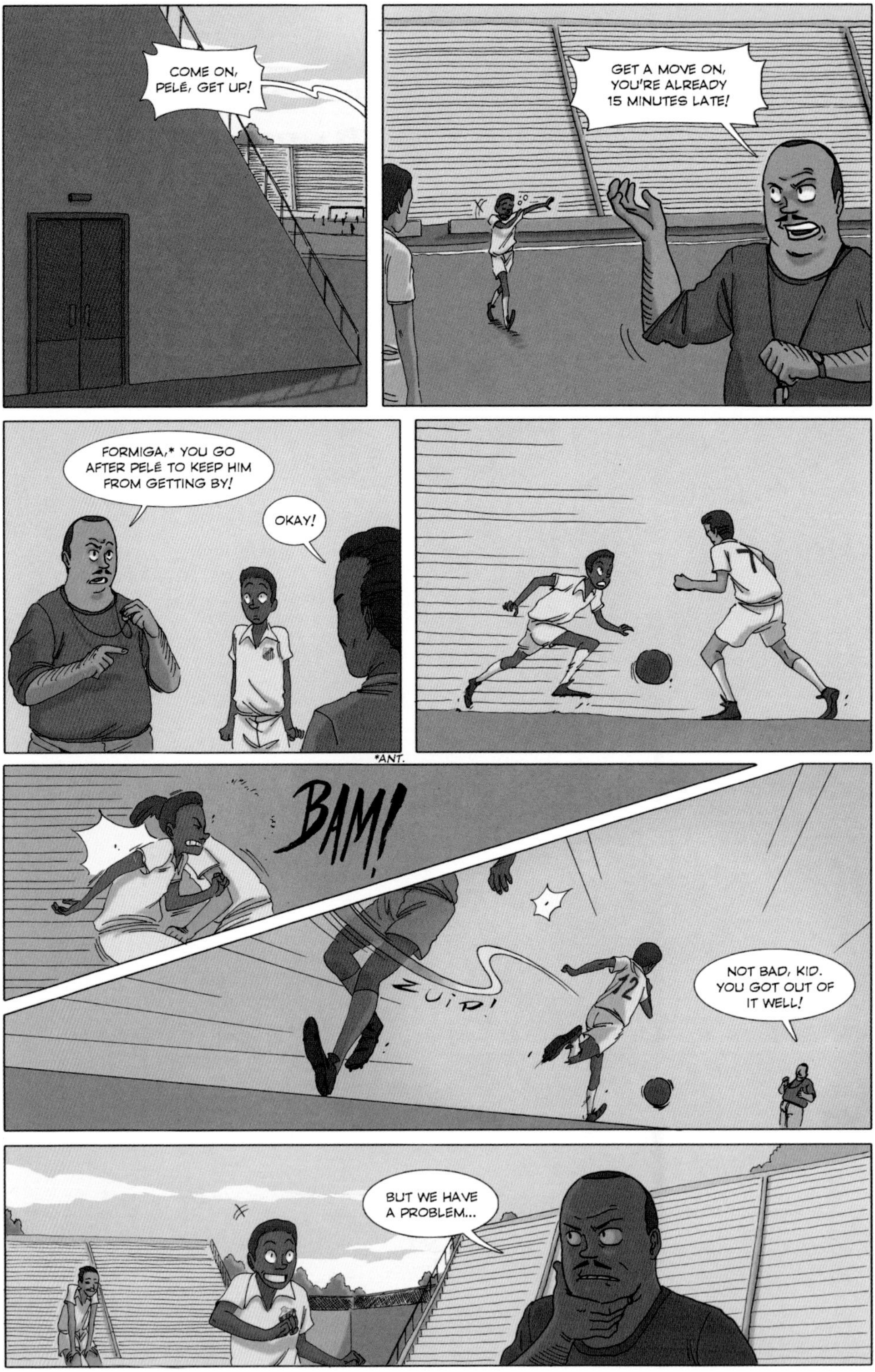
COME ON, PELÉ, GET UP!
GET A MOVE ON, YOU'RE ALREADY 15 MINUTES LATE!
FORMIGA,* YOU GO AFTER PELÉ TO KEEP HIM FROM GETTING BY!
OKAY!
*ANT.
BAM!
ZUiP!
NOT BAD, KID. YOU GOT OUT OF IT WELL!
BUT WE HAVE A PROBLEM...

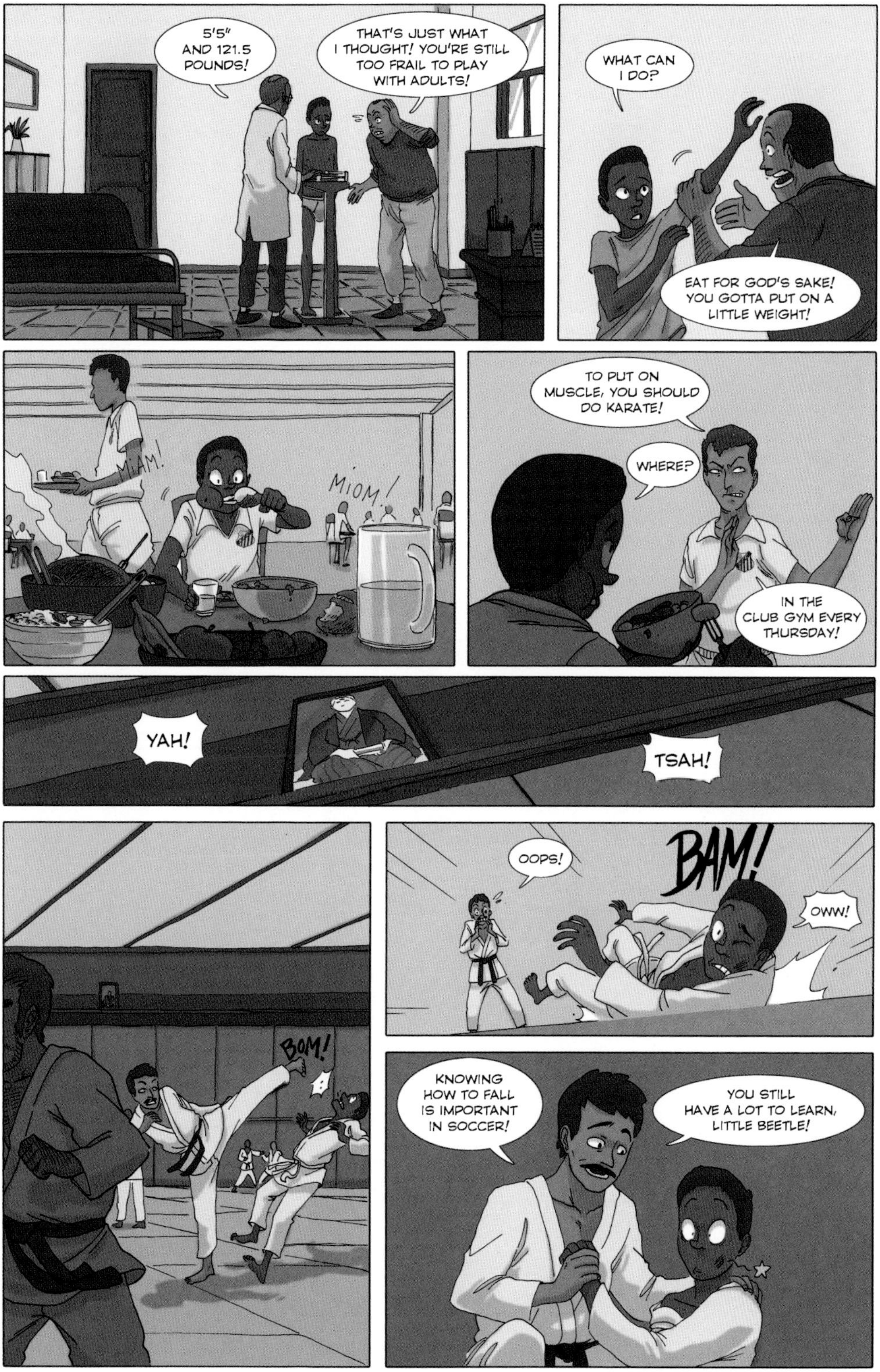
5'5" AND 121.5 POUNDS!
THAT'S JUST WHAT I THOUGHT! YOU'RE STILL TOO FRAIL TO PLAY WITH ADULTS!
WHAT CAN I DO?
EAT FOR GOD'S SAKE! YOU GOTTA PUT ON A LITTLE WEIGHT!
MIAM!
MIOM!
TO PUT ON MUSCLE, YOU SHOULD DO KARATE!
WHERE?
IN THE CLUB GYM EVERY THURSDAY!
YAH!
TSAH!
BOM!
OOPS!
BAM!
OWW!
KNOWING HOW TO FALL IS IMPORTANT IN SOCCER!
YOU STILL HAVE A LOT TO LEARN, LITTLE BEETLE!

DONDINHO ALWAYS TOLD HIS SON TALENT WAS OF LITTLE IMPORTANCE, YOU ALSO HAD TO KNOW HOW TO FORCE YOUR LUCK.

SHOWERS!

COMING!

PELÉ ENJOYS MAKING AN EFFORT. HE SPENDS HOURS ON THE FIELD HITTING THE BALL AGAIN AND AGAIN.

SUPPER!

FIVE MINUTES!

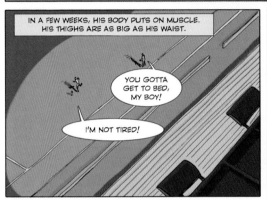

IN A FEW WEEKS, HIS BODY PUTS ON MUSCLE. HIS THIGHS ARE AS BIG AS HIS WAIST.

YOU GOTTA GET TO BED, MY BOY!

I'M NOT TIRED!

ALTHOUGH HE TRAINS WITH ADULTS, THE CLUB MAKES HIM PLAY WITH THE JUNIORS. WAS IT AN ILL OMEN?

AND THEN ONE FINE DAY—

YOUR TRIAL PERIOD'S OVER!

OH?! AND...

YOU HAVE BEAUTIFUL SKILLS AND YOU PERSEVERE!

HERE'S YOUR TEAM CONTRACT!

WELCOME TO THE BEST TEAM IN BRAZIL, CHAMP!

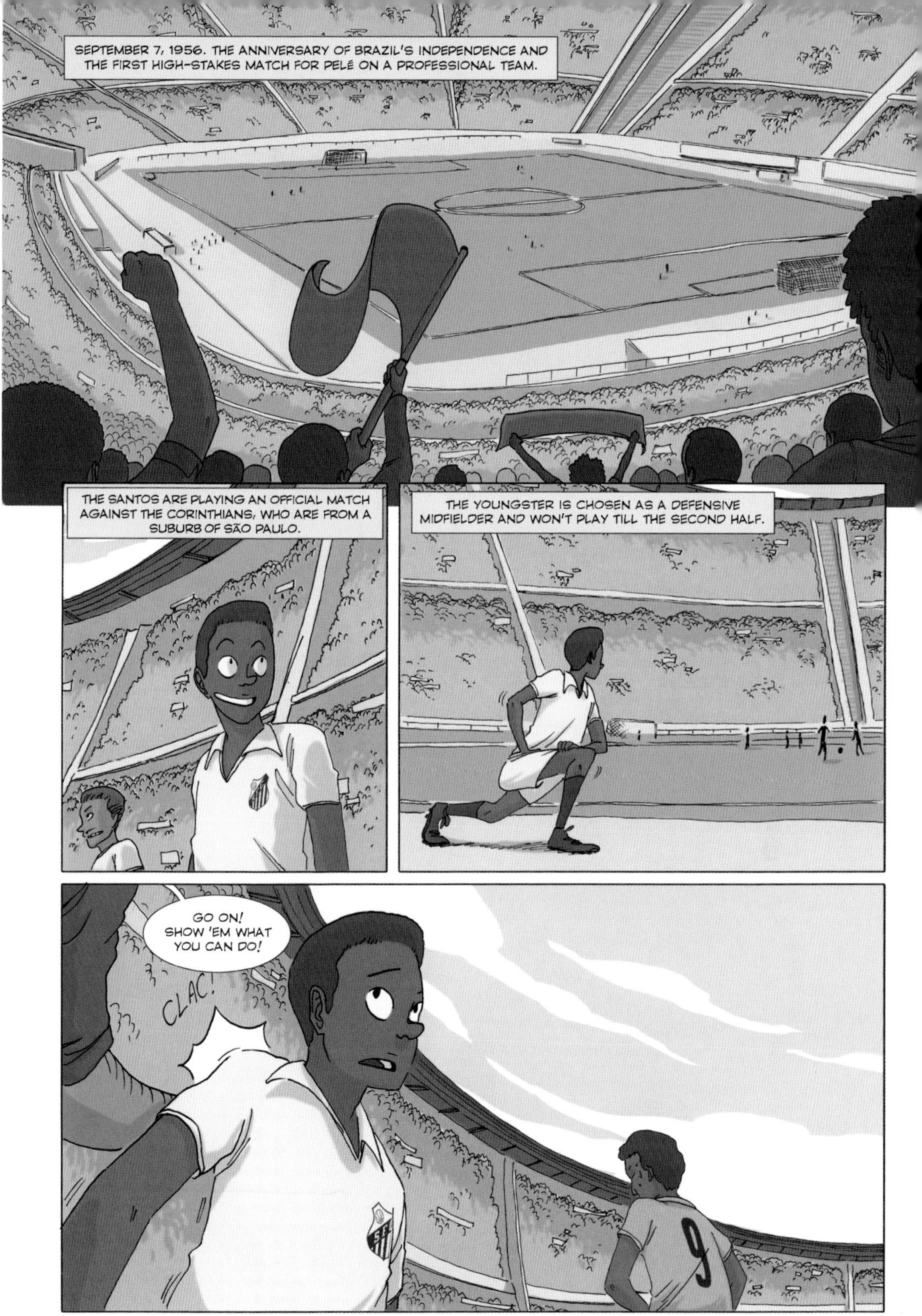

SEPTEMBER 7, 1956. THE ANNIVERSARY OF BRAZIL'S INDEPENDENCE AND THE FIRST HIGH-STAKES MATCH FOR PELÉ ON A PROFESSIONAL TEAM.
THE SANTOS ARE PLAYING AN OFFICIAL MATCH AGAINST THE CORINTHIANS, WHO ARE FROM A SUBURB OF SÃO PAULO.
THE YOUNGSTER IS CHOSEN AS A DEFENSIVE MIDFIELDER AND WON'T PLAY TILL THE SECOND HALF.
GO ON! SHOW 'EM WHAT YOU CAN DO!
CLAC!

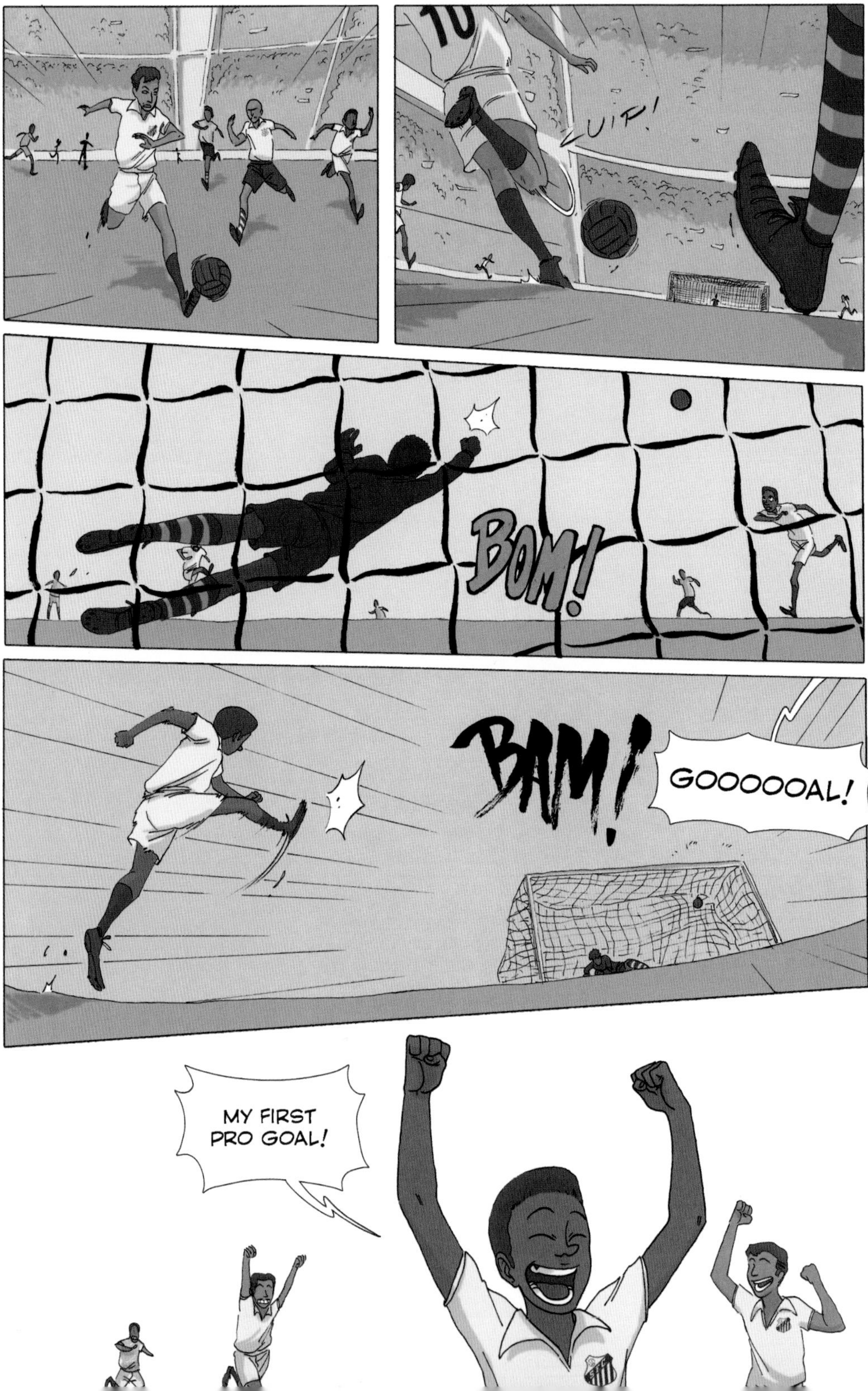
BOM!
BAM!
GOOOOOAL!
MY FIRST PRO GOAL!

Chapter 3
1958, the Birth of a King

"The Santos number 10 jersey was unquestionably mine—
until the arrival of a little black kid with legs as big as matchsticks,
who went down in history by the name of Pelé." —Vasco Vasconcelos

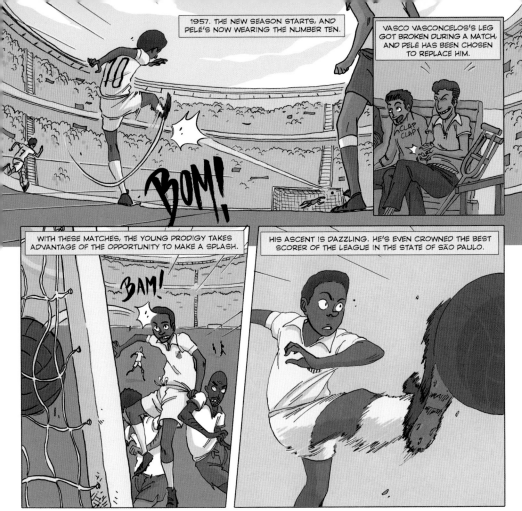

1957. THE NEW SEASON STARTS, AND PELÉ'S NOW WEARING THE NUMBER TEN.

VASCO VASCONCELOS'S LEG GOT BROKEN DURING A MATCH, AND PELÉ HAS BEEN CHOSEN TO REPLACE HIM.

BOM!

CLAP CLAP

WITH THESE MATCHES, THE YOUNG PRODIGY TAKES ADVANTAGE OF THE OPPORTUNITY TO MAKE A SPLASH.

BAM!

HIS ASCENT IS DAZZLING. HE'S EVEN CROWNED THE BEST SCORER OF THE LEAGUE IN THE STATE OF SÃO PAULO.

HIS NAME ENDLESSLY THUNDERS THROUGH THE STADIUM.

PELÉ! PELÉ!

GOOD JOB, KID! MY JERSEY'S IN GOOD HANDS FROM NOW ON!

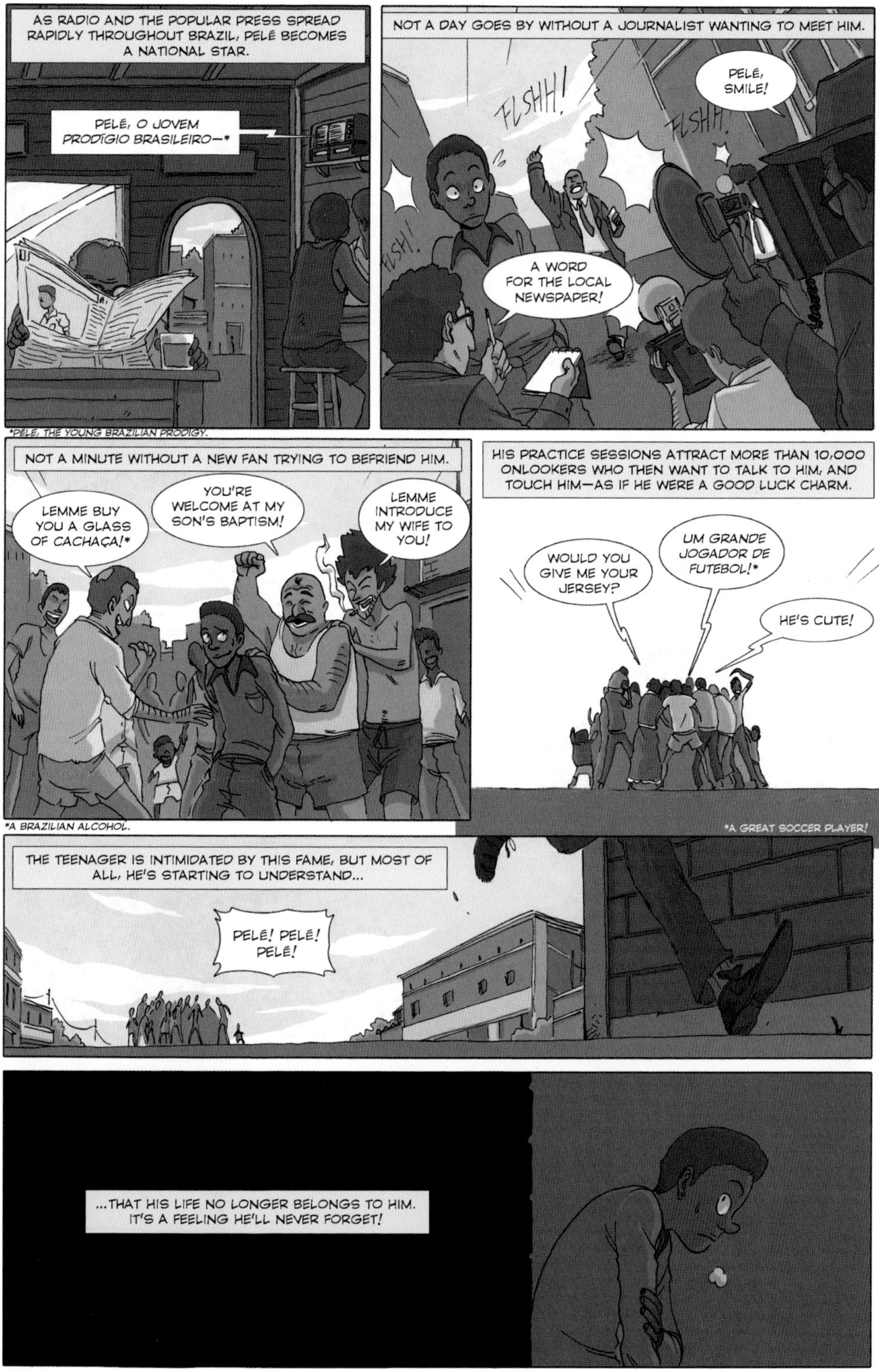

AS RADIO AND THE POPULAR PRESS SPREAD RAPIDLY THROUGHOUT BRAZIL, PELÉ BECOMES A NATIONAL STAR.
PELÉ, O JOVEM PRODÍGIO BRASILEIRO—*
*PELÉ, THE YOUNG BRAZILIAN PRODIGY.
NOT A DAY GOES BY WITHOUT A JOURNALIST WANTING TO MEET HIM.
FLSHH!
FLSHH!
PELÉ, SMILE!
FLSH!
A WORD FOR THE LOCAL NEWSPAPER!
NOT A MINUTE WITHOUT A NEW FAN TRYING TO BEFRIEND HIM.
LEMME BUY YOU A GLASS OF CACHAÇA!*
YOU'RE WELCOME AT MY SON'S BAPTISM!
LEMME INTRODUCE MY WIFE TO YOU!
*A BRAZILIAN ALCOHOL.
HIS PRACTICE SESSIONS ATTRACT MORE THAN 10,000 ONLOOKERS WHO THEN WANT TO TALK TO HIM, AND TOUCH HIM—AS IF HE WERE A GOOD LUCK CHARM.
WOULD YOU GIVE ME YOUR JERSEY?
UM GRANDE JOGADOR DE FUTEBOL!*
HE'S CUTE!
*A GREAT SOCCER PLAYER!
THE TEENAGER IS INTIMIDATED BY THIS FAME, BUT MOST OF ALL, HE'S STARTING TO UNDERSTAND...
PELÉ! PELÉ! PELÉ!
...THAT HIS LIFE NO LONGER BELONGS TO HIM. IT'S A FEELING HE'LL NEVER FORGET!

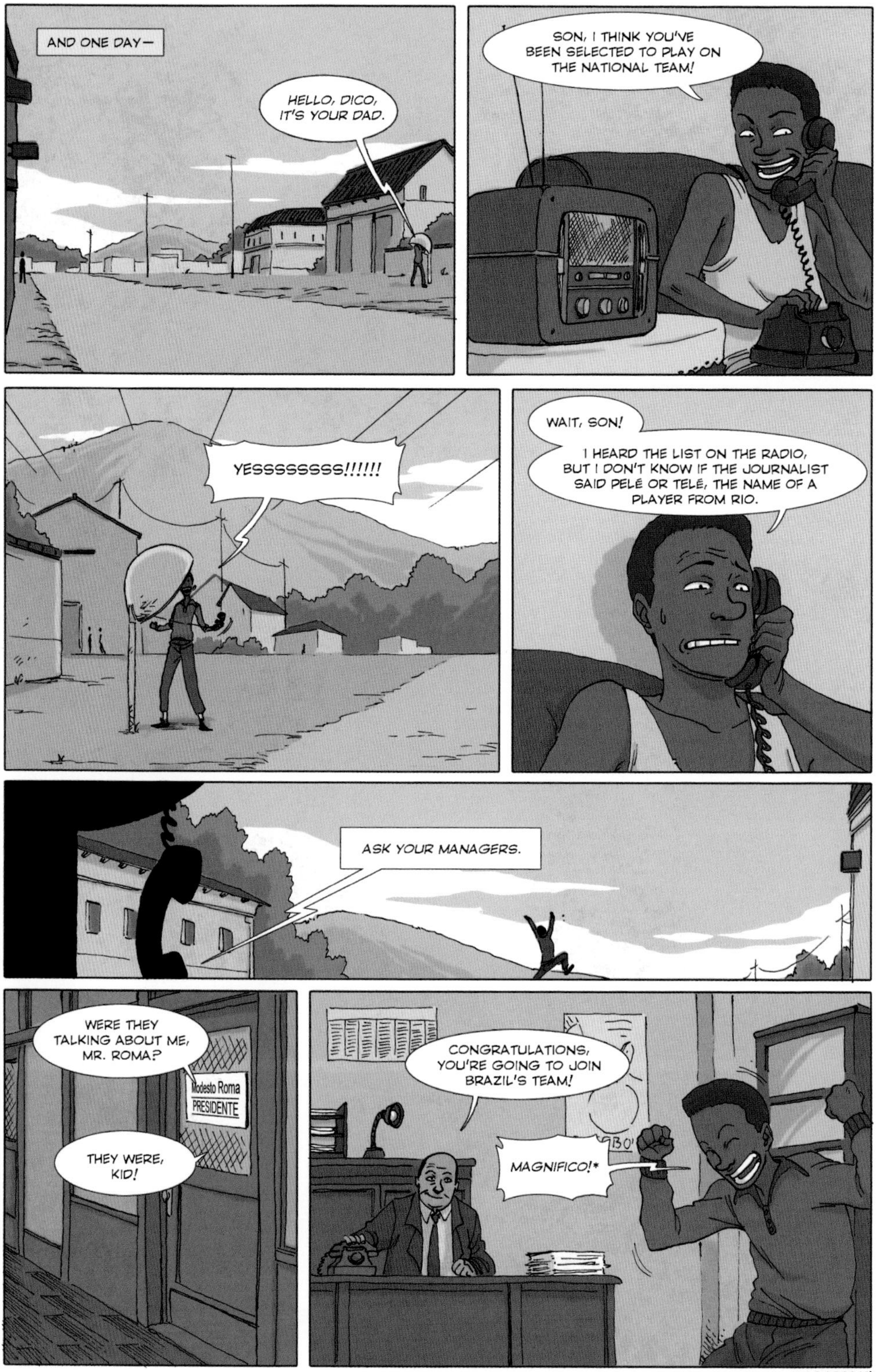
AND ONE DAY—
HELLO, DICO, IT'S YOUR DAD.
SON, I THINK YOU'VE BEEN SELECTED TO PLAY ON THE NATIONAL TEAM!
YESSSSSSSS!!!!!!
WAIT, SON!
I HEARD THE LIST ON THE RADIO, BUT I DON'T KNOW IF THE JOURNALIST SAID PELÉ OR TELÉ, THE NAME OF A PLAYER FROM RIO.
ASK YOUR MANAGERS.
WERE THEY TALKING ABOUT ME, MR. ROMA?
Modesto Roma PRESIDENTE
THEY WERE, KID!
CONGRATULATIONS, YOU'RE GOING TO JOIN BRAZIL'S TEAM!
MAGNIFICO!*

*MAGNIFICENT!

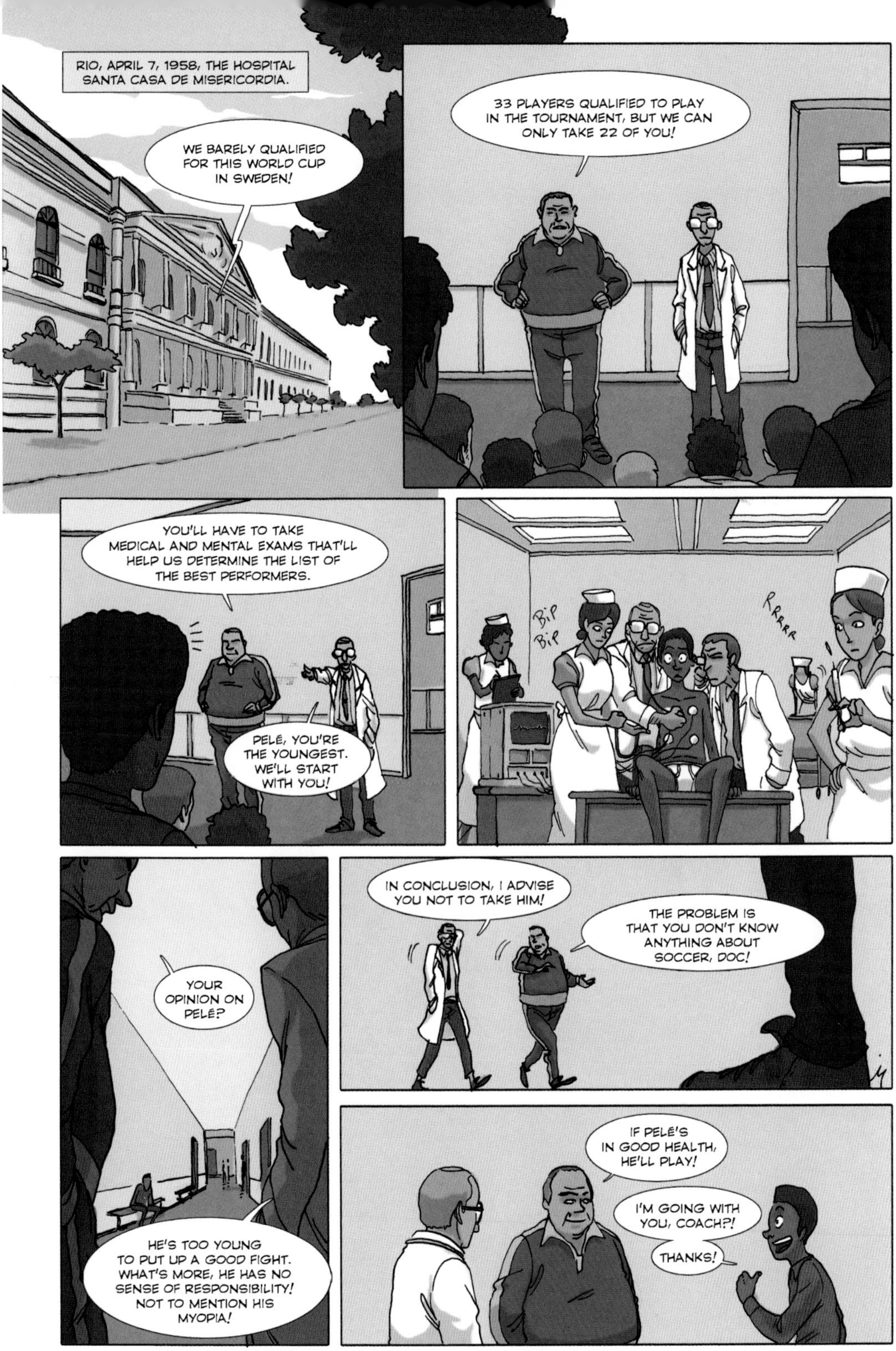
RIO, APRIL 7, 1958, THE HOSPITAL SANTA CASA DE MISERICORDIA.
WE BARELY QUALIFIED FOR THIS WORLD CUP IN SWEDEN!
33 PLAYERS QUALIFIED TO PLAY IN THE TOURNAMENT, BUT WE CAN ONLY TAKE 22 OF YOU!
YOU'LL HAVE TO TAKE MEDICAL AND MENTAL EXAMS THAT'LL HELP US DETERMINE THE LIST OF THE BEST PERFORMERS.
PELÉ, YOU'RE THE YOUNGEST. WE'LL START WITH YOU!
BIP BIP
RRRRR
YOUR OPINION ON PELÉ?
HE'S TOO YOUNG TO PUT UP A GOOD FIGHT. WHAT'S MORE, HE HAS NO SENSE OF RESPONSIBILITY! NOT TO MENTION HIS MYOPIA!
IN CONCLUSION, I ADVISE YOU NOT TO TAKE HIM!
THE PROBLEM IS THAT YOU DON'T KNOW ANYTHING ABOUT SOCCER, DOC!
IF PELÉ'S IN GOOD HEALTH, HE'LL PLAY!
I'M GOING WITH YOU, COACH?!
THANKS!

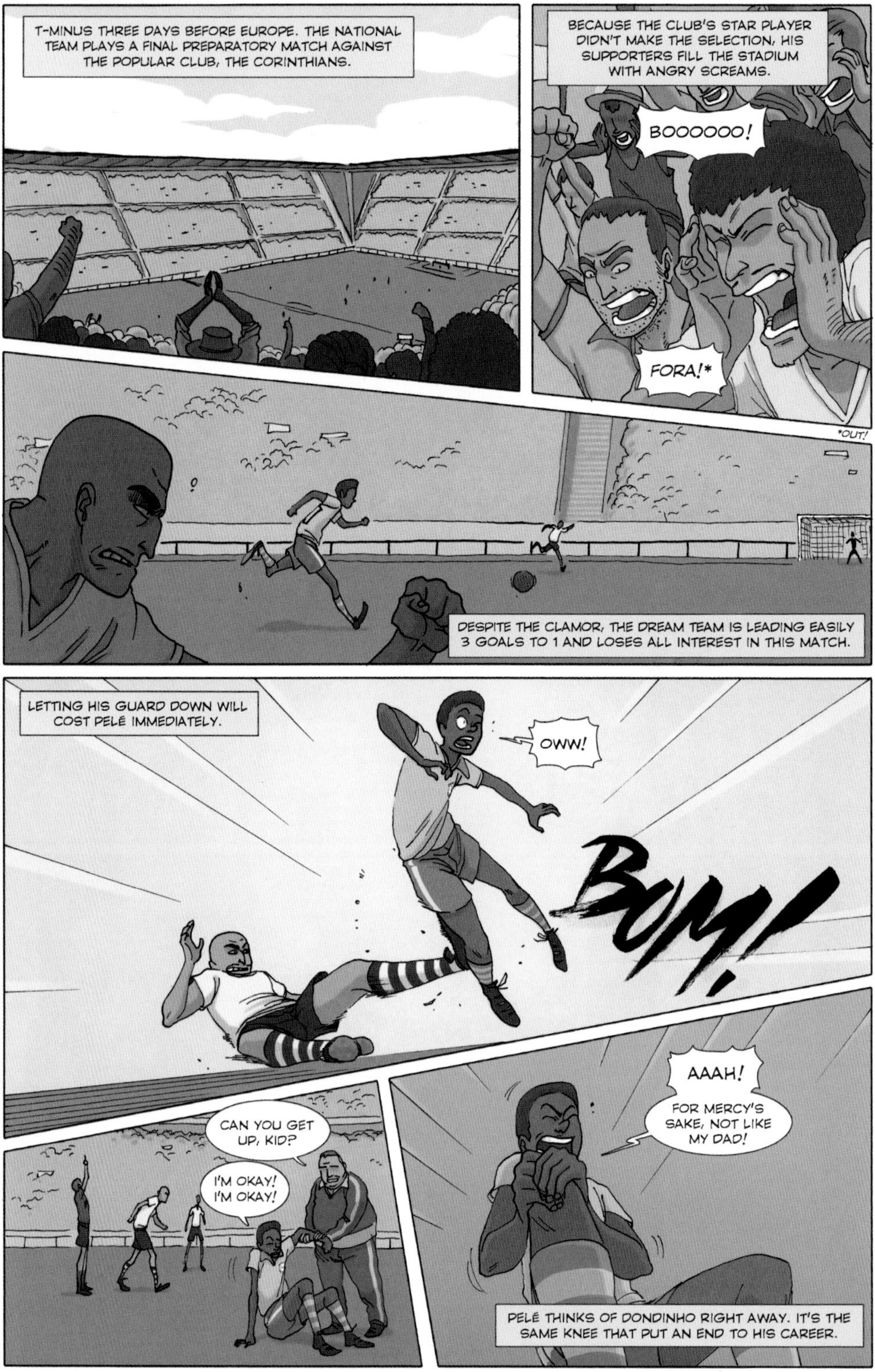
T-MINUS THREE DAYS BEFORE EUROPE. THE NATIONAL TEAM PLAYS A FINAL PREPARATORY MATCH AGAINST THE POPULAR CLUB, THE CORINTHIANS.
BECAUSE THE CLUB'S STAR PLAYER DIDN'T MAKE THE SELECTION, HIS SUPPORTERS FILL THE STADIUM WITH ANGRY SCREAMS.
BOOOOOO!
FORA!*
*OUT!
DESPITE THE CLAMOR, THE DREAM TEAM IS LEADING EASILY 3 GOALS TO 1 AND LOSES ALL INTEREST IN THIS MATCH.
LETTING HIS GUARD DOWN WILL COST PELÉ IMMEDIATELY.
OWW!
BUM!
CAN YOU GET UP, KID?
I'M OKAY! I'M OKAY!
AAAH!
FOR MERCY'S SAKE, NOT LIKE MY DAD!
PELÉ THINKS OF DONDINHO RIGHT AWAY. IT'S THE SAME KNEE THAT PUT AN END TO HIS CAREER.

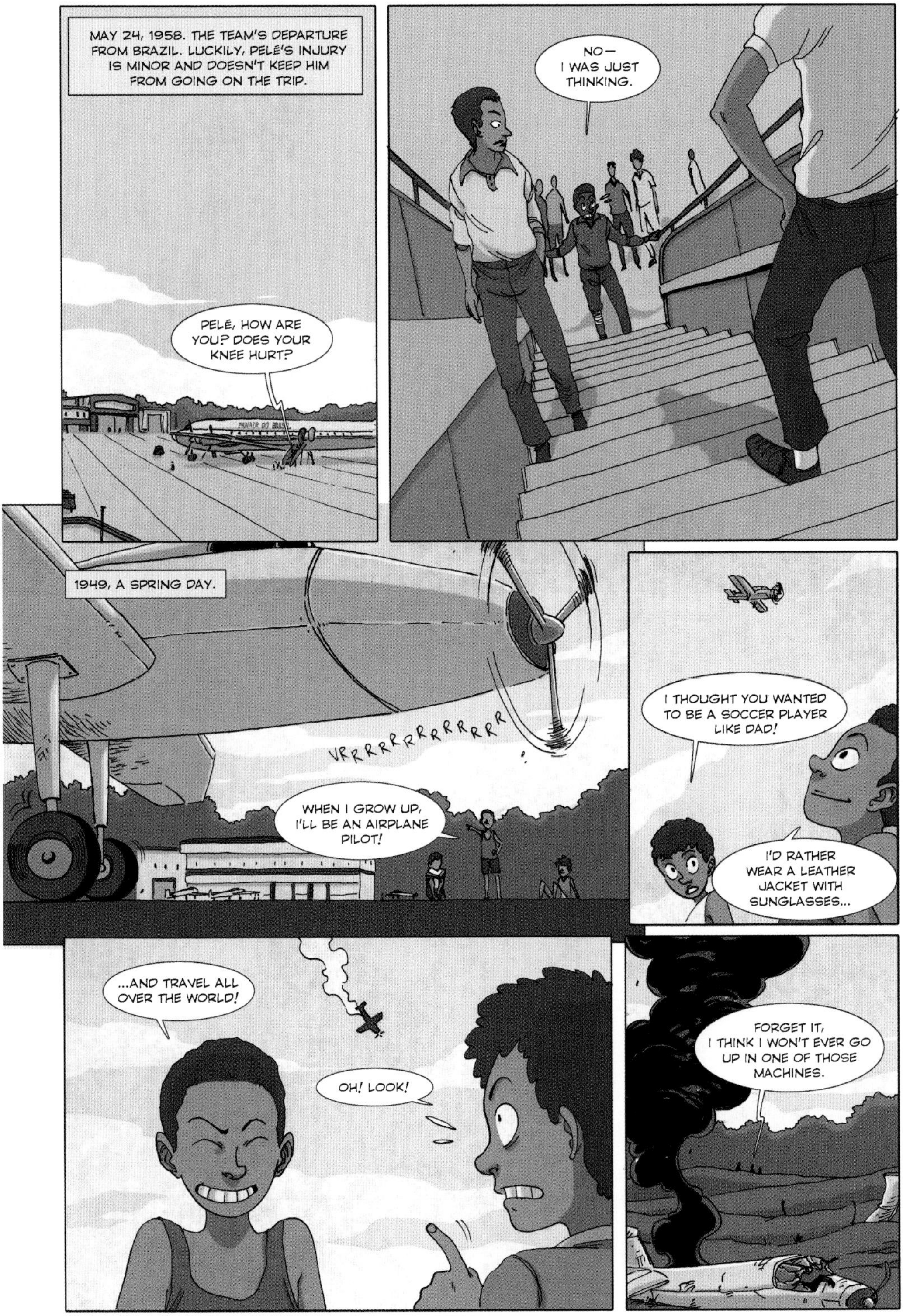
MAY 24, 1958. THE TEAM'S DEPARTURE FROM BRAZIL. LUCKILY, PELÉ'S INJURY IS MINOR AND DOESN'T KEEP HIM FROM GOING ON THE TRIP.
PELÉ, HOW ARE YOU? DOES YOUR KNEE HURT?
NO— I WAS JUST THINKING.
1949, A SPRING DAY.
VRRRRRRRRRRRRRR
WHEN I GROW UP, I'LL BE AN AIRPLANE PILOT!
I THOUGHT YOU WANTED TO BE A SOCCER PLAYER LIKE DAD!
I'D RATHER WEAR A LEATHER JACKET WITH SUNGLASSES...
...AND TRAVEL ALL OVER THE WORLD!
OH! LOOK!
FORGET IT, I THINK I WON'T EVER GO UP IN ONE OF THOSE MACHINES.

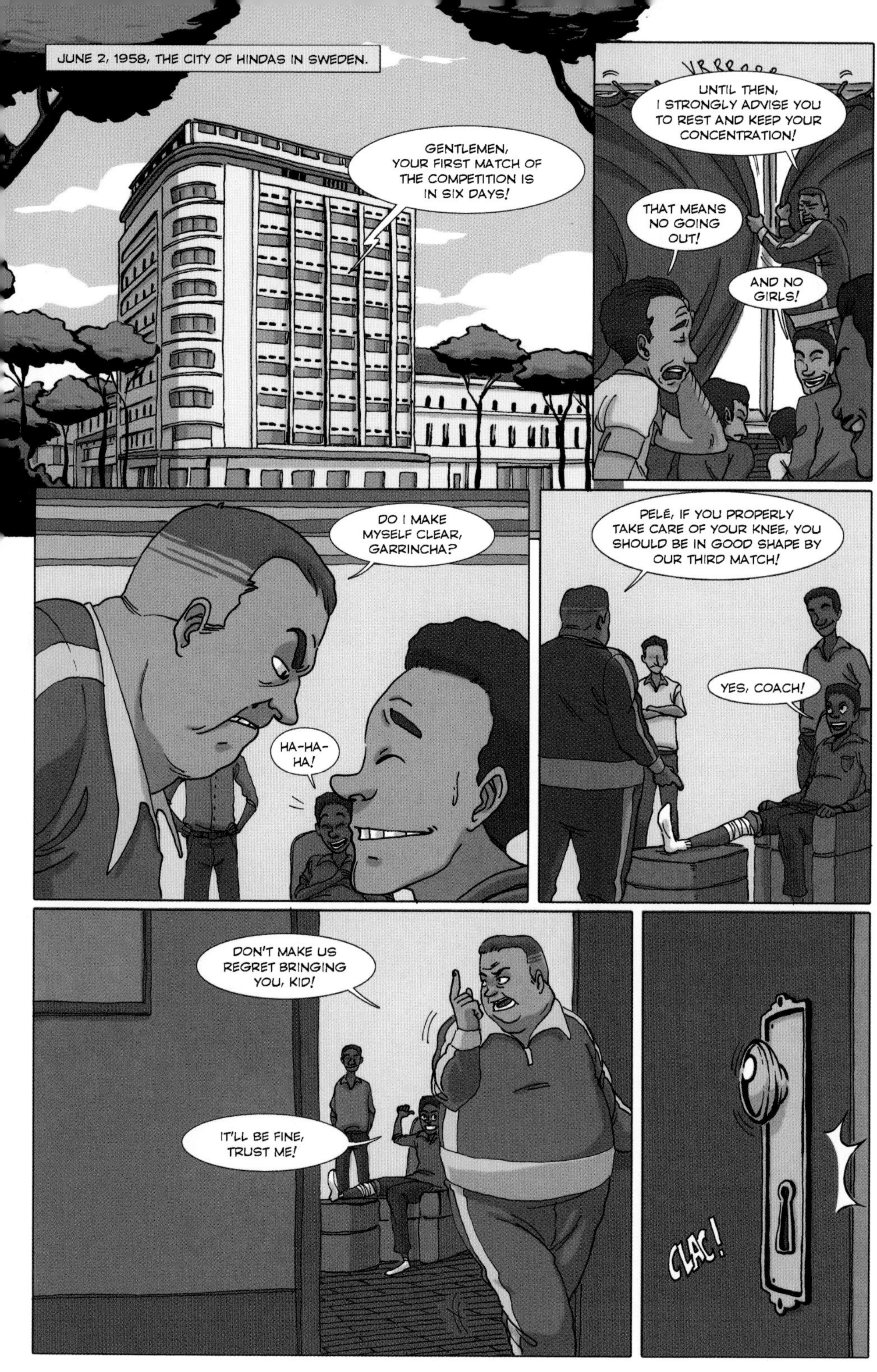

JUNE 2, 1958, THE CITY OF HINDAS IN SWEDEN.
GENTLEMEN, YOUR FIRST MATCH OF THE COMPETITION IS IN SIX DAYS!
VRRRooo
UNTIL THEN, I STRONGLY ADVISE YOU TO REST AND KEEP YOUR CONCENTRATION!
THAT MEANS NO GOING OUT!
AND NO GIRLS!
DO I MAKE MYSELF CLEAR, GARRINCHA?
HA-HA-HA!
PELÉ, IF YOU PROPERLY TAKE CARE OF YOUR KNEE, YOU SHOULD BE IN GOOD SHAPE BY OUR THIRD MATCH!
YES, COACH!
DON'T MAKE US REGRET BRINGING YOU, KID!
IT'LL BE FINE, TRUST ME!
CLAC!

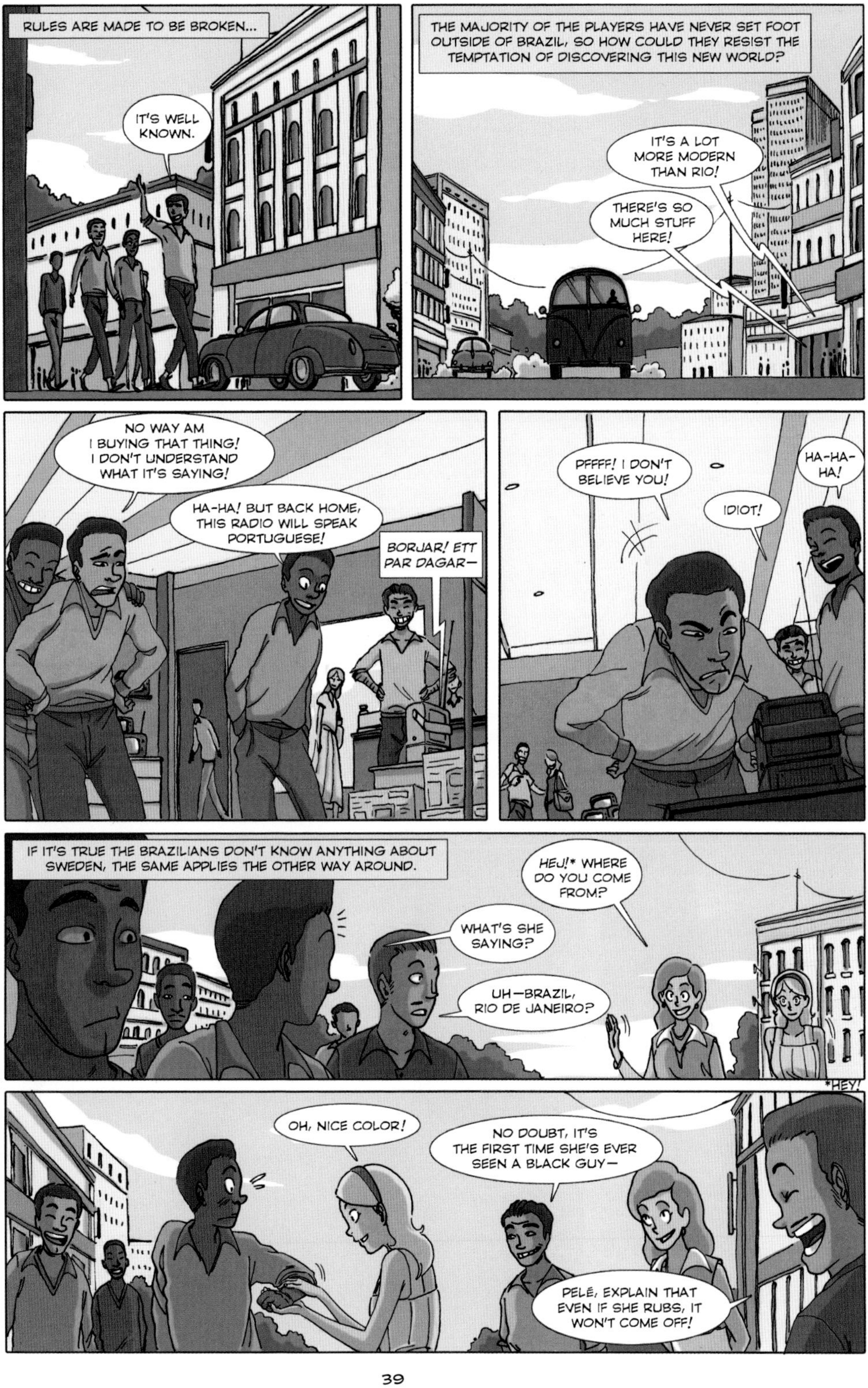
RULES ARE MADE TO BE BROKEN...
IT'S WELL KNOWN.
THE MAJORITY OF THE PLAYERS HAVE NEVER SET FOOT OUTSIDE OF BRAZIL, SO HOW COULD THEY RESIST THE TEMPTATION OF DISCOVERING THIS NEW WORLD?
IT'S A LOT MORE MODERN THAN RIO!
THERE'S SO MUCH STUFF HERE!
NO WAY AM I BUYING THAT THING! I DON'T UNDERSTAND WHAT IT'S SAYING!
HA-HA! BUT BACK HOME, THIS RADIO WILL SPEAK PORTUGUESE!
BORJAR! ETT PAR DAGAR—
PFFFF! I DON'T BELIEVE YOU!
IDIOT!
HA-HA-HA!
IF IT'S TRUE THE BRAZILIANS DON'T KNOW ANYTHING ABOUT SWEDEN, THE SAME APPLIES THE OTHER WAY AROUND.
HEJ!* WHERE DO YOU COME FROM?
WHAT'S SHE SAYING?
UH—BRAZIL, RIO DE JANEIRO?
*HEY!
OH, NICE COLOR!
NO DOUBT, IT'S THE FIRST TIME SHE'S EVER SEEN A BLACK GUY—
PELÉ, EXPLAIN THAT EVEN IF SHE RUBS, IT WON'T COME OFF!

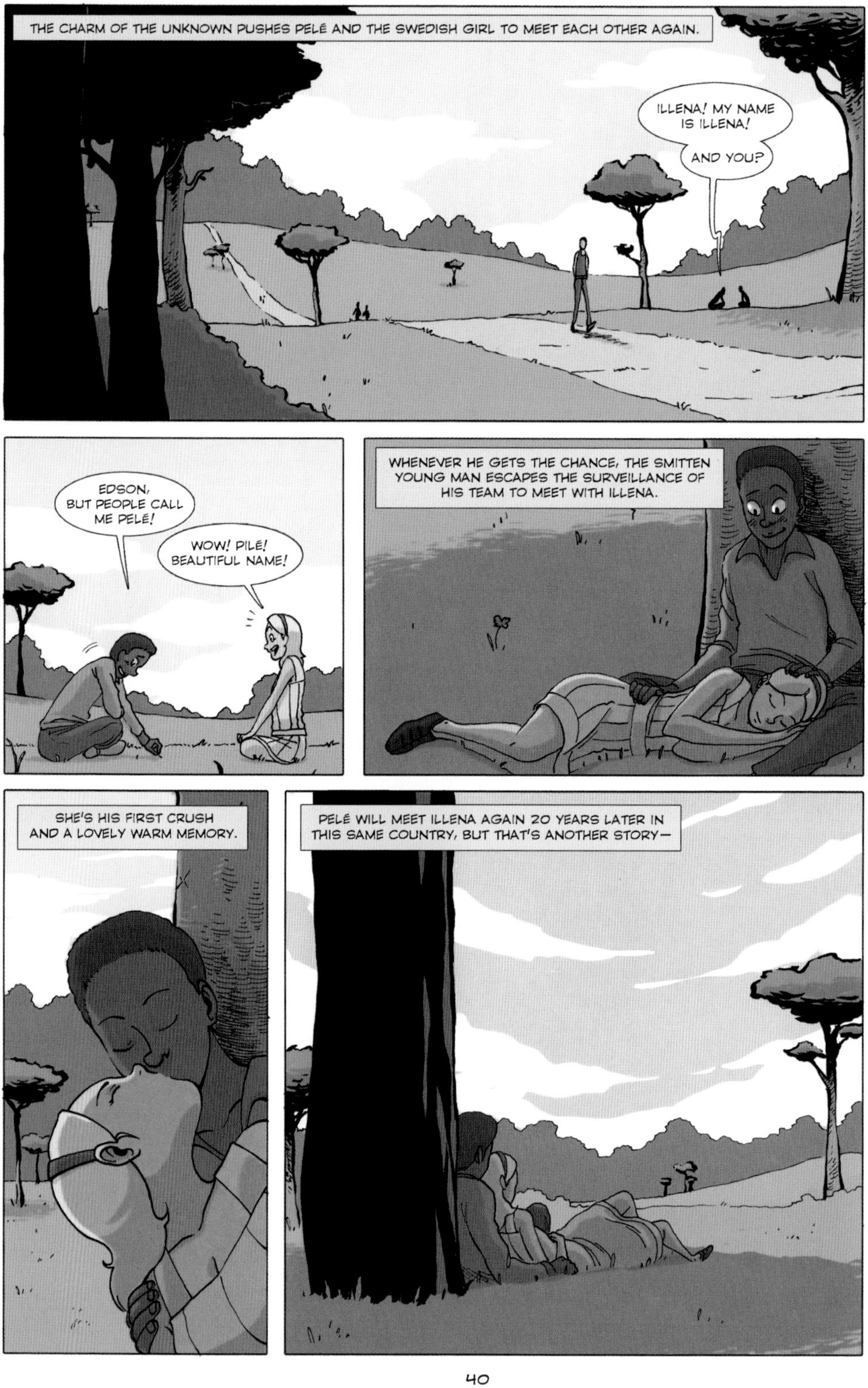
THE CHARM OF THE UNKNOWN PUSHES PELÉ AND THE SWEDISH GIRL TO MEET EACH OTHER AGAIN.
ILLENA! MY NAME IS ILLENA!
AND YOU?
EDSON, BUT PEOPLE CALL ME PELÉ!
WOW! PILÉ! BEAUTIFUL NAME!
WHENEVER HE GETS THE CHANCE, THE SMITTEN YOUNG MAN ESCAPES THE SURVEILLANCE OF HIS TEAM TO MEET WITH ILLENA.
SHE'S HIS FIRST CRUSH AND A LOVELY WARM MEMORY.
PELÉ WILL MEET ILLENA AGAIN 20 YEARS LATER IN THIS SAME COUNTRY, BUT THAT'S ANOTHER STORY—

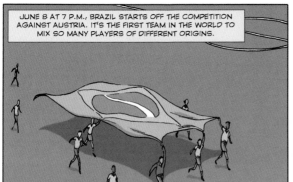

JUNE 8 AT 7 P.M., BRAZIL STARTS OFF THE COMPETITION AGAINST AUSTRIA. IT'S THE FIRST TEAM IN THE WORLD TO MIX SO MANY PLAYERS OF DIFFERENT ORIGINS.

THE 3—0 VICTORY DEFINITIVELY BONDS THE GROUP WHO IMPRESS ONLOOKERS WITH THEIR CREATIVE STYLE.

ON JUNE 11, THE BRAZILIANS MUST CONTENT THEMSELVES WITH A DISAPPOINTING 0—0 AGAINST ENGLAND.

WHEN DO I PLAY, MISTER FEOLA?

YOUR TIME WILL COME, KID!

AFTER THIS DRAW, YOU GOTTA LET GARRINCHA, PELÉ, AND ME PLAY, OR ELSE WE'RE HEADING FOR A DISASTER LIKE IN 1950!

WE'RE NOT HERE TO JUST WARM THE BENCH!

CALM DOWN, I HAVE A PLAN!

ON JUNE 15, THE OPPONENT IS THE USSR. IT'S THEIR FIRST TIME IN A WORLD CUP!

THE RUSSIANS HAVE JUST REELED OFF TWO CONSECUTIVE WINS. THEIR ATTACKERS ARE DANGEROUS AND UNPREDICTABLE!

WE NEED THREE STARS TO SHINE FOR US AND GET US THAT WIN!

I THINK THE MOMENT HAS COME FOR US!

HUH?

DIDI! PELÉ! GARRINCHA! IT'S UP TO YOU TO SPARK THE FLAME!

ABOUT TIME!

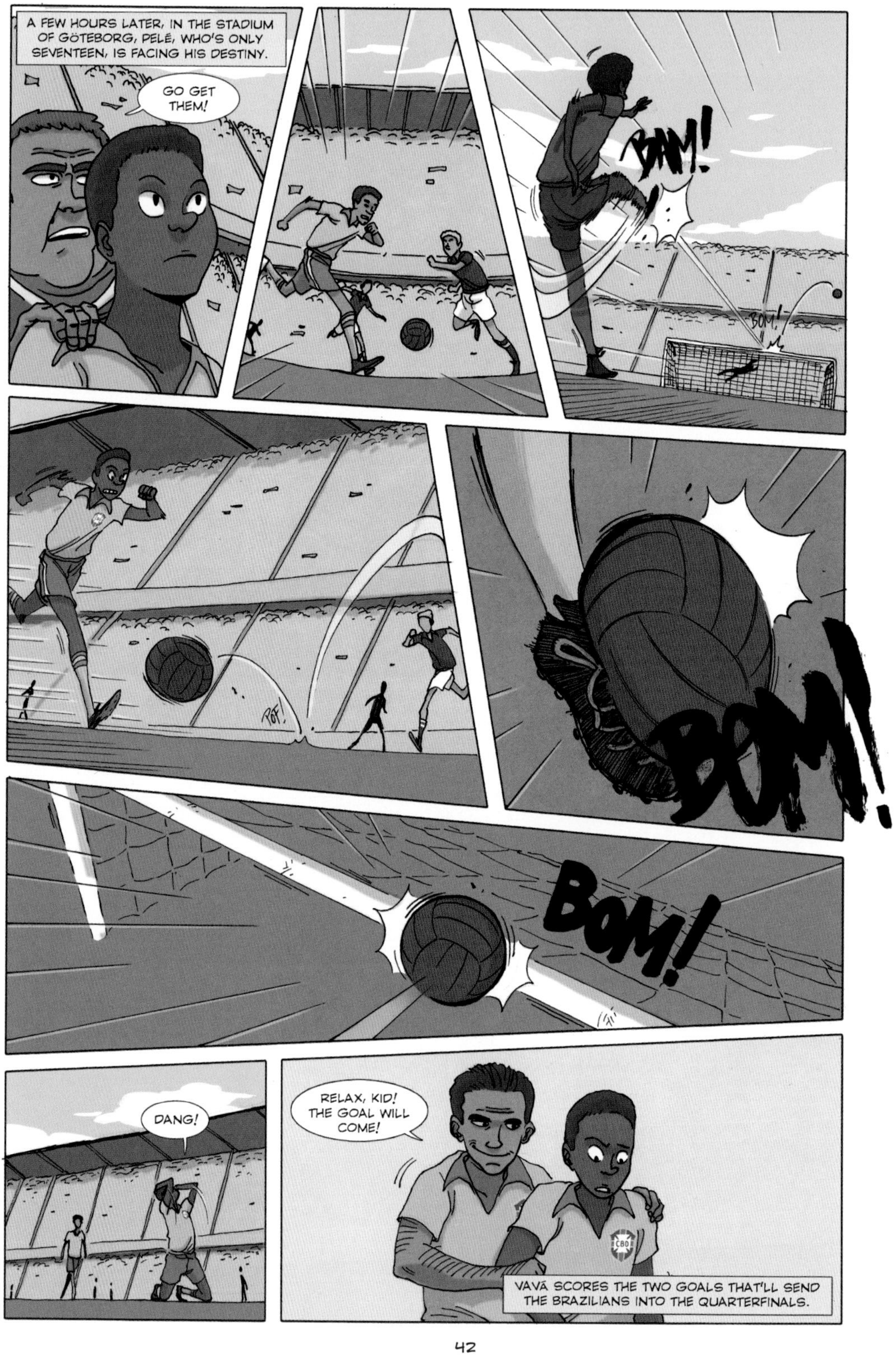
A FEW HOURS LATER, IN THE STADIUM OF GÖTEBORG, PELÉ, WHO'S ONLY SEVENTEEN, IS FACING HIS DESTINY.
GO GET THEM!
BAM!
BOM!
POF!
BOM!
BOM!
DANG!
RELAX, KID! THE GOAL WILL COME!
VAVÁ SCORES THE TWO GOALS THAT'LL SEND THE BRAZILIANS INTO THE QUARTERFINALS.

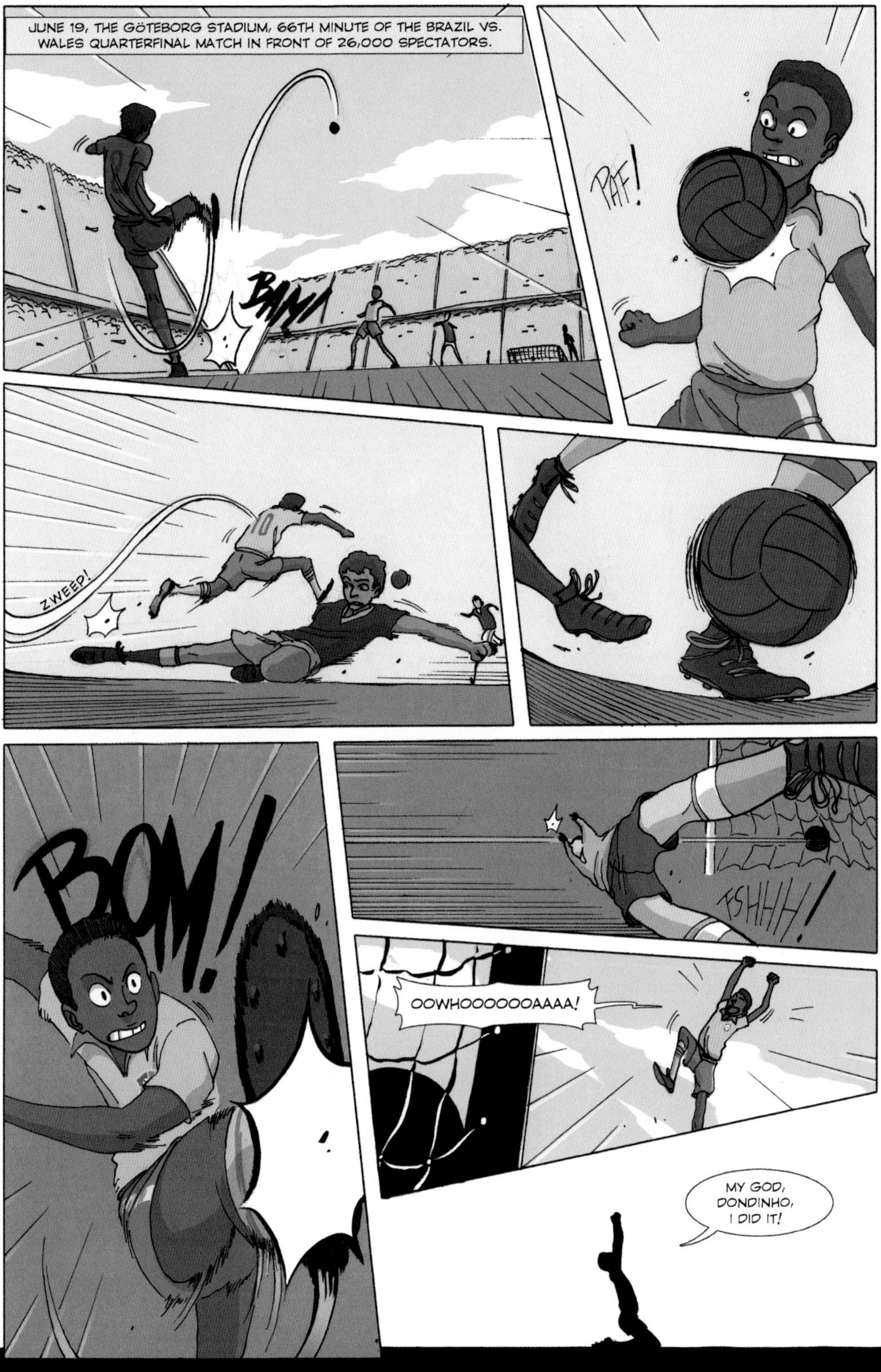
JUNE 19, THE GÖTEBORG STADIUM, 66TH MINUTE OF THE BRAZIL VS. WALES QUARTERFINAL MATCH IN FRONT OF 26,000 SPECTATORS.
BAM!
PAF!
ZWEEP!
BOM!
TSHHH!
OOWHOOOOOOAAAA!
MY GOD, DONDINHO, I DID IT!

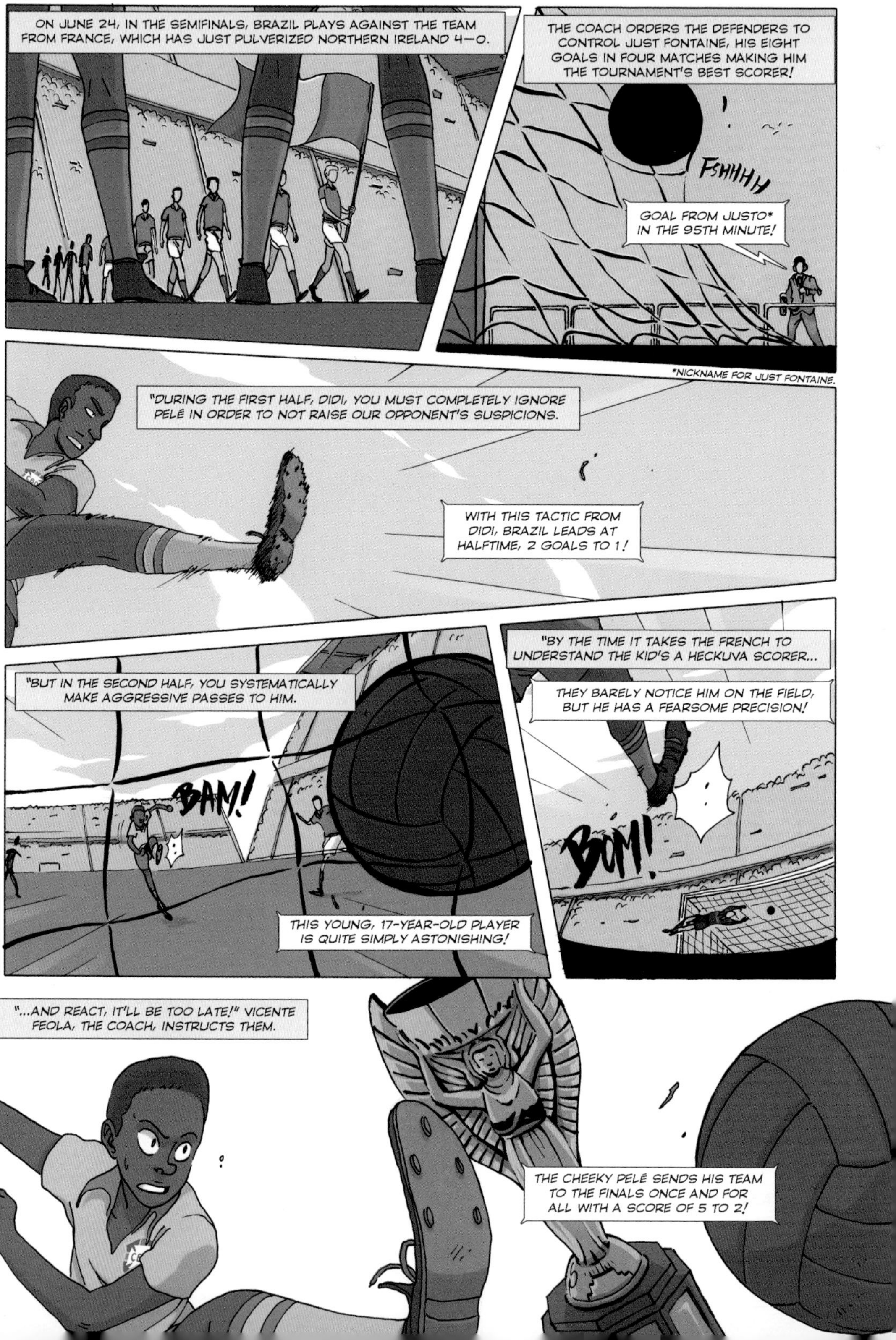

ON JUNE 24, IN THE SEMIFINALS, BRAZIL PLAYS AGAINST THE TEAM FROM FRANCE, WHICH HAS JUST PULVERIZED NORTHERN IRELAND 4–0.
THE COACH ORDERS THE DEFENDERS TO CONTROL JUST FONTAINE, HIS EIGHT GOALS IN FOUR MATCHES MAKING HIM THE TOURNAMENT'S BEST SCORER!
FSHHHH
GOAL FROM JUSTO* IN THE 95TH MINUTE!
*NICKNAME FOR JUST FONTAINE.
"DURING THE FIRST HALF, DIDI, YOU MUST COMPLETELY IGNORE PELÉ IN ORDER TO NOT RAISE OUR OPPONENT'S SUSPICIONS.
WITH THIS TACTIC FROM DIDI, BRAZIL LEADS AT HALFTIME, 2 GOALS TO 1!
"BUT IN THE SECOND HALF, YOU SYSTEMATICALLY MAKE AGGRESSIVE PASSES TO HIM.
BAM!
THIS YOUNG, 17-YEAR-OLD PLAYER IS QUITE SIMPLY ASTONISHING!
"BY THE TIME IT TAKES THE FRENCH TO UNDERSTAND THE KID'S A HECKUVA SCORER...
THEY BARELY NOTICE HIM ON THE FIELD, BUT HE HAS A FEARSOME PRECISION!
BOM!
"...AND REACT, IT'LL BE TOO LATE!" VICENTE FEOLA, THE COACH, INSTRUCTS THEM.
THE CHEEKY PELÉ SENDS HIS TEAM TO THE FINALS ONCE AND FOR ALL WITH A SCORE OF 5 TO 2!

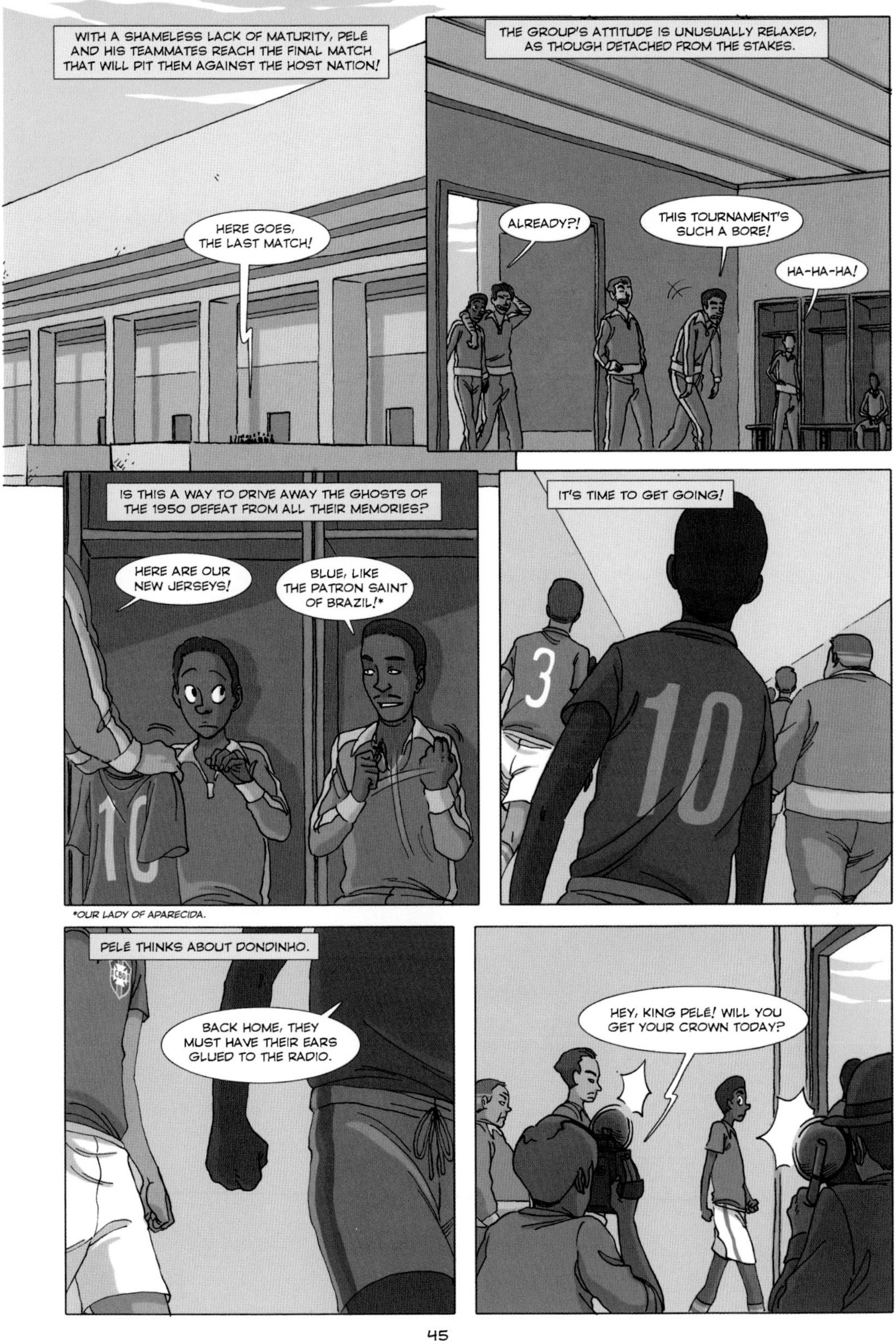
WITH A SHAMELESS LACK OF MATURITY, PELÉ AND HIS TEAMMATES REACH THE FINAL MATCH THAT WILL PIT THEM AGAINST THE HOST NATION!
HERE GOES, THE LAST MATCH!
THE GROUP'S ATTITUDE IS UNUSUALLY RELAXED, AS THOUGH DETACHED FROM THE STAKES.
ALREADY?!
THIS TOURNAMENT'S SUCH A BORE!
HA-HA-HA!
IS THIS A WAY TO DRIVE AWAY THE GHOSTS OF THE 1950 DEFEAT FROM ALL THEIR MEMORIES?
HERE ARE OUR NEW JERSEYS!
BLUE, LIKE THE PATRON SAINT OF BRAZIL!*
IT'S TIME TO GET GOING!
*OUR LADY OF APARECIDA.
PELÉ THINKS ABOUT DONDINHO.
BACK HOME, THEY MUST HAVE THEIR EARS GLUED TO THE RADIO.
HEY, KING PELÉ! WILL YOU GET YOUR CROWN TODAY?

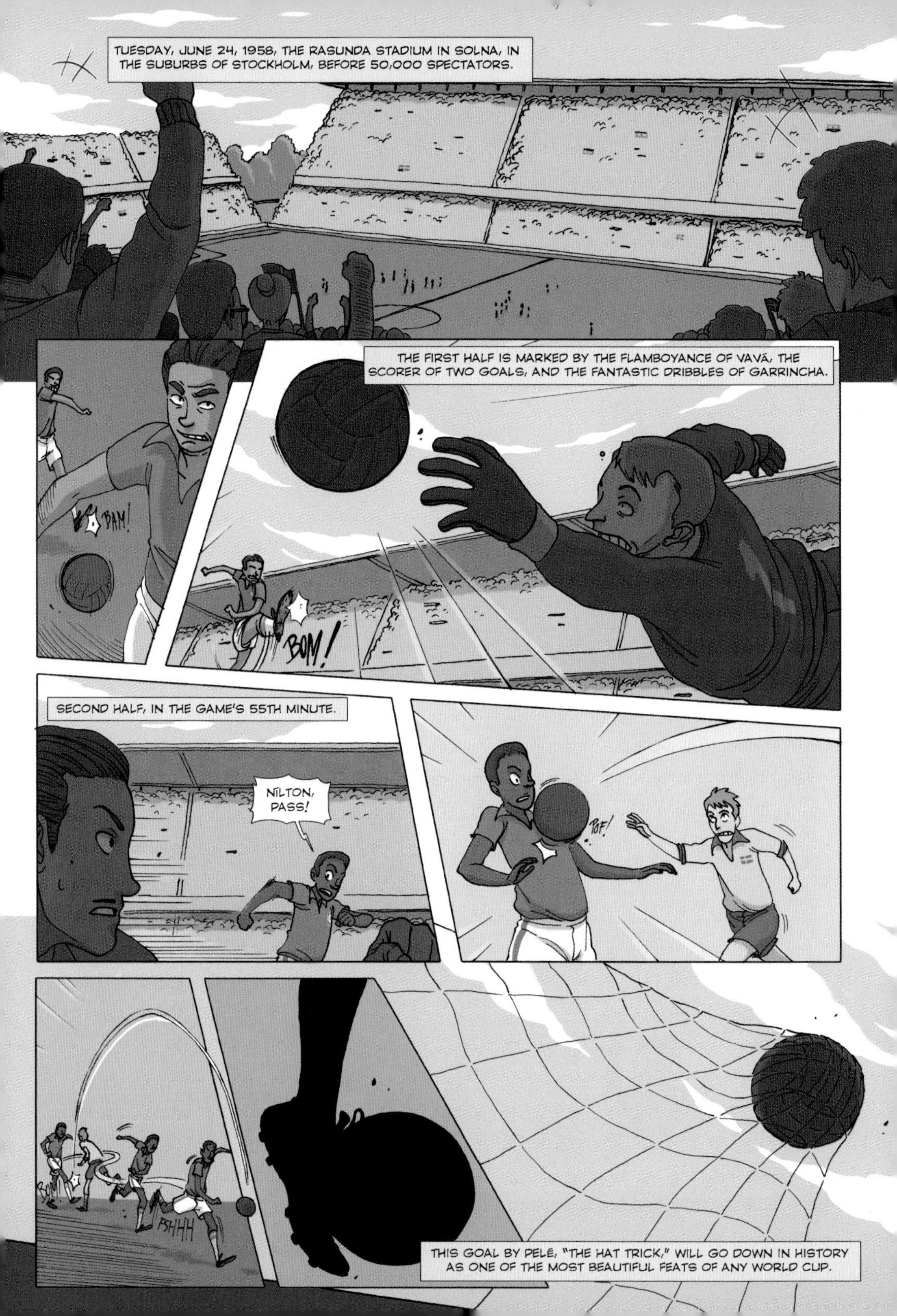
TUESDAY, JUNE 24, 1958, THE RASUNDA STADIUM IN SOLNA, IN THE SUBURBS OF STOCKHOLM, BEFORE 50,000 SPECTATORS.
BAM!
THE FIRST HALF IS MARKED BY THE FLAMBOYANCE OF VAVÁ, THE SCORER OF TWO GOALS, AND THE FANTASTIC DRIBBLES OF GARRINCHA.
BOM!
SECOND HALF, IN THE GAME'S 55TH MINUTE.
NILTON, PASS!
POF!
BOM!
FSHHH
THIS GOAL BY PELÉ, "THE HAT TRICK," WILL GO DOWN IN HISTORY AS ONE OF THE MOST BEAUTIFUL FEATS OF ANY WORLD CUP.

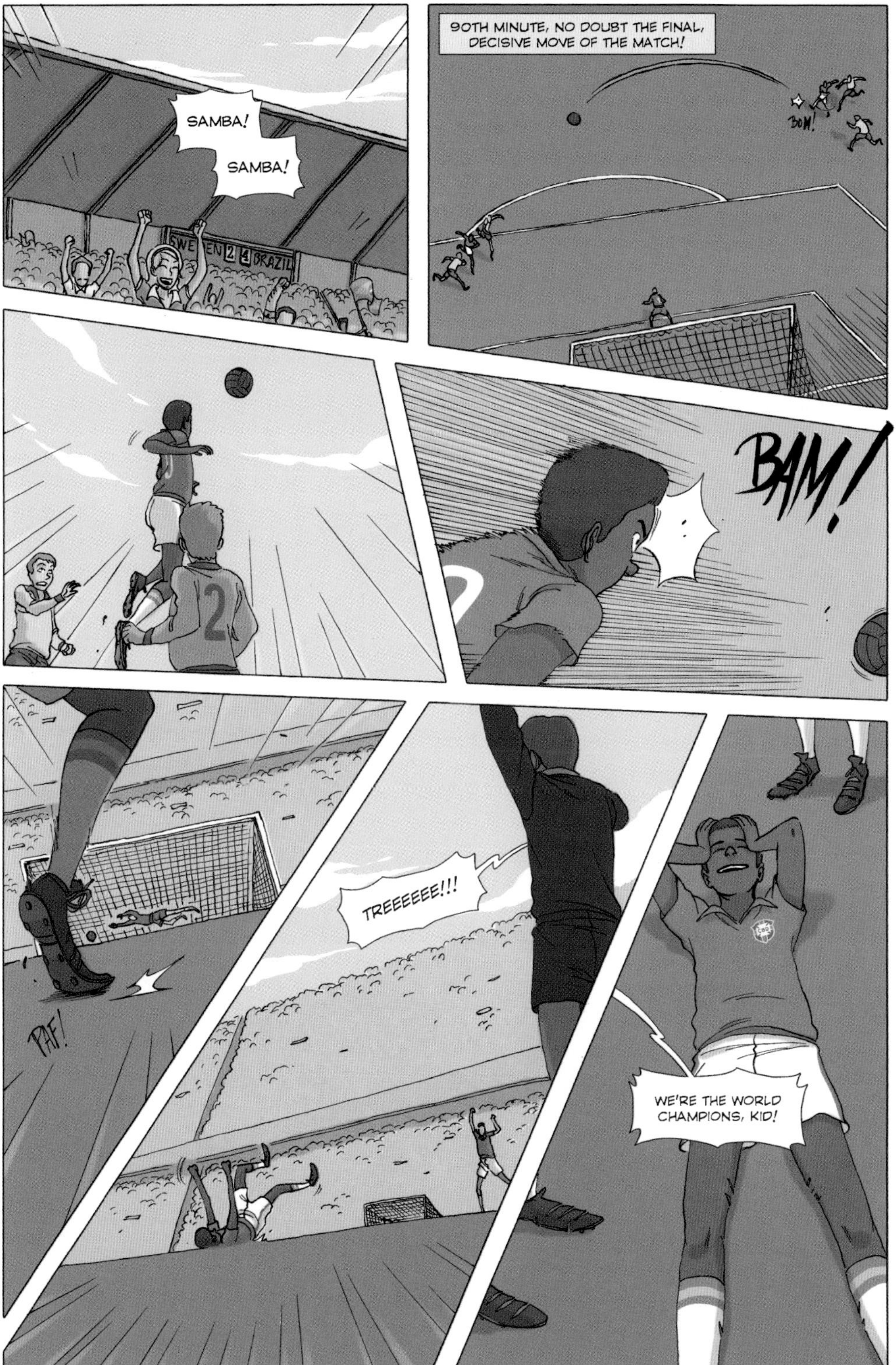
SAMBA!
SAMBA!
90TH MINUTE, NO DOUBT THE FINAL, DECISIVE MOVE OF THE MATCH!
BAM!
PAF!
TREEEEEE!!!
WE'RE THE WORLD CHAMPIONS, KID!

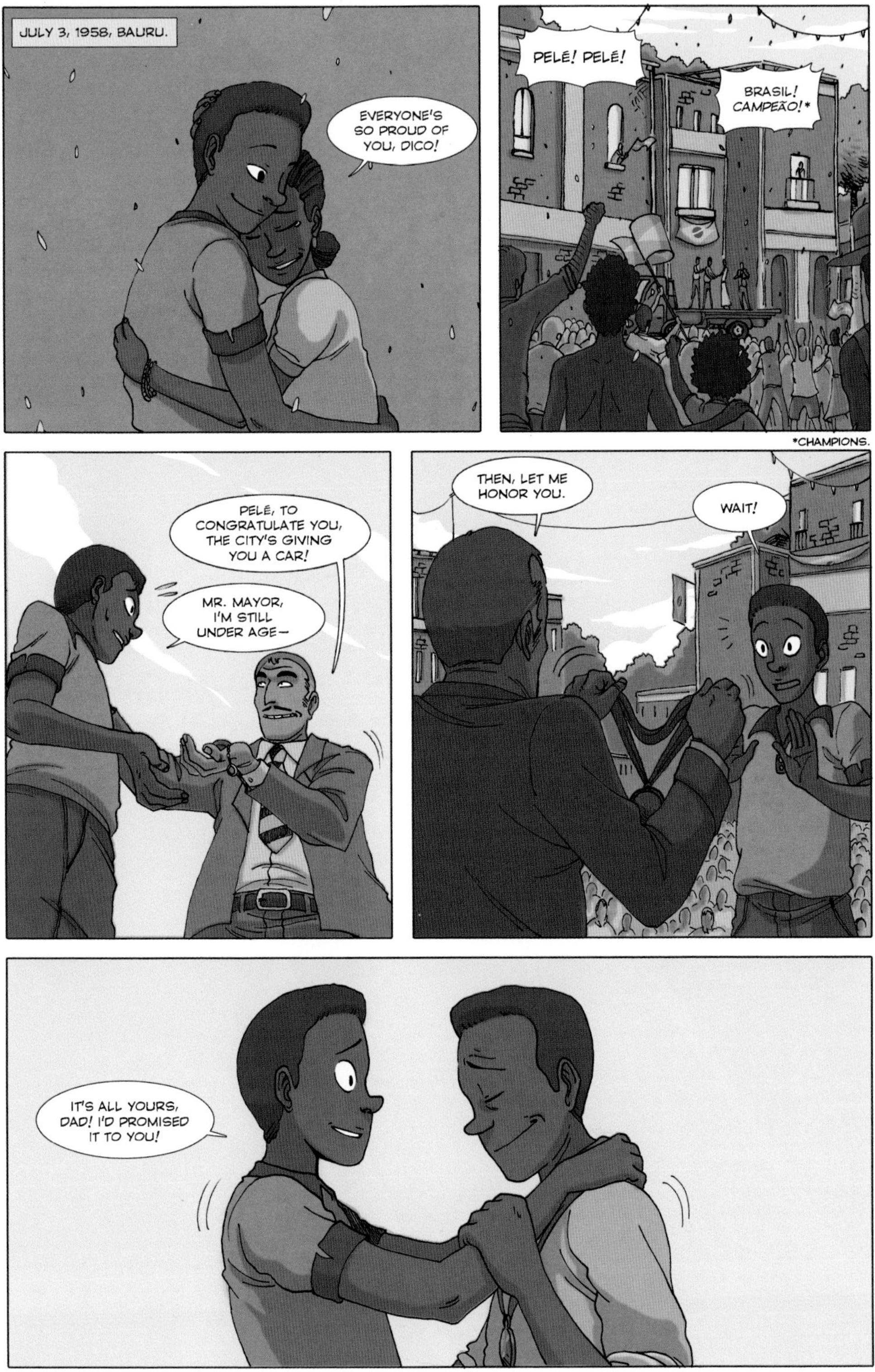
JULY 3, 1958, BAURU.
EVERYONE'S SO PROUD OF YOU, DICO!
PELÉ! PELÉ!
BRASIL! CAMPEÃO!*
*CHAMPIONS.
PELÉ, TO CONGRATULATE YOU, THE CITY'S GIVING YOU A CAR!
MR. MAYOR, I'M STILL UNDER AGE—
THEN, LET ME HONOR YOU.
WAIT!
IT'S ALL YOURS, DAD! I'D PROMISED IT TO YOU!

Chapter 4

A Path Strewn with Rose(s)

"Edson is the person who has feelings, a family, and who works hard. Pelé is the idol." —Pelé, 2003

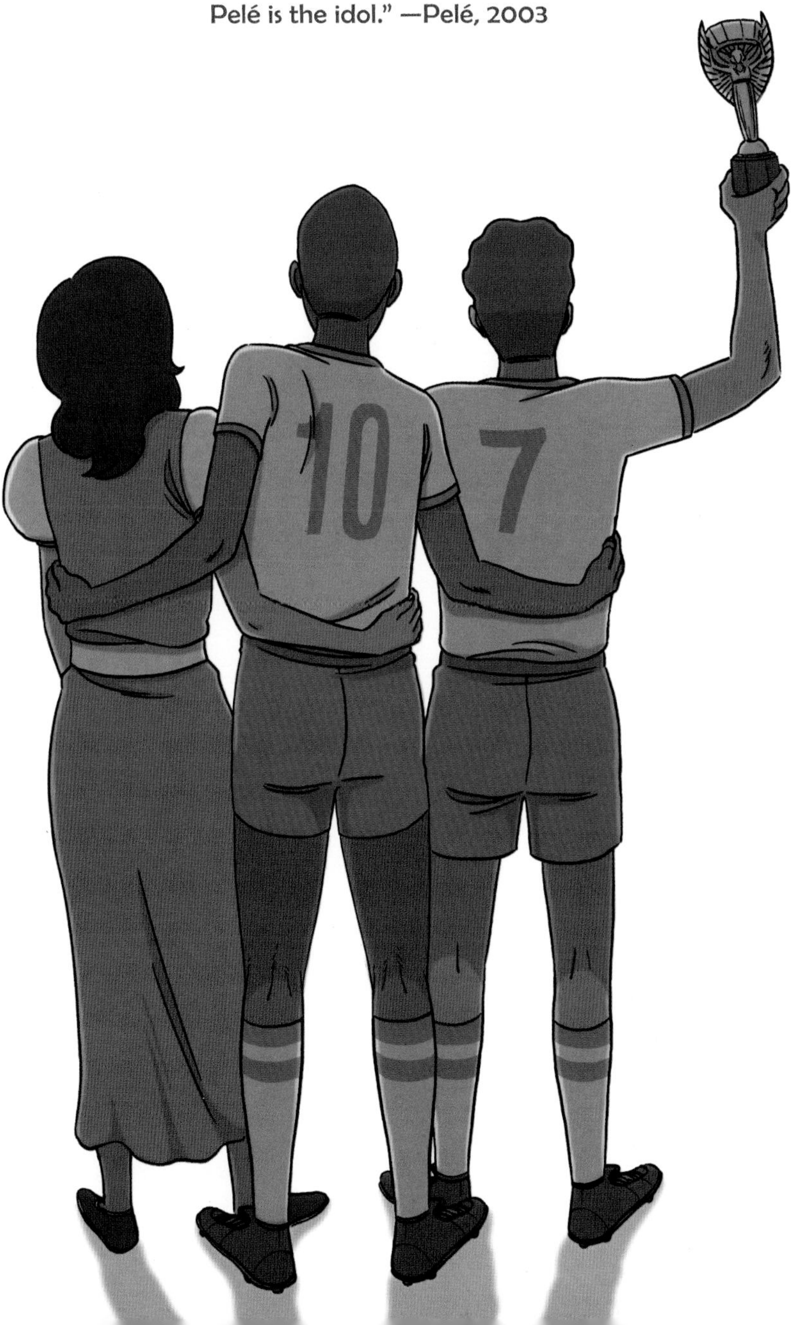

10
7

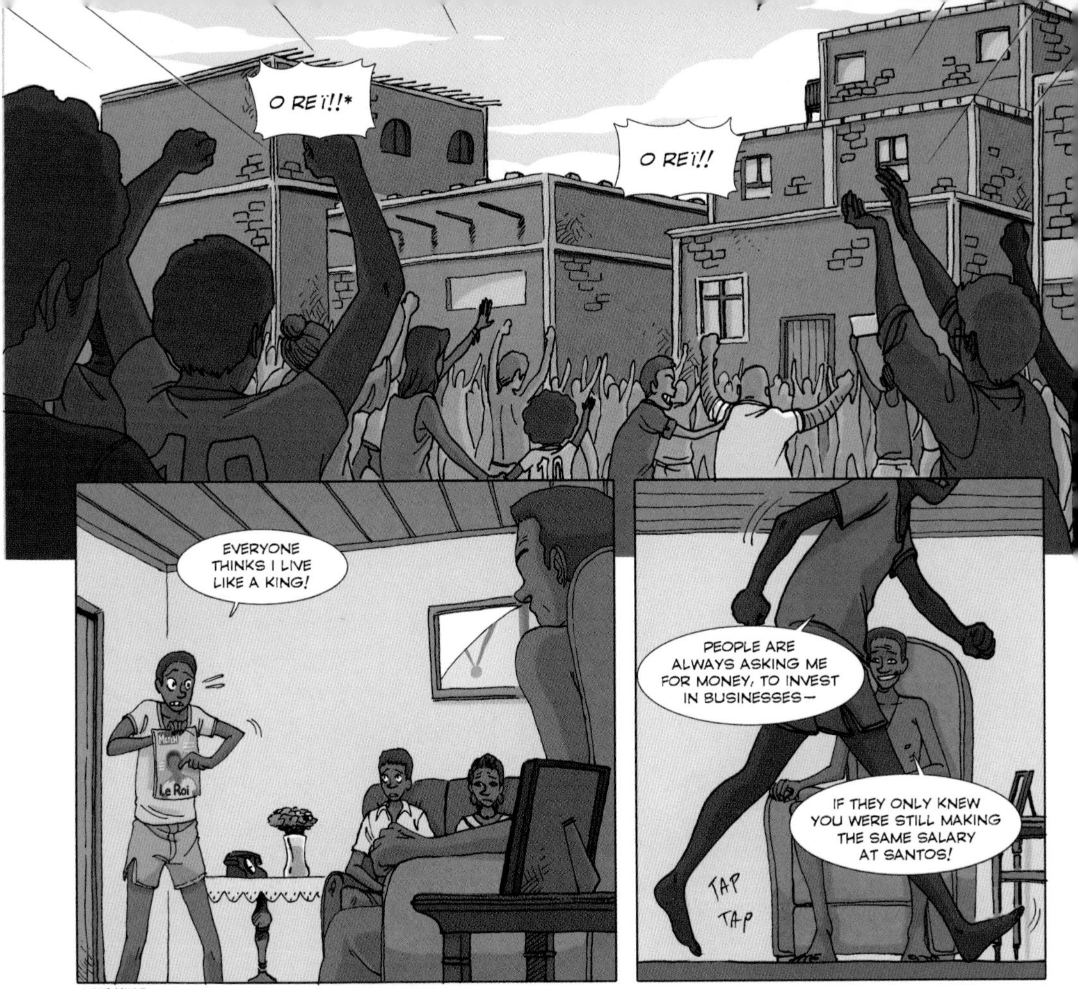
O REÏ!!*
O REÏ!!
EVERYONE THINKS I LIVE LIKE A KING!
Le Roi
PEOPLE ARE ALWAYS ASKING ME FOR MONEY, TO INVEST IN BUSINESSES—
IF THEY ONLY KNEW YOU WERE STILL MAKING THE SAME SALARY AT SANTOS!
TAP
TAP

*THE KING.

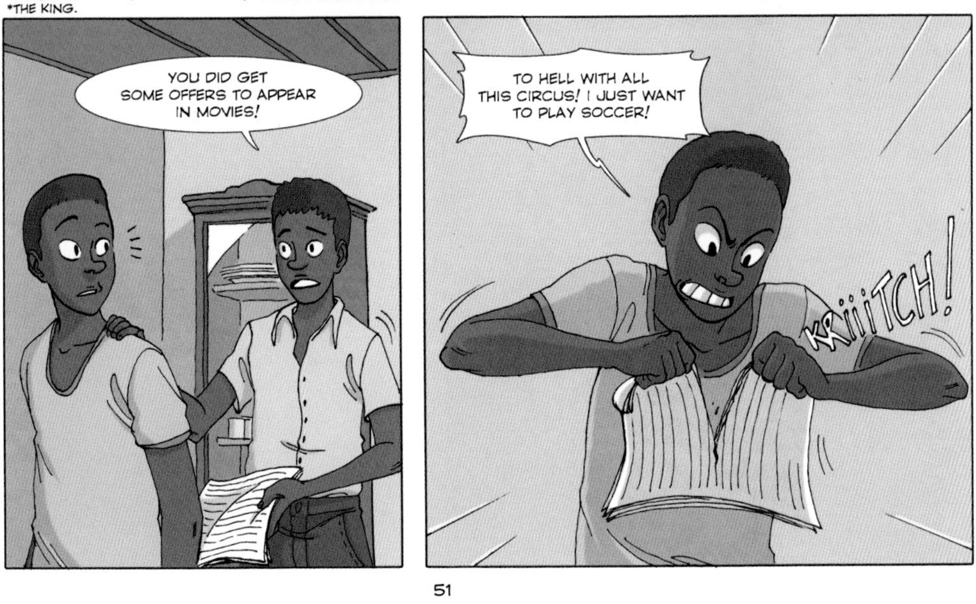
YOU DID GET SOME OFFERS TO APPEAR IN MOVIES!
TO HELL WITH ALL THIS CIRCUS! I JUST WANT TO PLAY SOCCER!
KRiiiTCH!

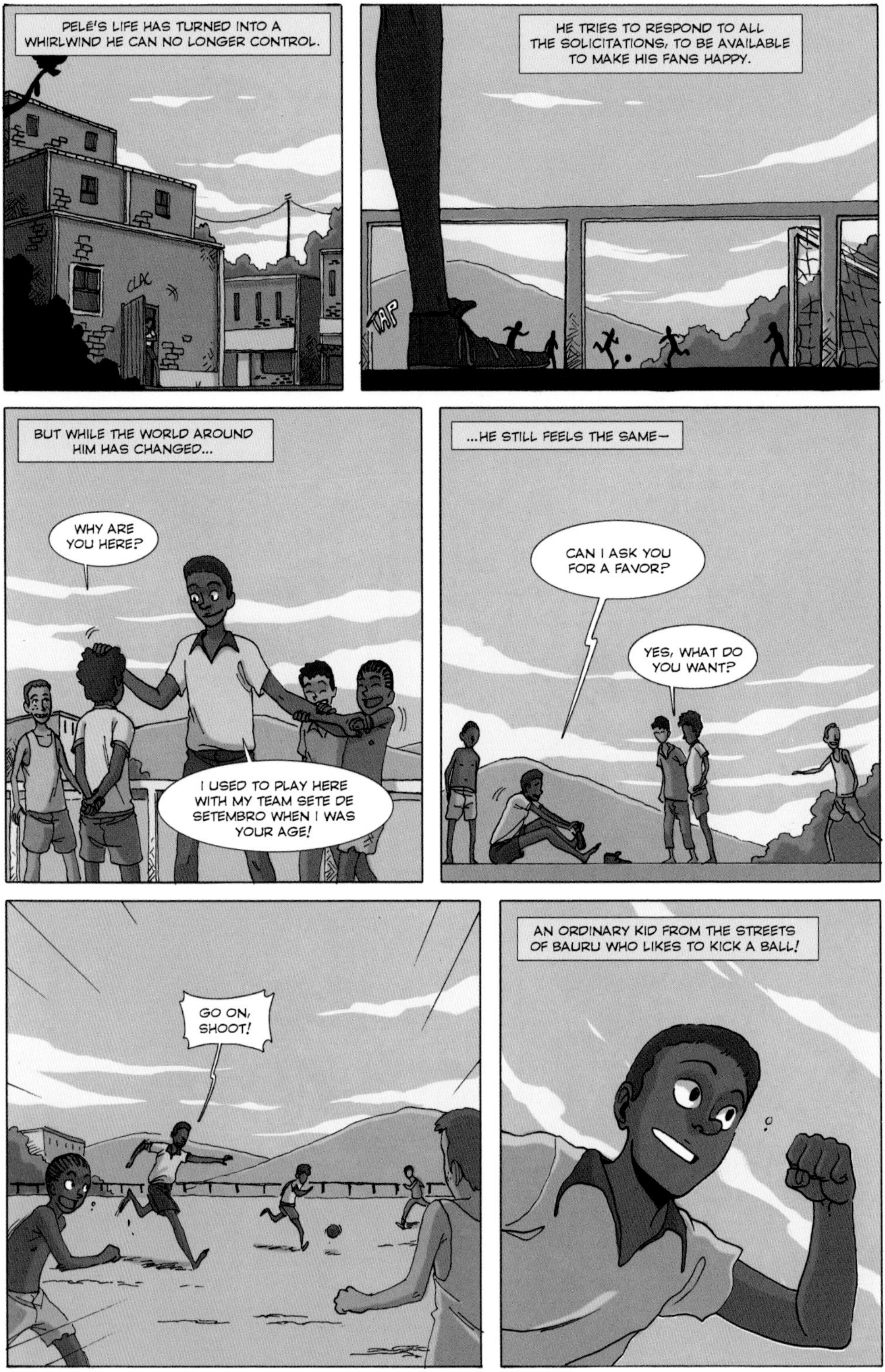

PELÉ'S LIFE HAS TURNED INTO A WHIRLWIND HE CAN NO LONGER CONTROL.
CLAC
HE TRIES TO RESPOND TO ALL THE SOLICITATIONS, TO BE AVAILABLE TO MAKE HIS FANS HAPPY.
TAP
BUT WHILE THE WORLD AROUND HIM HAS CHANGED...
WHY ARE YOU HERE?
I USED TO PLAY HERE WITH MY TEAM SETE DE SETEMBRO WHEN I WAS YOUR AGE!
...HE STILL FEELS THE SAME—
CAN I ASK YOU FOR A FAVOR?
YES, WHAT DO YOU WANT?
GO ON, SHOOT!
AN ORDINARY KID FROM THE STREETS OF BAURU WHO LIKES TO KICK A BALL!

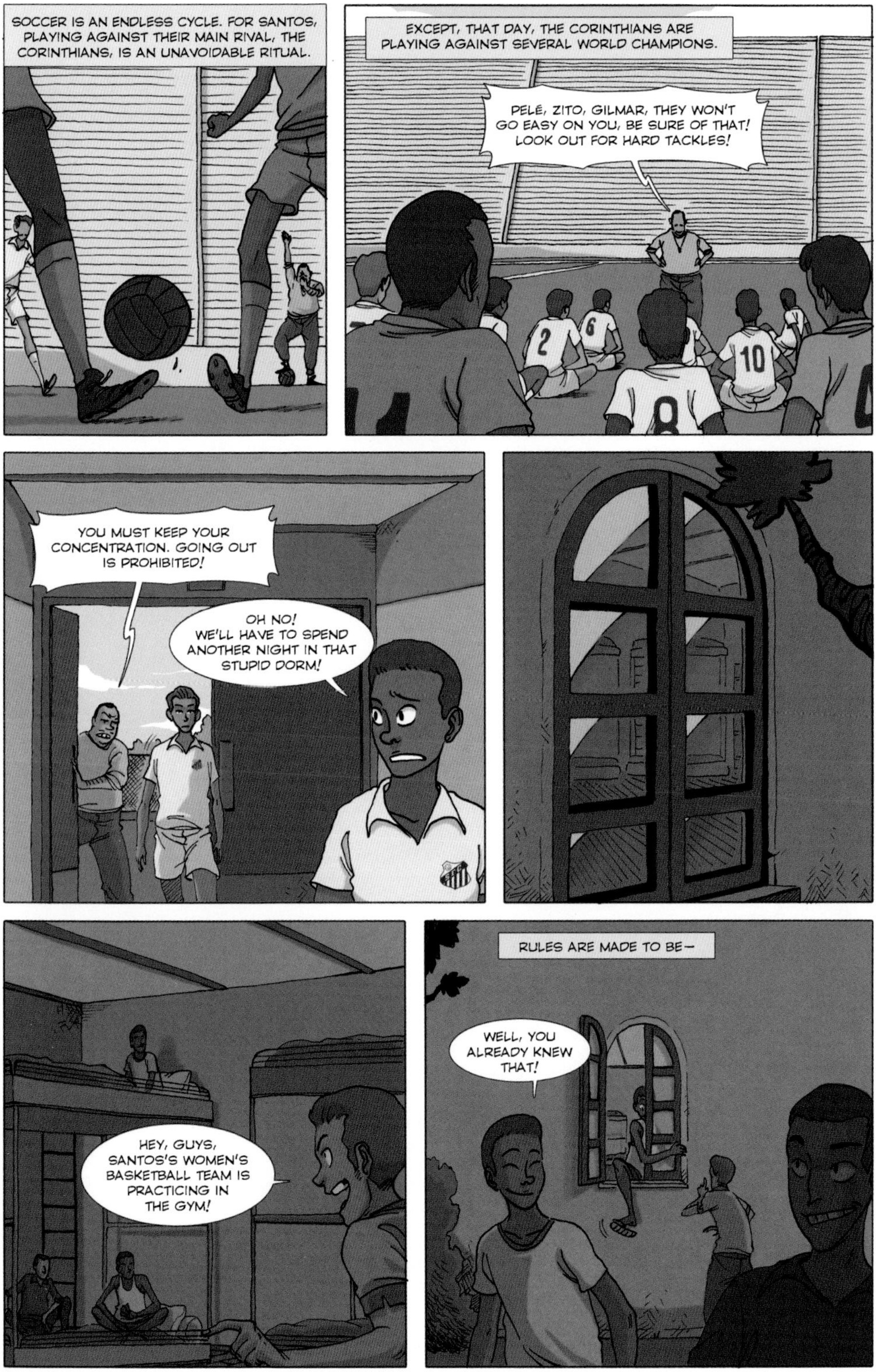
SOCCER IS AN ENDLESS CYCLE. FOR SANTOS, PLAYING AGAINST THEIR MAIN RIVAL, THE CORINTHIANS, IS AN UNAVOIDABLE RITUAL.
EXCEPT, THAT DAY, THE CORINTHIANS ARE PLAYING AGAINST SEVERAL WORLD CHAMPIONS.
PELÉ, ZITO, GILMAR, THEY WON'T GO EASY ON YOU, BE SURE OF THAT! LOOK OUT FOR HARD TACKLES!
YOU MUST KEEP YOUR CONCENTRATION. GOING OUT IS PROHIBITED!
OH NO! WE'LL HAVE TO SPEND ANOTHER NIGHT IN THAT STUPID DORM!
HEY, GUYS, SANTOS'S WOMEN'S BASKETBALL TEAM IS PRACTICING IN THE GYM!
RULES ARE MADE TO BE—
WELL, YOU ALREADY KNEW THAT!

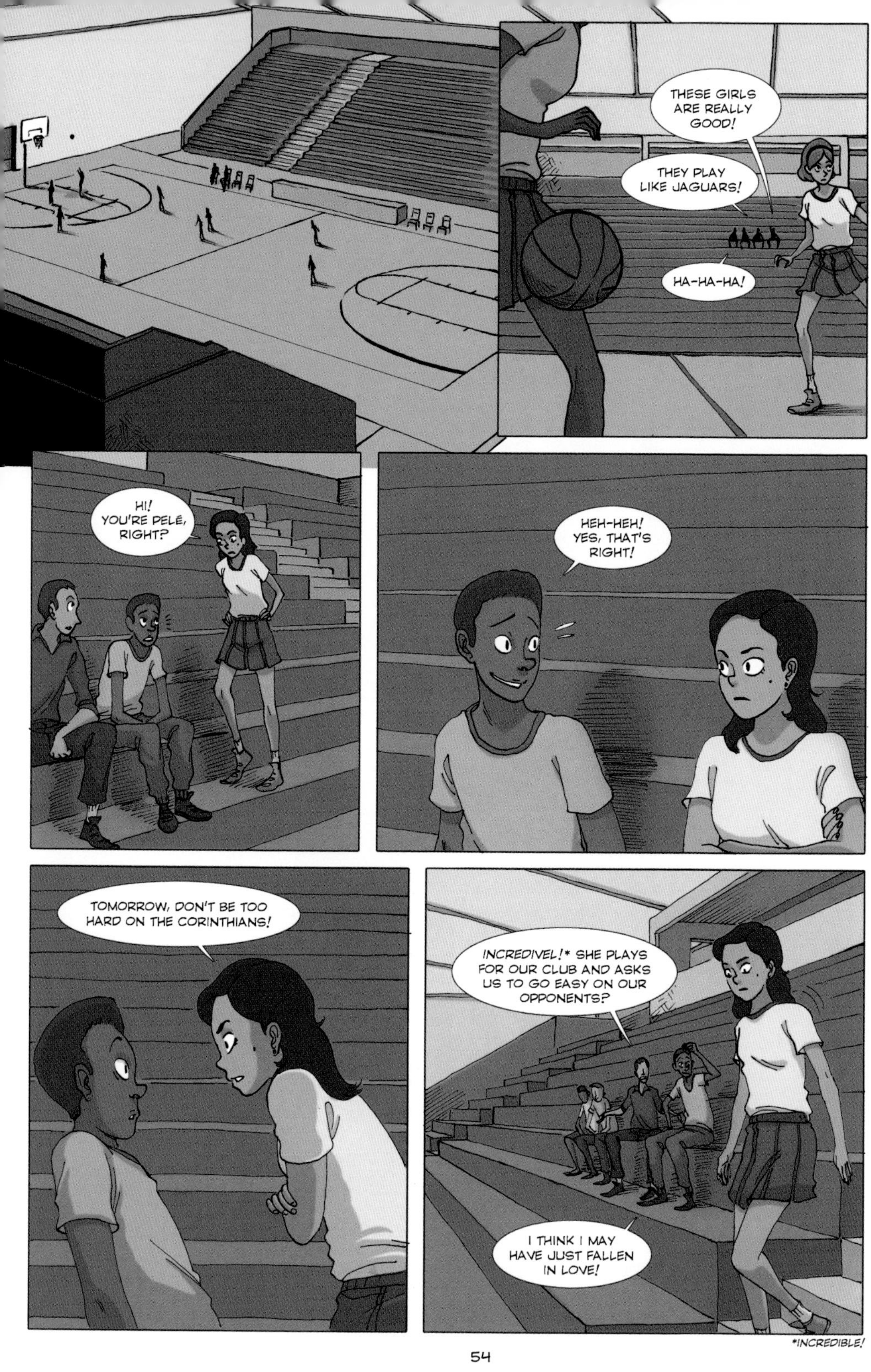
THESE GIRLS ARE REALLY GOOD!
THEY PLAY LIKE JAGUARS!
HA-HA-HA!
HI! YOU'RE PELÉ, RIGHT?
HEH-HEH! YES, THAT'S RIGHT!
TOMORROW, DON'T BE TOO HARD ON THE CORINTHIANS!
*INCREDIVEL!** SHE PLAYS FOR OUR CLUB AND ASKS US TO GO EASY ON OUR OPPONENTS?
I THINK I MAY HAVE JUST FALLEN IN LOVE!

**INCREDIBLE!*

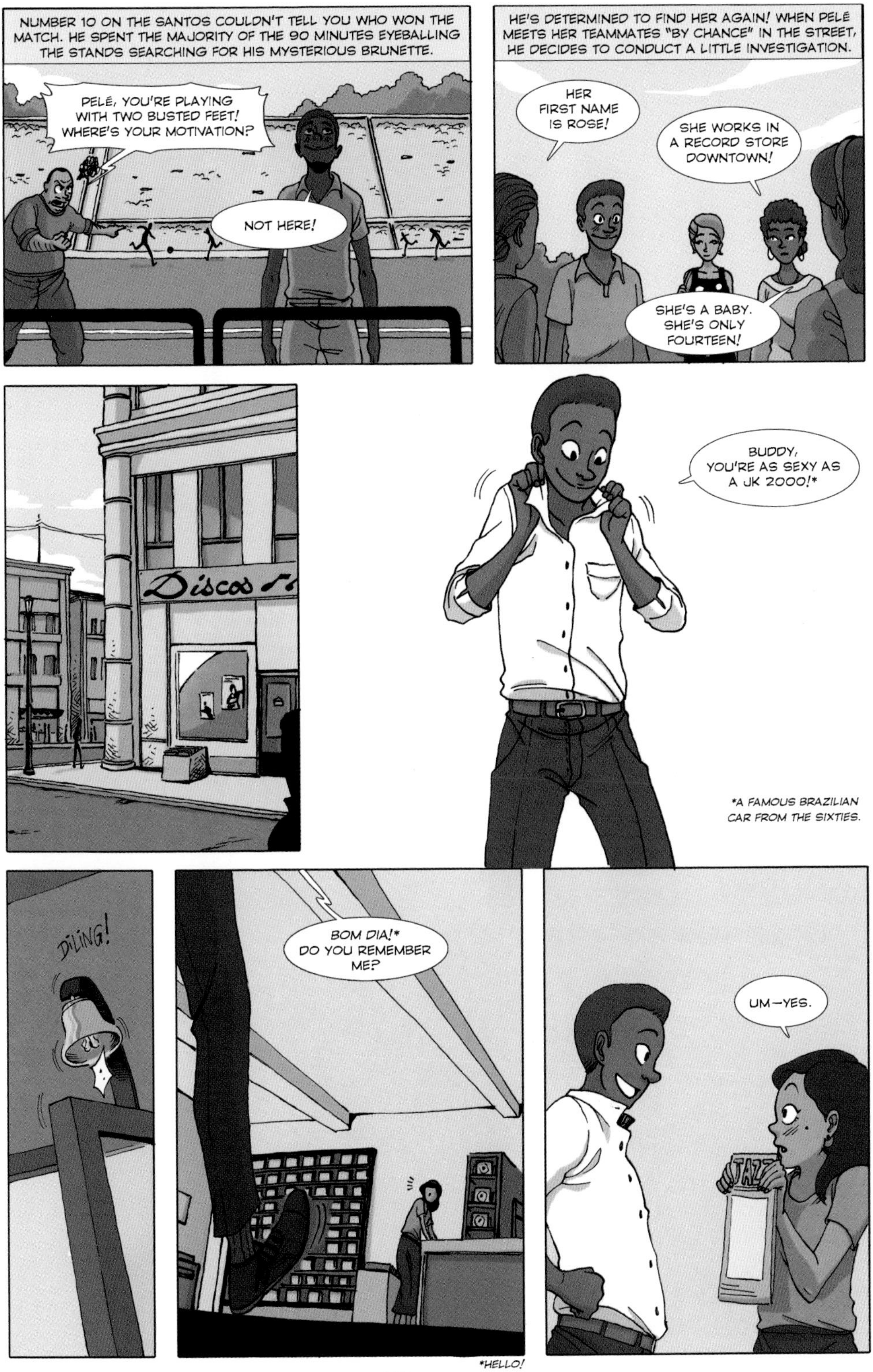
NUMBER 10 ON THE SANTOS COULDN'T TELL YOU WHO WON THE MATCH. HE SPENT THE MAJORITY OF THE 90 MINUTES EYEBALLING THE STANDS SEARCHING FOR HIS MYSTERIOUS BRUNETTE.
PELÉ, YOU'RE PLAYING WITH TWO BUSTED FEET! WHERE'S YOUR MOTIVATION?
NOT HERE!
HE'S DETERMINED TO FIND HER AGAIN! WHEN PELÉ MEETS HER TEAMMATES "BY CHANCE" IN THE STREET, HE DECIDES TO CONDUCT A LITTLE INVESTIGATION.
HER FIRST NAME IS ROSE!
SHE WORKS IN A RECORD STORE DOWNTOWN!
SHE'S A BABY. SHE'S ONLY FOURTEEN!
Discos
BUDDY, YOU'RE AS SEXY AS A JK 2000!*
*A FAMOUS BRAZILIAN CAR FROM THE SIXTIES.
DILING!
BOM DIA!* DO YOU REMEMBER ME?
UM—YES.
JAZZ
*HELLO!

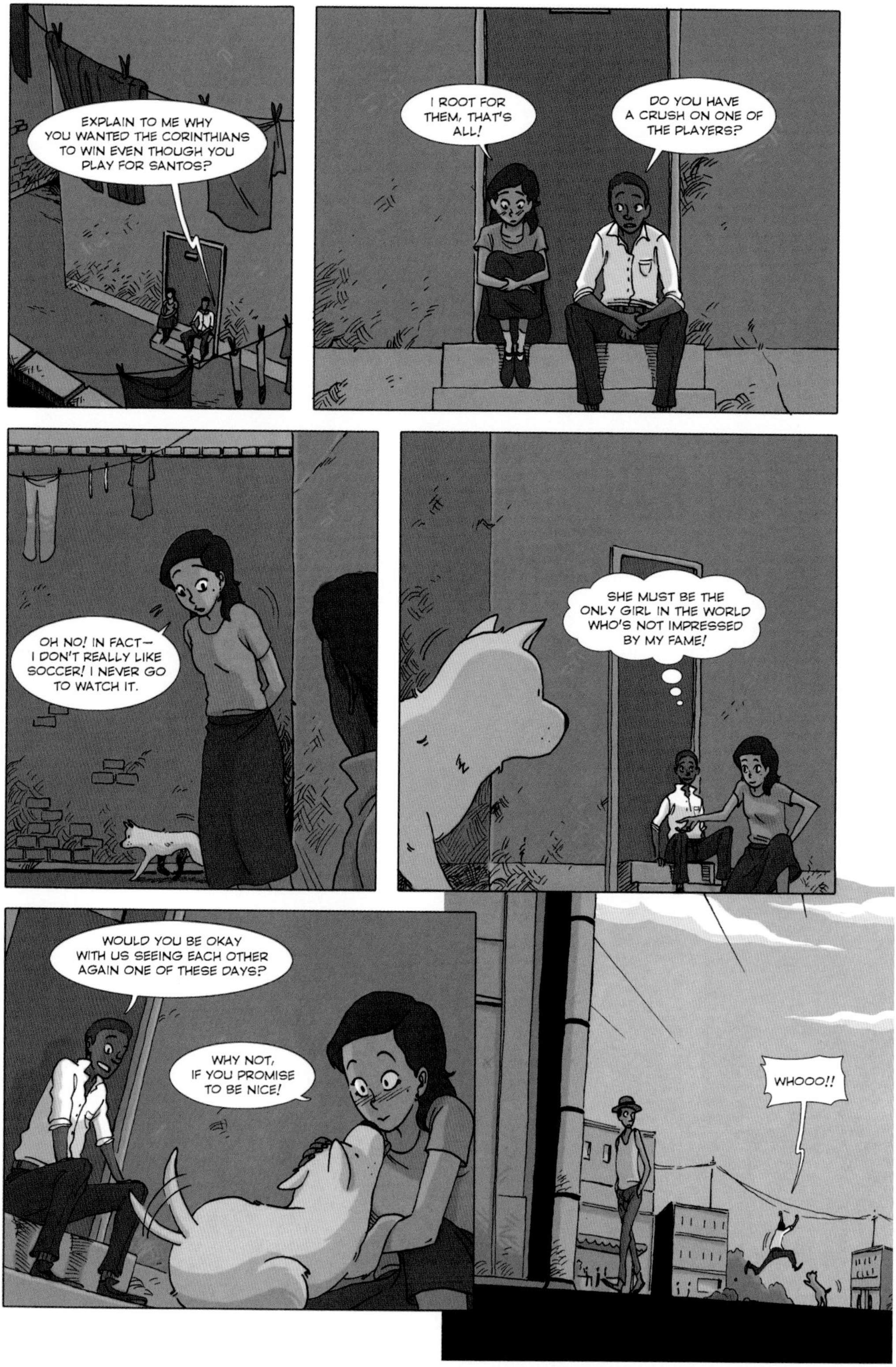
EXPLAIN TO ME WHY YOU WANTED THE CORINTHIANS TO WIN EVEN THOUGH YOU PLAY FOR SANTOS?
I ROOT FOR THEM, THAT'S ALL!
DO YOU HAVE A CRUSH ON ONE OF THE PLAYERS?
OH NO! IN FACT— I DON'T REALLY LIKE SOCCER! I NEVER GO TO WATCH IT.
SHE MUST BE THE ONLY GIRL IN THE WORLD WHO'S NOT IMPRESSED BY MY FAME!
WOULD YOU BE OKAY WITH US SEEING EACH OTHER AGAIN ONE OF THESE DAYS?
WHY NOT, IF YOU PROMISE TO BE NICE!
WHOOO!!

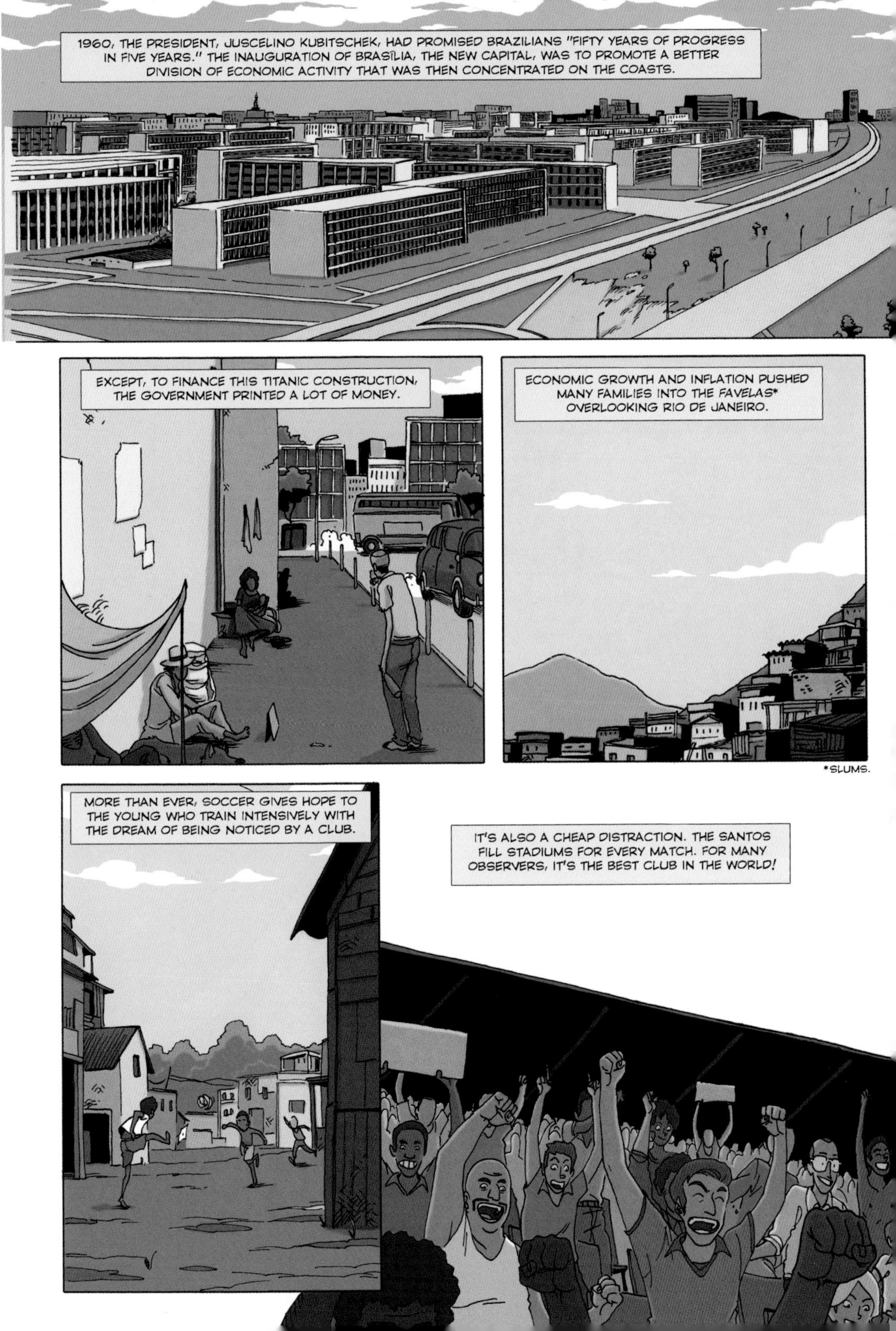
1960, THE PRESIDENT, JUSCELINO KUBITSCHEK, HAD PROMISED BRAZILIANS "FIFTY YEARS OF PROGRESS IN FIVE YEARS." THE INAUGURATION OF BRASÍLIA, THE NEW CAPITAL, WAS TO PROMOTE A BETTER DIVISION OF ECONOMIC ACTIVITY THAT WAS THEN CONCENTRATED ON THE COASTS.
EXCEPT, TO FINANCE THIS TITANIC CONSTRUCTION, THE GOVERNMENT PRINTED A LOT OF MONEY.
ECONOMIC GROWTH AND INFLATION PUSHED MANY FAMILIES INTO THE *FAVELAS** OVERLOOKING RIO DE JANEIRO.
*SLUMS.
MORE THAN EVER, SOCCER GIVES HOPE TO THE YOUNG WHO TRAIN INTENSIVELY WITH THE DREAM OF BEING NOTICED BY A CLUB.
IT'S ALSO A CHEAP DISTRACTION. THE SANTOS FILL STADIUMS FOR EVERY MATCH. FOR MANY OBSERVERS, IT'S THE BEST CLUB IN THE WORLD!

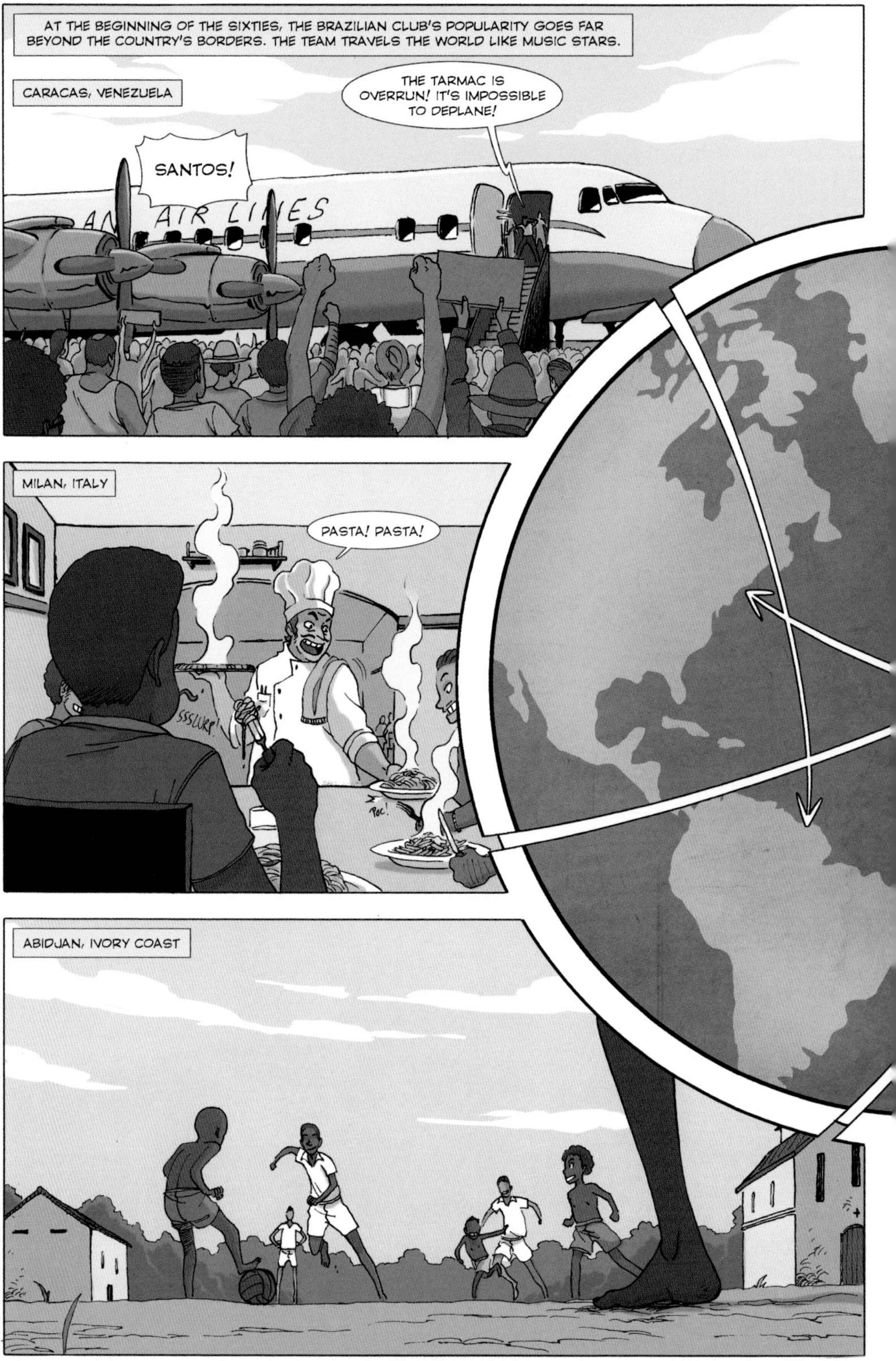
AT THE BEGINNING OF THE SIXTIES, THE BRAZILIAN CLUB'S POPULARITY GOES FAR BEYOND THE COUNTRY'S BORDERS. THE TEAM TRAVELS THE WORLD LIKE MUSIC STARS.
CARACAS, VENEZUELA
SANTOS!
THE TARMAC IS OVERRUN! IT'S IMPOSSIBLE TO DEPLANE!
AIR LINES
MILAN, ITALY
PASTA! PASTA!
SSSLURP!
Poc!
ABIDJAN, IVORY COAST

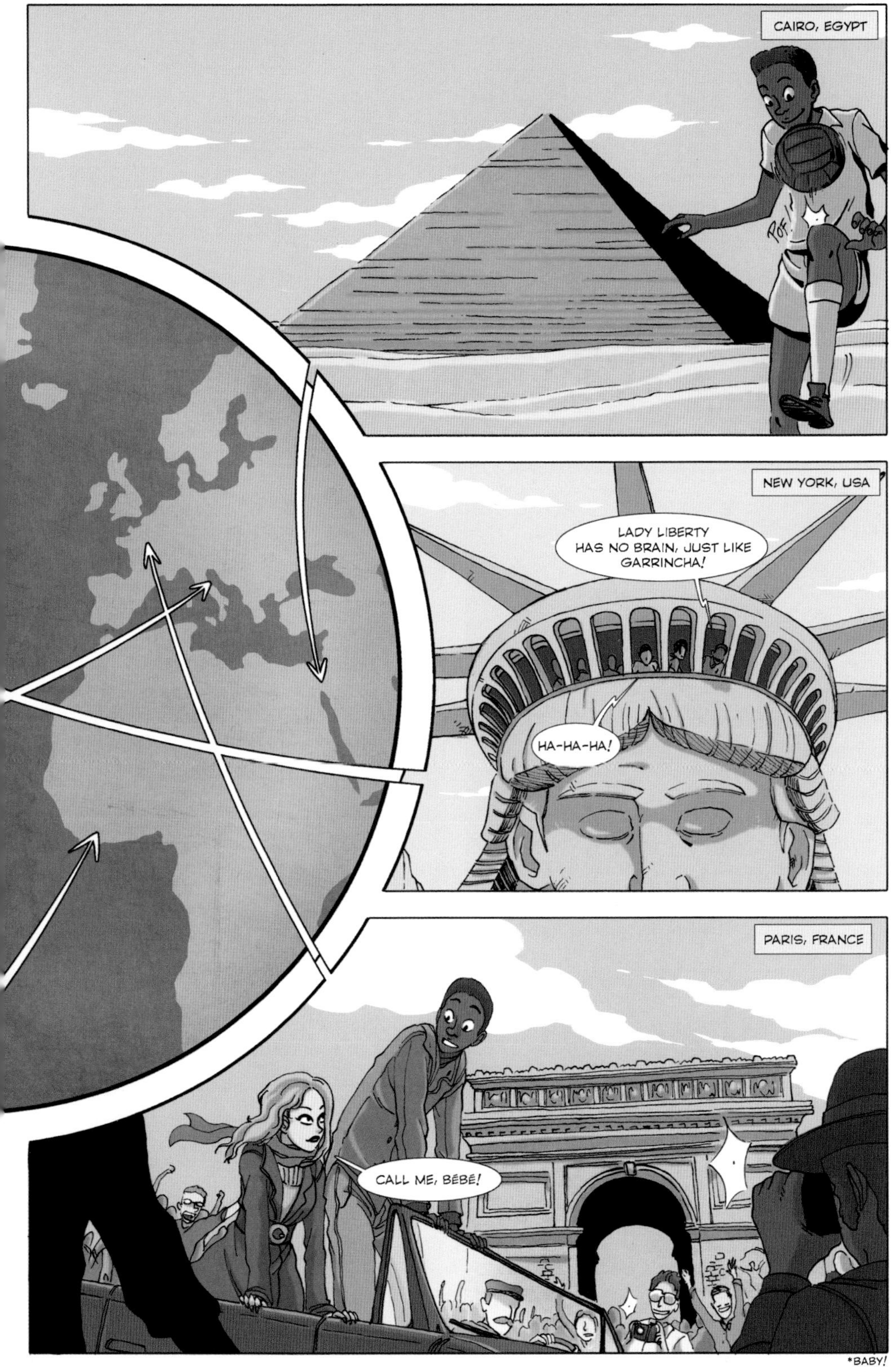
CAIRO, EGYPT
POF!
NEW YORK, USA
LADY LIBERTY HAS NO BRAIN, JUST LIKE GARRINCHA!
HA-HA-HA!
PARIS, FRANCE
CALL ME, BÉBÉ!

*BABY!

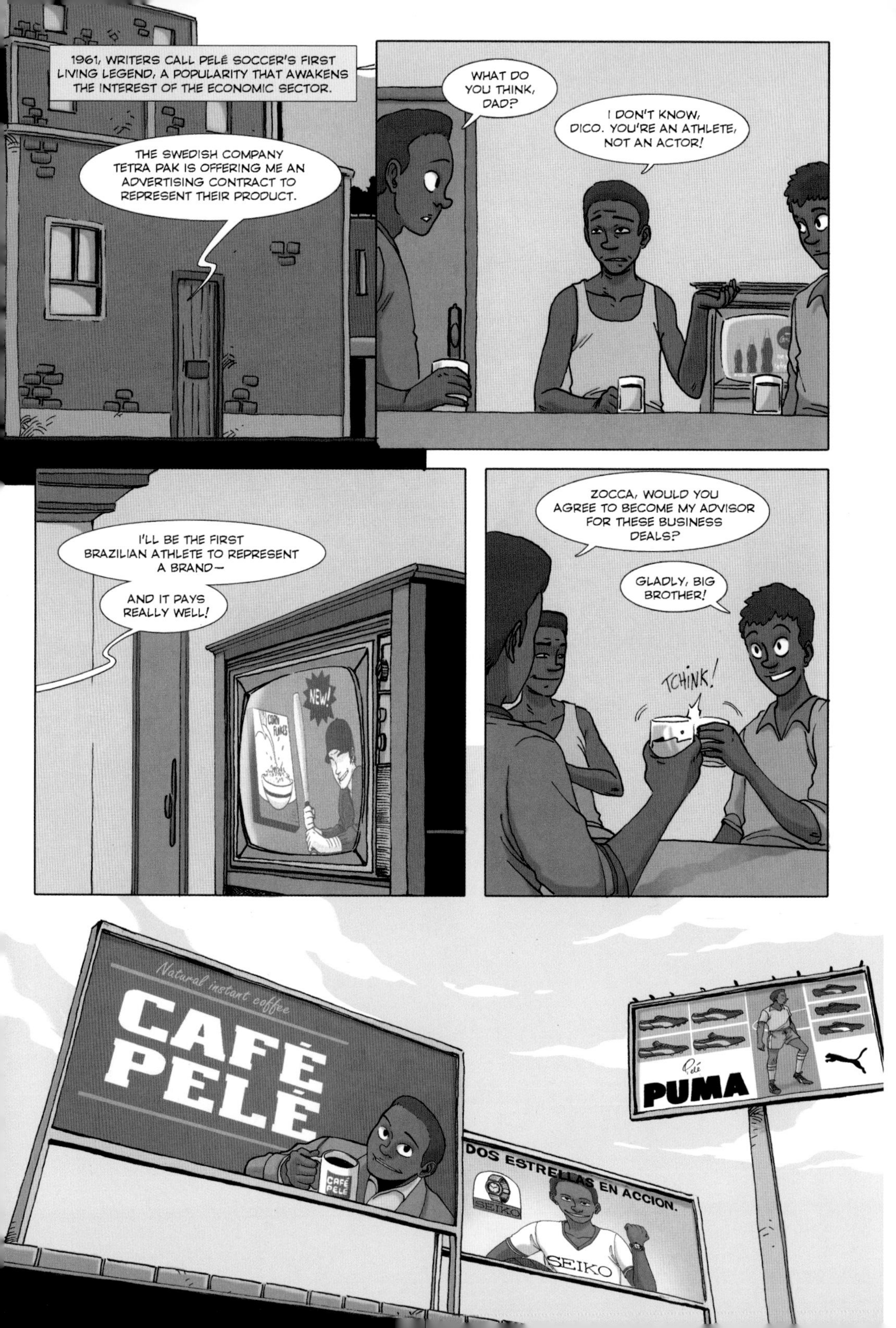
1961, WRITERS CALL PELÉ SOCCER'S FIRST LIVING LEGEND, A POPULARITY THAT AWAKENS THE INTEREST OF THE ECONOMIC SECTOR.
THE SWEDISH COMPANY TETRA PAK IS OFFERING ME AN ADVERTISING CONTRACT TO REPRESENT THEIR PRODUCT.
WHAT DO YOU THINK, DAD?
I DON'T KNOW, DICO. YOU'RE AN ATHLETE, NOT AN ACTOR!
I'LL BE THE FIRST BRAZILIAN ATHLETE TO REPRESENT A BRAND—
AND IT PAYS REALLY WELL!
NEW!
CORN FLAKES
ZOCCA, WOULD YOU AGREE TO BECOME MY ADVISOR FOR THESE BUSINESS DEALS?
GLADLY, BIG BROTHER!
TCHINK!
Natural instant coffee
CAFÉ PELÉ
CAFÉ PELÉ
DOS ESTRELLAS EN ACCION.
SEIKO
SEIKO
Pelé
PUMA

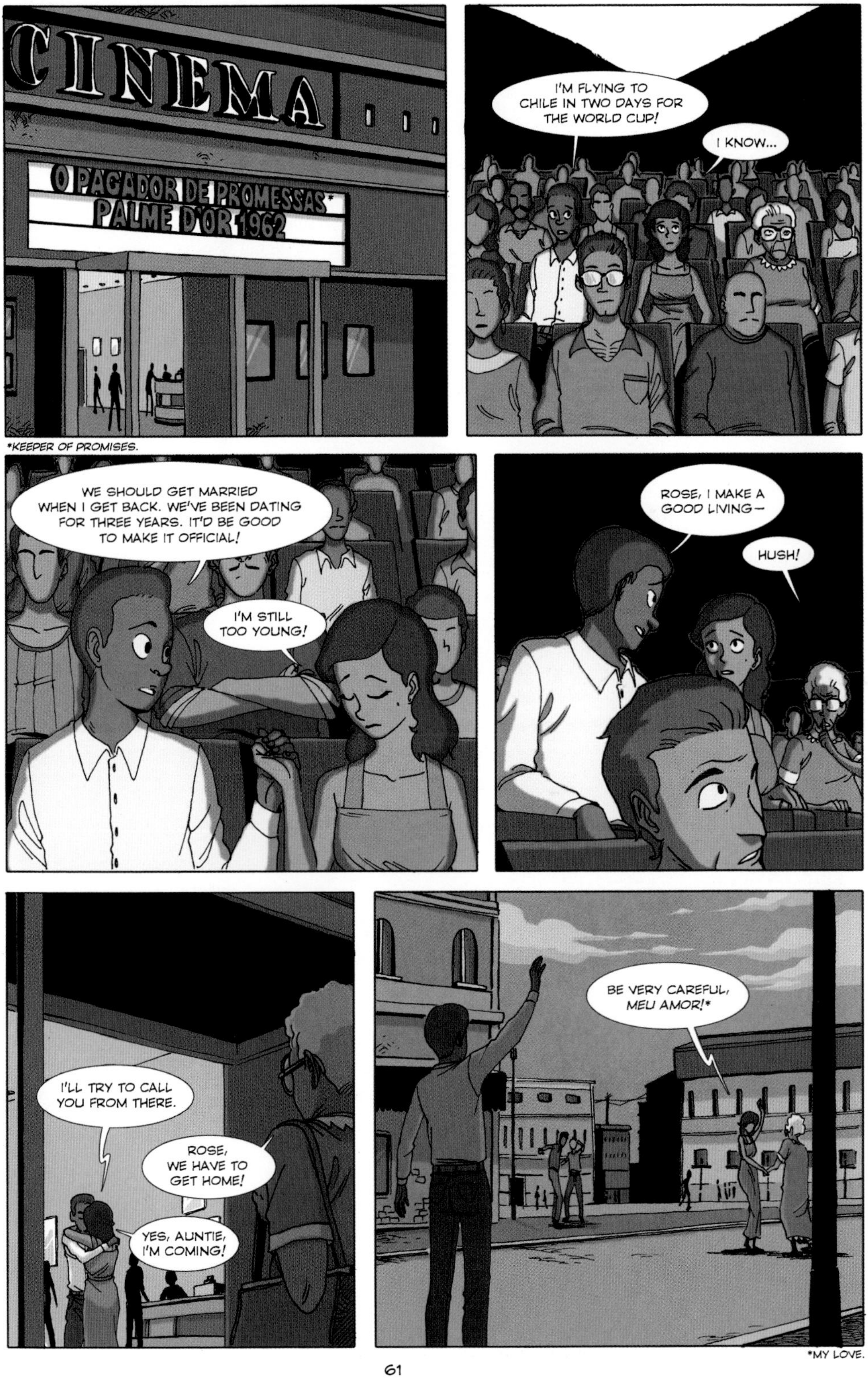
CINEMA
O PAGADOR DE PROMESSAS*
PALME D'OR 1962
*KEEPER OF PROMISES.
I'M FLYING TO CHILE IN TWO DAYS FOR THE WORLD CUP!
I KNOW...
WE SHOULD GET MARRIED WHEN I GET BACK. WE'VE BEEN DATING FOR THREE YEARS. IT'D BE GOOD TO MAKE IT OFFICIAL!
I'M STILL TOO YOUNG!
ROSE, I MAKE A GOOD LIVING—
HUSH!
I'LL TRY TO CALL YOU FROM THERE.
ROSE, WE HAVE TO GET HOME!
YES, AUNTIE, I'M COMING!
BE VERY CAREFUL, MEU AMOR!*
*MY LOVE.

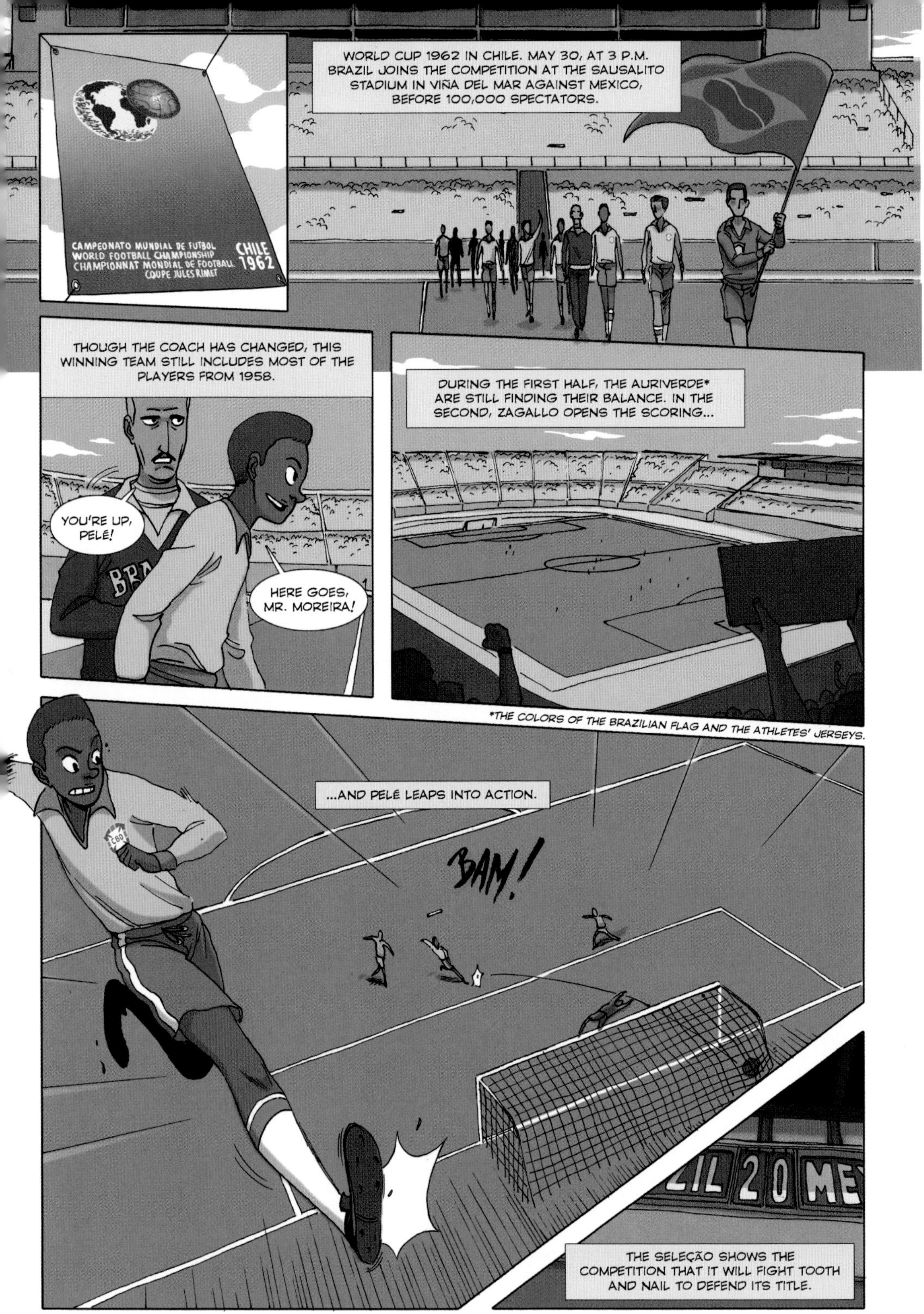
CAMPEONATO MUNDIAL DE FUTBOL
WORLD FOOTBALL CHAMPIONSHIP
CHAMPIONNAT MONDIAL DE FOOTBALL
COUPE JULES RIMET
CHILE 1962
WORLD CUP 1962 IN CHILE. MAY 30, AT 3 P.M. BRAZIL JOINS THE COMPETITION AT THE SAUSALITO STADIUM IN VIÑA DEL MAR AGAINST MEXICO, BEFORE 100,000 SPECTATORS.
THOUGH THE COACH HAS CHANGED, THIS WINNING TEAM STILL INCLUDES MOST OF THE PLAYERS FROM 1958.
YOU'RE UP, PELÉ!
HERE GOES, MR. MOREIRA!
DURING THE FIRST HALF, THE AURIVERDE* ARE STILL FINDING THEIR BALANCE. IN THE SECOND, ZAGALLO OPENS THE SCORING...
...AND PELÉ LEAPS INTO ACTION.
BAM!
THE SELEÇÃO SHOWS THE COMPETITION THAT IT WILL FIGHT TOOTH AND NAIL TO DEFEND ITS TITLE.

*THE COLORS OF THE BRAZILIAN FLAG AND THE ATHLETES' JERSEYS.

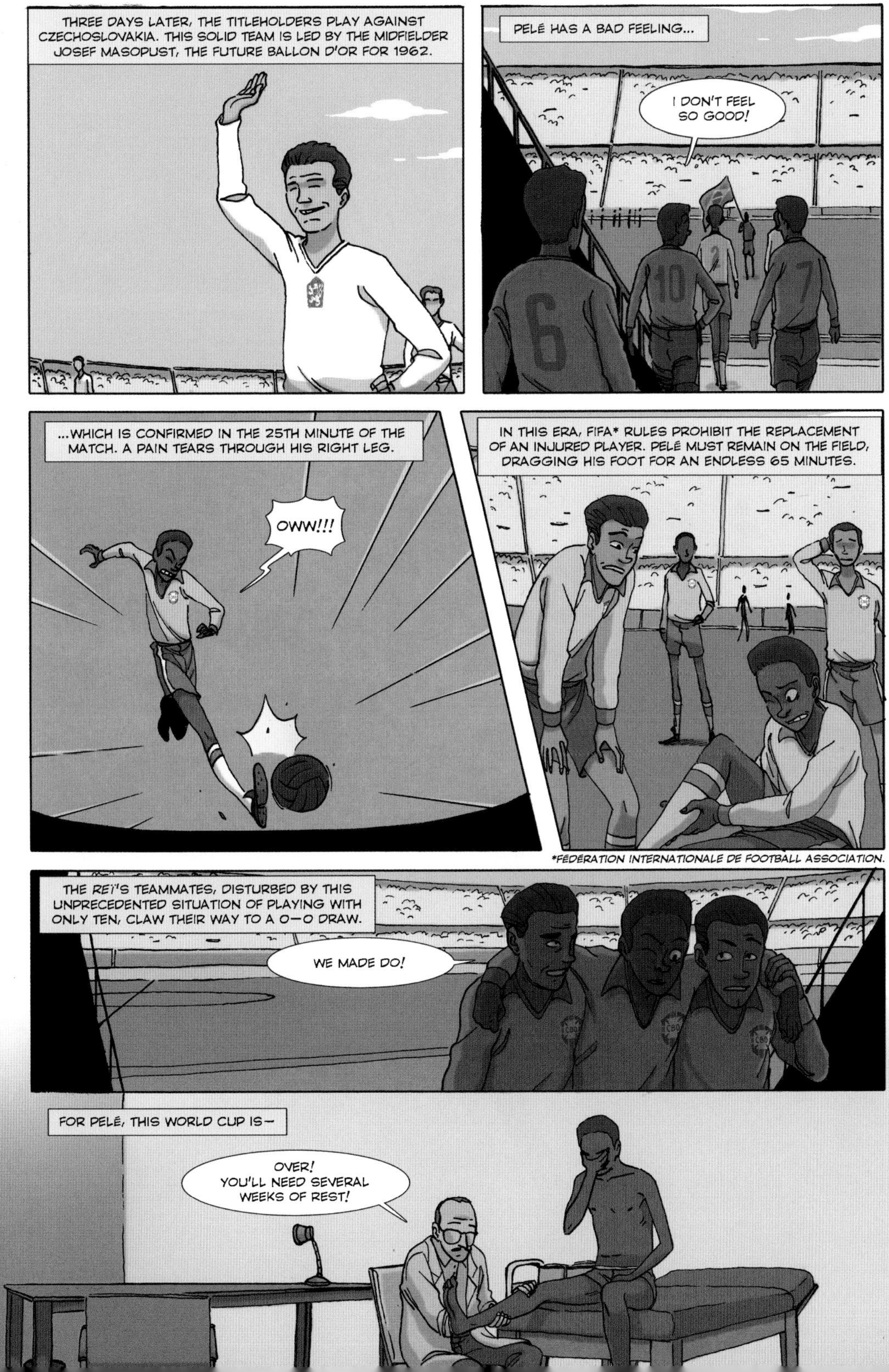
THREE DAYS LATER, THE TITLEHOLDERS PLAY AGAINST CZECHOSLOVAKIA. THIS SOLID TEAM IS LED BY THE MIDFIELDER JOSEF MASOPUST, THE FUTURE BALLON D'OR FOR 1962.
PELÉ HAS A BAD FEELING...
I DON'T FEEL SO GOOD!
...WHICH IS CONFIRMED IN THE 25TH MINUTE OF THE MATCH. A PAIN TEARS THROUGH HIS RIGHT LEG.
OWW!!!
IN THIS ERA, FIFA* RULES PROHIBIT THE REPLACEMENT OF AN INJURED PLAYER. PELÉ MUST REMAIN ON THE FIELD, DRAGGING HIS FOOT FOR AN ENDLESS 65 MINUTES.
*FÉDÉRATION INTERNATIONALE DE FOOTBALL ASSOCIATION.
THE REI'S TEAMMATES, DISTURBED BY THIS UNPRECEDENTED SITUATION OF PLAYING WITH ONLY TEN, CLAW THEIR WAY TO A 0—0 DRAW.
WE MADE DO!
FOR PELÉ, THIS WORLD CUP IS—
OVER! YOU'LL NEED SEVERAL WEEKS OF REST!

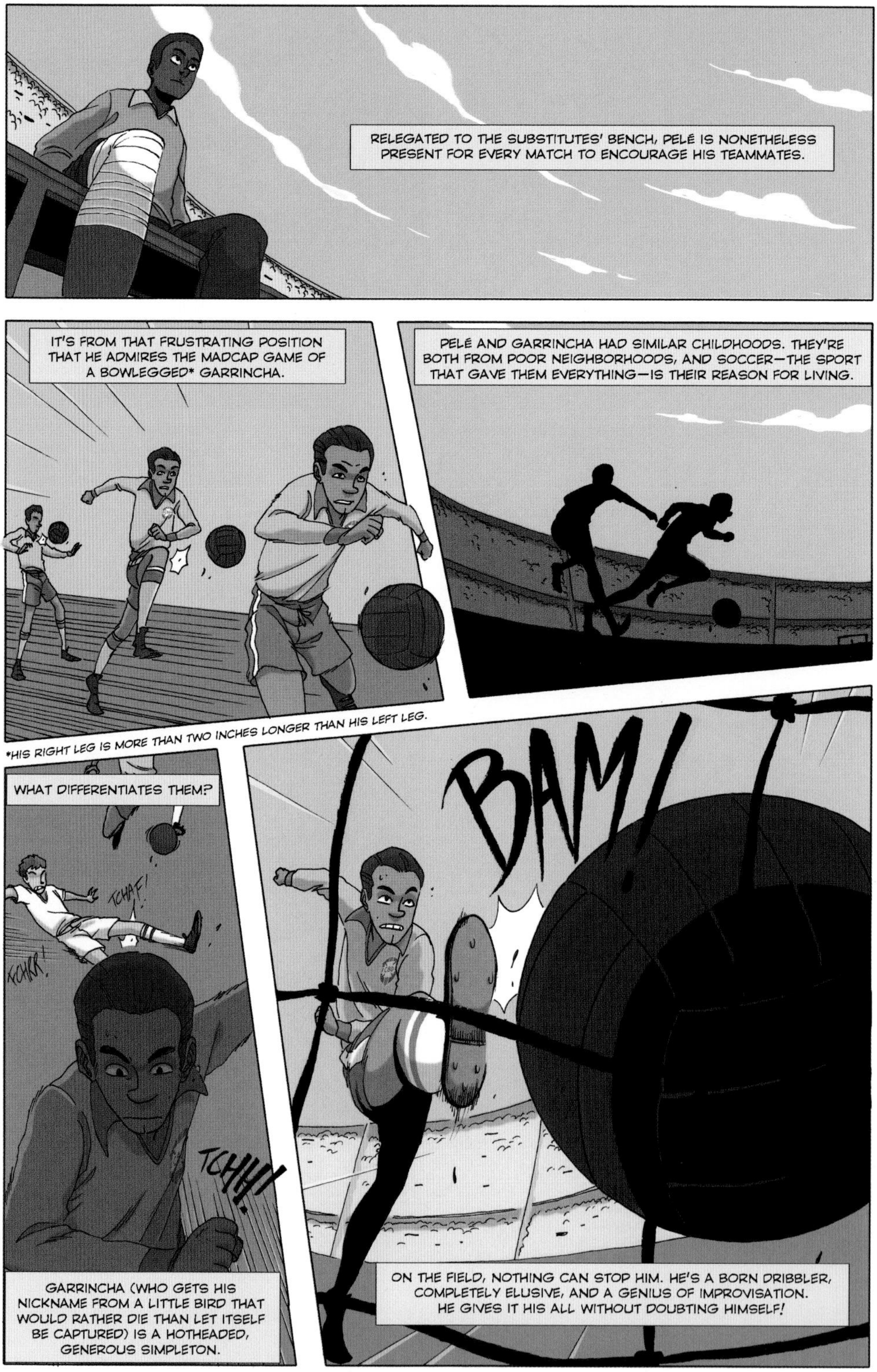
RELEGATED TO THE SUBSTITUTES' BENCH, PELÉ IS NONETHELESS PRESENT FOR EVERY MATCH TO ENCOURAGE HIS TEAMMATES.
IT'S FROM THAT FRUSTRATING POSITION THAT HE ADMIRES THE MADCAP GAME OF A BOWLEGGED* GARRINCHA.
PELÉ AND GARRINCHA HAD SIMILAR CHILDHOODS. THEY'RE BOTH FROM POOR NEIGHBORHOODS, AND SOCCER—THE SPORT THAT GAVE THEM EVERYTHING—IS THEIR REASON FOR LIVING.
*HIS RIGHT LEG IS MORE THAN TWO INCHES LONGER THAN HIS LEFT LEG.
WHAT DIFFERENTIATES THEM?
TCHAF!
GARRINCHA (WHO GETS HIS NICKNAME FROM A LITTLE BIRD THAT WOULD RATHER DIE THAN LET ITSELF BE CAPTURED) IS A HOTHEADED, GENEROUS SIMPLETON.
BAM!
ON THE FIELD, NOTHING CAN STOP HIM. HE'S A BORN DRIBBLER, COMPLETELY ELUSIVE, AND A GENIUS OF IMPROVISATION. HE GIVES IT HIS ALL WITHOUT DOUBTING HIMSELF!

PELÉ!

NO, GARRINCHA!

LE DOUBLÉ DE GARRINCHA!

3-1

FOR SEVERAL MONTHS, A DEBATE RAGES IN THE WORLD OF SOCCER TO DECIDE WHICH OF THE TWO BRAZILIAN STARS IS THE BETTER PLAYER.

IN NO WAY DOES THIS "FRIENDLY" POLEMIC CLOUD THE FRIENDSHIP OF THE TWO TEAMMATES, WHO FEEL A TRUE RESPECT FOR ONE ANOTHER.

VIVA GARRINCHA!

BAM!

TCHH!

AND ALSO, THE REALITY OF THE MOMENT IS INARGUABLE—

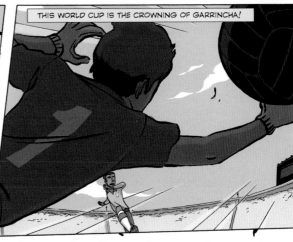

THIS WORLD CUP IS THE CROWNING OF GARRINCHA!

BRAZIL WINS THE SUPREME TITLE FOR A SECOND CONSECUTIVE TIME ON JUNE 17, 1962, AGAINST CZECHOSLOVAKIA.

IT'S THANKS TO YOU, AMIGO!

UNFORTUNATELY, THE MAN WHO IS AFFECTIONATELY NICKNAMED "ALEGRIA DO POVO"* WILL DIE TWENTY YEARS LATER, CONSUMED BY ALCOHOL AND IN POVERTY.

*THE PEOPLE'S JOY.

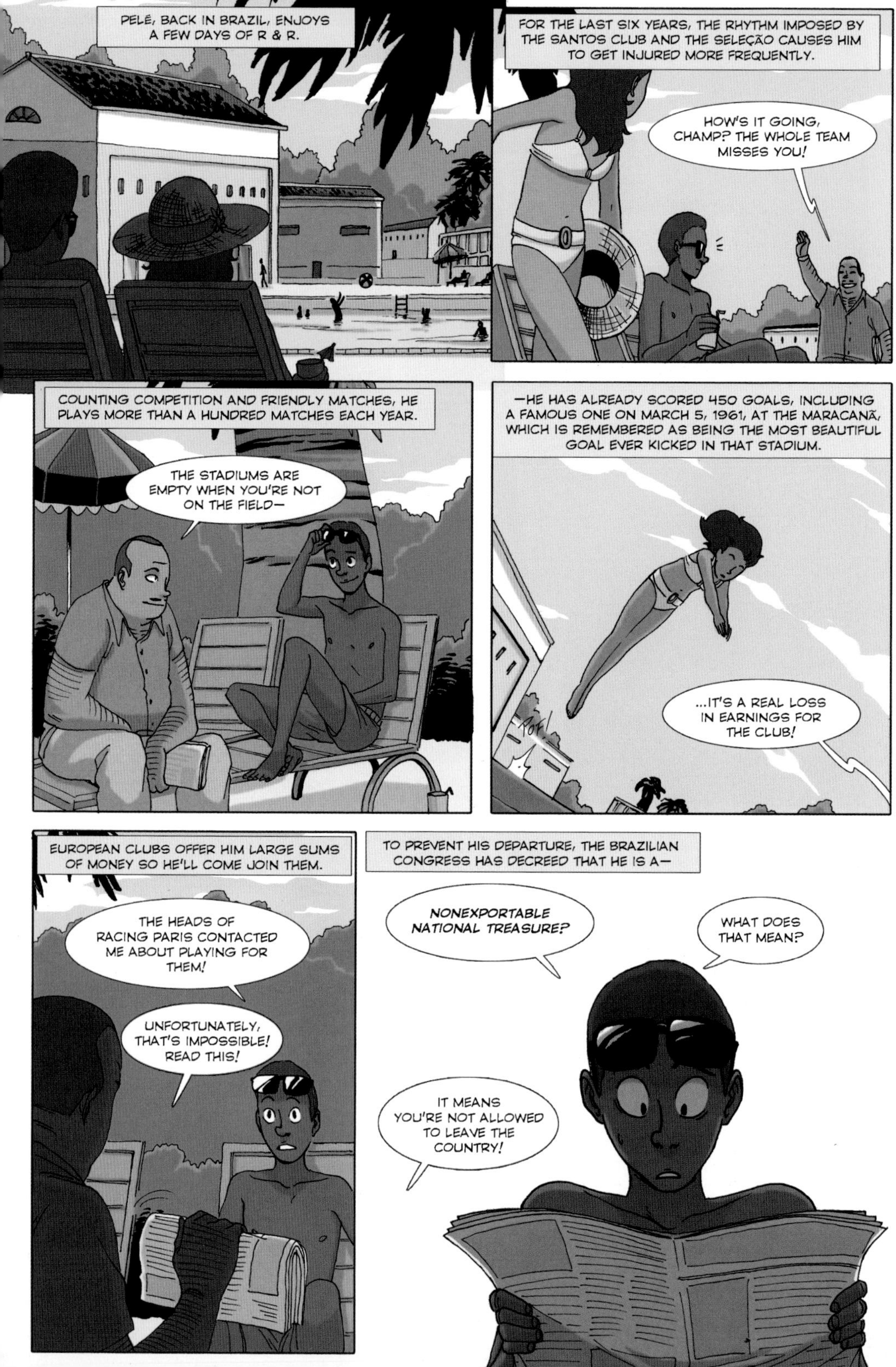

PELÉ, BACK IN BRAZIL, ENJOYS A FEW DAYS OF R & R.
FOR THE LAST SIX YEARS, THE RHYTHM IMPOSED BY THE SANTOS CLUB AND THE SELEÇÃO CAUSES HIM TO GET INJURED MORE FREQUENTLY.
HOW'S IT GOING, CHAMP? THE WHOLE TEAM MISSES YOU!
COUNTING COMPETITION AND FRIENDLY MATCHES, HE PLAYS MORE THAN A HUNDRED MATCHES EACH YEAR.
THE STADIUMS ARE EMPTY WHEN YOU'RE NOT ON THE FIELD—
—HE HAS ALREADY SCORED 450 GOALS, INCLUDING A FAMOUS ONE ON MARCH 5, 1961, AT THE MARACANÃ, WHICH IS REMEMBERED AS BEING THE MOST BEAUTIFUL GOAL EVER KICKED IN THAT STADIUM.
...IT'S A REAL LOSS IN EARNINGS FOR THE CLUB!
EUROPEAN CLUBS OFFER HIM LARGE SUMS OF MONEY SO HE'LL COME JOIN THEM.
THE HEADS OF RACING PARIS CONTACTED ME ABOUT PLAYING FOR THEM!
UNFORTUNATELY, THAT'S IMPOSSIBLE! READ THIS!
TO PREVENT HIS DEPARTURE, THE BRAZILIAN CONGRESS HAS DECREED THAT HE IS A—
NONEXPORTABLE NATIONAL TREASURE?
WHAT DOES THAT MEAN?
IT MEANS YOU'RE NOT ALLOWED TO LEAVE THE COUNTRY!

Chapter 5
O Reï!

"Pelé has extraordinary physical abilities, but he also has intelligence. Few people know he has an IQ above 160. He thinks like a mathematician."
—Professor Julio Mazzei, Pelé's confidant and advisor

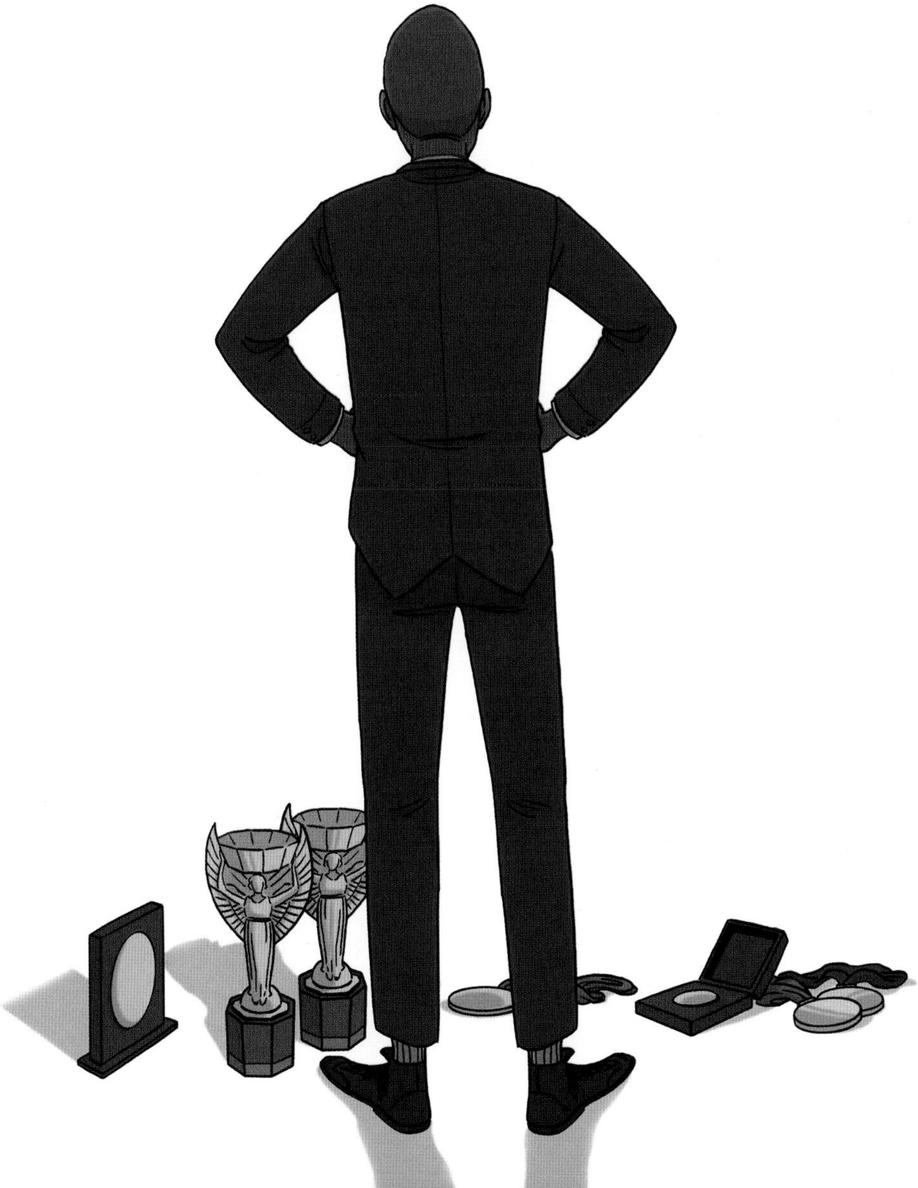

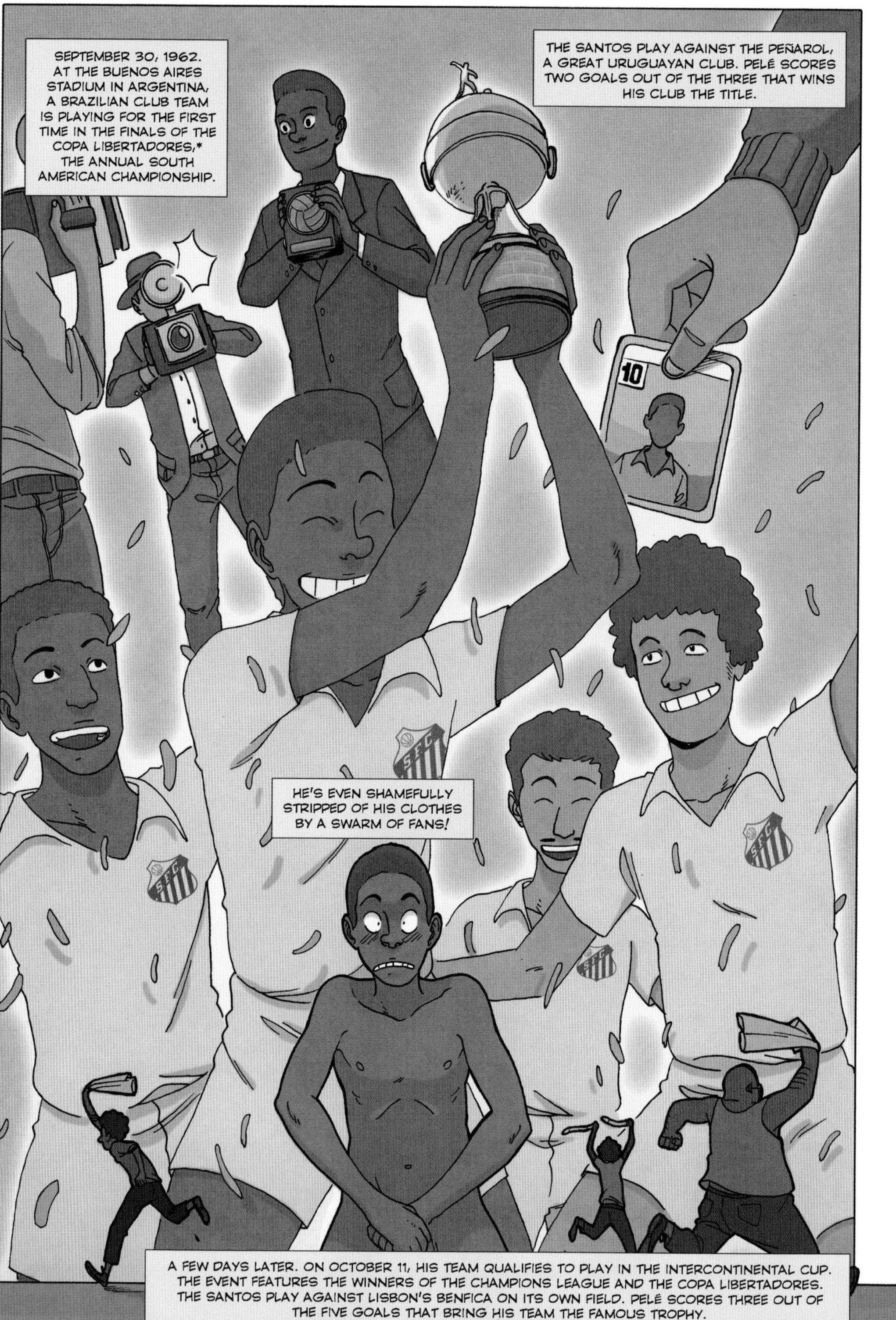
SEPTEMBER 30, 1962. AT THE BUENOS AIRES STADIUM IN ARGENTINA, A BRAZILIAN CLUB TEAM IS PLAYING FOR THE FIRST TIME IN THE FINALS OF THE COPA LIBERTADORES,* THE ANNUAL SOUTH AMERICAN CHAMPIONSHIP.
THE SANTOS PLAY AGAINST THE PEÑAROL, A GREAT URUGUAYAN CLUB. PELÉ SCORES TWO GOALS OUT OF THE THREE THAT WINS HIS CLUB THE TITLE.
10
HE'S EVEN SHAMEFULLY STRIPPED OF HIS CLOTHES BY A SWARM OF FANS!
A FEW DAYS LATER. ON OCTOBER 11, HIS TEAM QUALIFIES TO PLAY IN THE INTERCONTINENTAL CUP. THE EVENT FEATURES THE WINNERS OF THE CHAMPIONS LEAGUE AND THE COPA LIBERTADORES. THE SANTOS PLAY AGAINST LISBON'S BENFICA ON ITS OWN FIELD. PELÉ SCORES THREE OUT OF THE FIVE GOALS THAT BRING HIS TEAM THE FAMOUS TROPHY.

*THE LIBERATORS CUP.

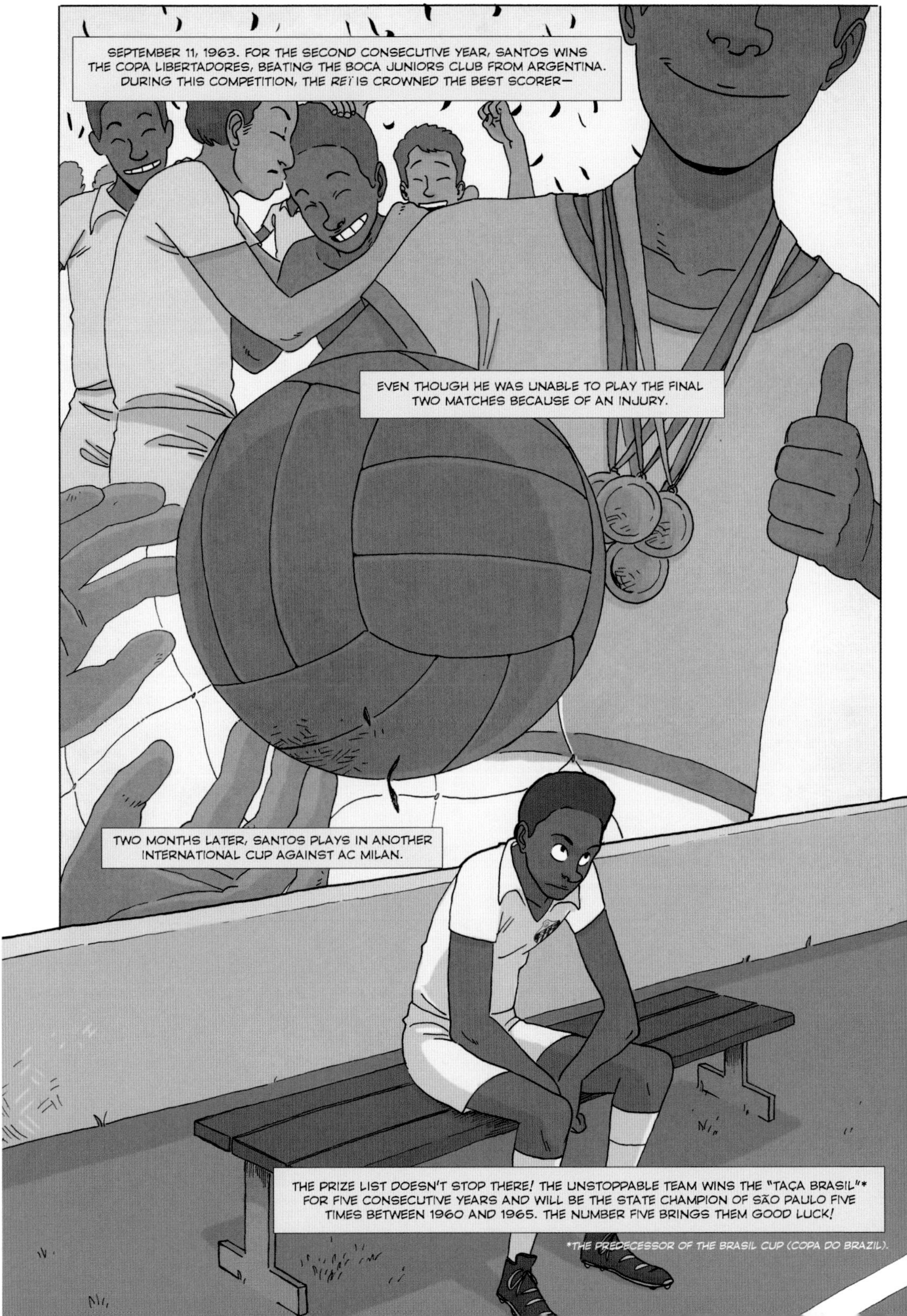
SEPTEMBER 11, 1963. FOR THE SECOND CONSECUTIVE YEAR, SANTOS WINS THE COPA LIBERTADORES, BEATING THE BOCA JUNIORS CLUB FROM ARGENTINA. DURING THIS COMPETITION, THE *REI* IS CROWNED THE BEST SCORER—
EVEN THOUGH HE WAS UNABLE TO PLAY THE FINAL TWO MATCHES BECAUSE OF AN INJURY.
TWO MONTHS LATER, SANTOS PLAYS IN ANOTHER INTERNATIONAL CUP AGAINST AC MILAN.
THE PRIZE LIST DOESN'T STOP THERE! THE UNSTOPPABLE TEAM WINS THE "TAÇA BRASIL"* FOR FIVE CONSECUTIVE YEARS AND WILL BE THE STATE CHAMPION OF SÃO PAULO FIVE TIMES BETWEEN 1960 AND 1965. THE NUMBER FIVE BRINGS THEM GOOD LUCK!
*THE PREDECESSOR OF THE BRASIL CUP (COPA DO BRAZIL).

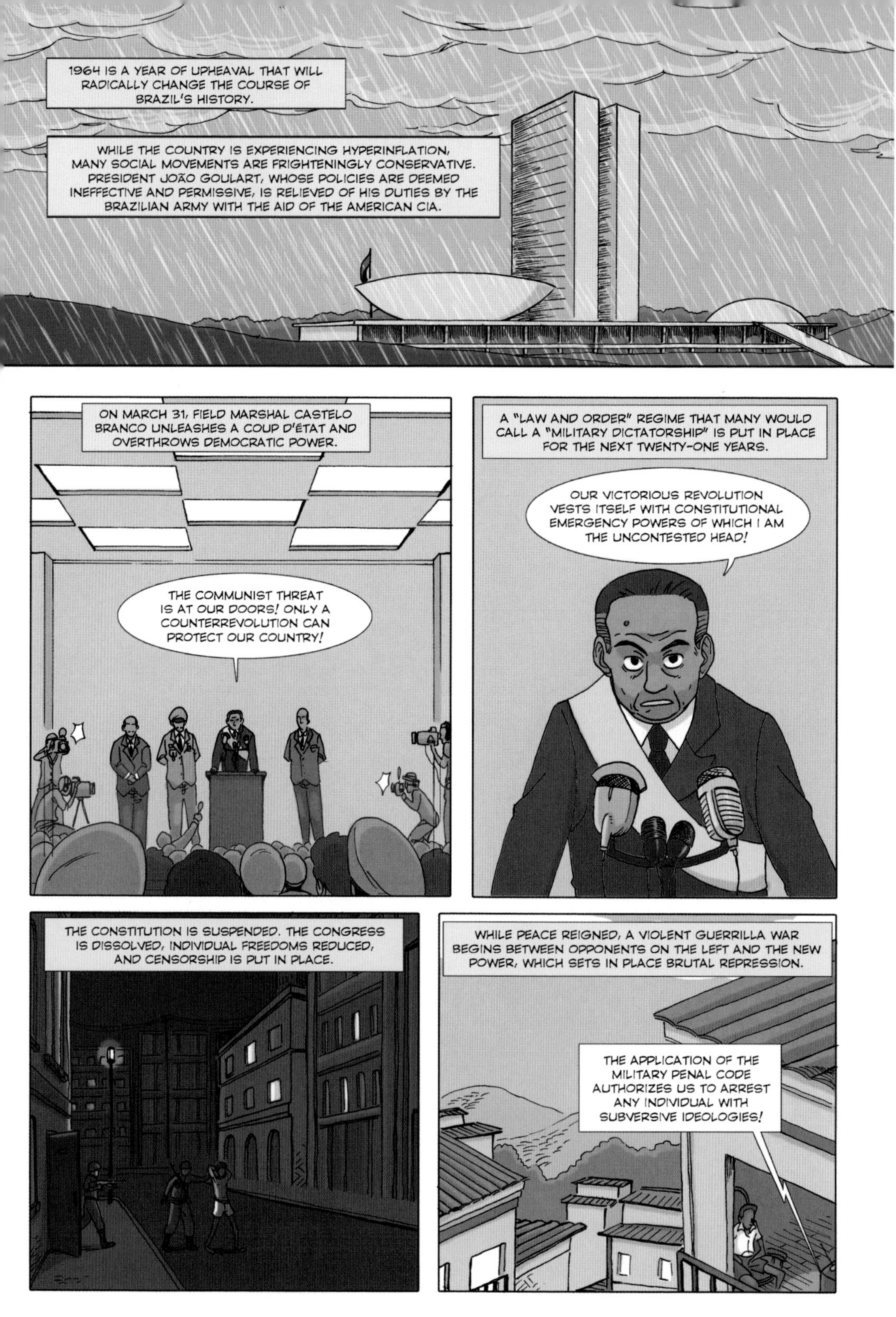
1964 IS A YEAR OF UPHEAVAL THAT WILL RADICALLY CHANGE THE COURSE OF BRAZIL'S HISTORY.
WHILE THE COUNTRY IS EXPERIENCING HYPERINFLATION, MANY SOCIAL MOVEMENTS ARE FRIGHTENINGLY CONSERVATIVE. PRESIDENT JOÃO GOULART, WHOSE POLICIES ARE DEEMED INEFFECTIVE AND PERMISSIVE, IS RELIEVED OF HIS DUTIES BY THE BRAZILIAN ARMY WITH THE AID OF THE AMERICAN CIA.
ON MARCH 31, FIELD MARSHAL CASTELO BRANCO UNLEASHES A COUP D'ÉTAT AND OVERTHROWS DEMOCRATIC POWER.
THE COMMUNIST THREAT IS AT OUR DOORS! ONLY A COUNTERREVOLUTION CAN PROTECT OUR COUNTRY!
A "LAW AND ORDER" REGIME THAT MANY WOULD CALL A "MILITARY DICTATORSHIP" IS PUT IN PLACE FOR THE NEXT TWENTY-ONE YEARS.
OUR VICTORIOUS REVOLUTION VESTS ITSELF WITH CONSTITUTIONAL EMERGENCY POWERS OF WHICH I AM THE UNCONTESTED HEAD!
THE CONSTITUTION IS SUSPENDED. THE CONGRESS IS DISSOLVED, INDIVIDUAL FREEDOMS REDUCED, AND CENSORSHIP IS PUT IN PLACE.
WHILE PEACE REIGNED, A VIOLENT GUERRILLA WAR BEGINS BETWEEN OPPONENTS ON THE LEFT AND THE NEW POWER, WHICH SETS IN PLACE BRUTAL REPRESSION.
THE APPLICATION OF THE MILITARY PENAL CODE AUTHORIZES US TO ARREST ANY INDIVIDUAL WITH SUBVERSIVE IDEOLOGIES!

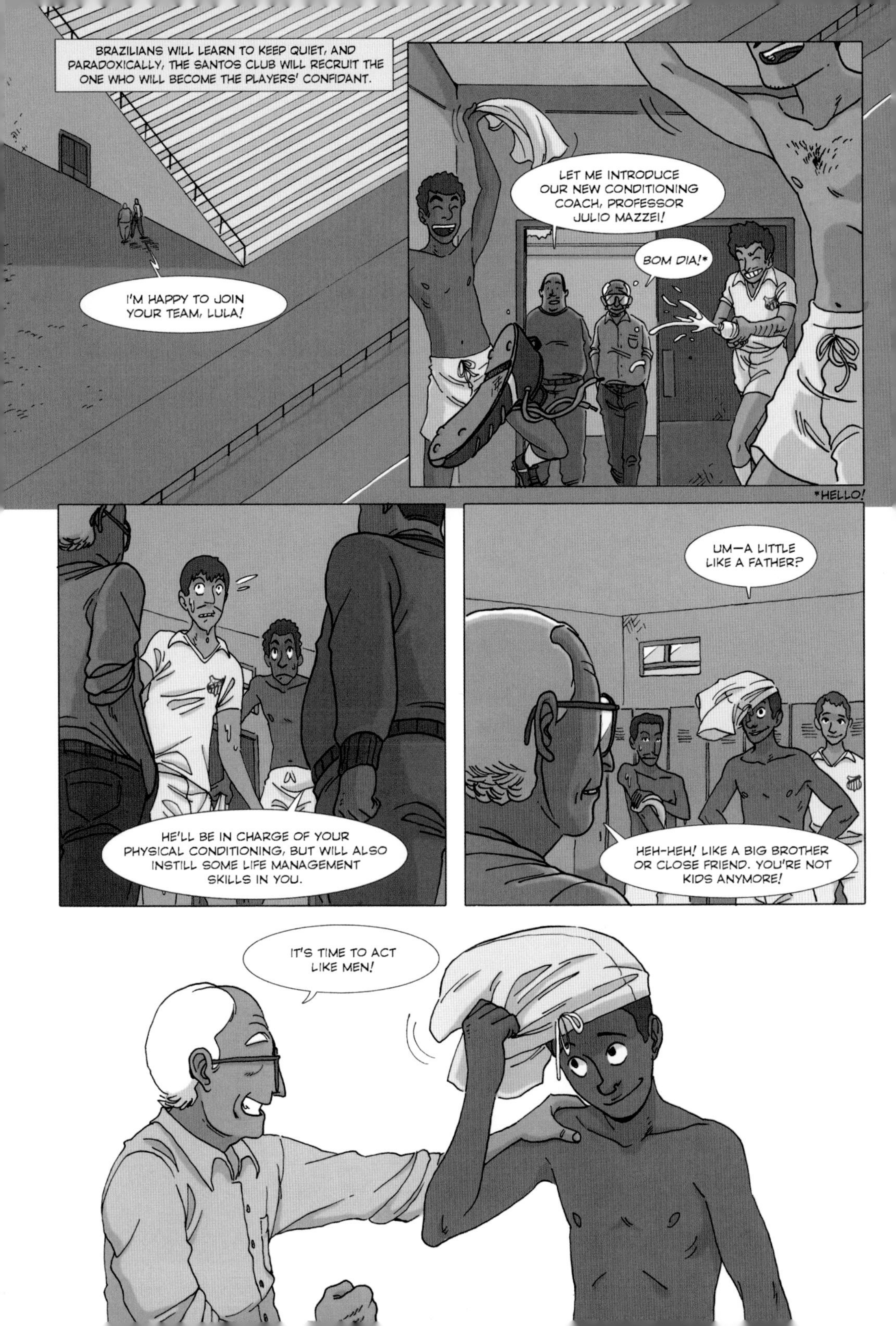
BRAZILIANS WILL LEARN TO KEEP QUIET, AND PARADOXICALLY, THE SANTOS CLUB WILL RECRUIT THE ONE WHO WILL BECOME THE PLAYERS' CONFIDANT.
I'M HAPPY TO JOIN YOUR TEAM, LULA!
LET ME INTRODUCE OUR NEW CONDITIONING COACH, PROFESSOR JULIO MAZZEI!
BOM DIA!*
*HELLO!
HE'LL BE IN CHARGE OF YOUR PHYSICAL CONDITIONING, BUT WILL ALSO INSTILL SOME LIFE MANAGEMENT SKILLS IN YOU.
UM—A LITTLE LIKE A FATHER?
HEH-HEH! LIKE A BIG BROTHER OR CLOSE FRIEND. YOU'RE NOT KIDS ANYMORE!
IT'S TIME TO ACT LIKE MEN!

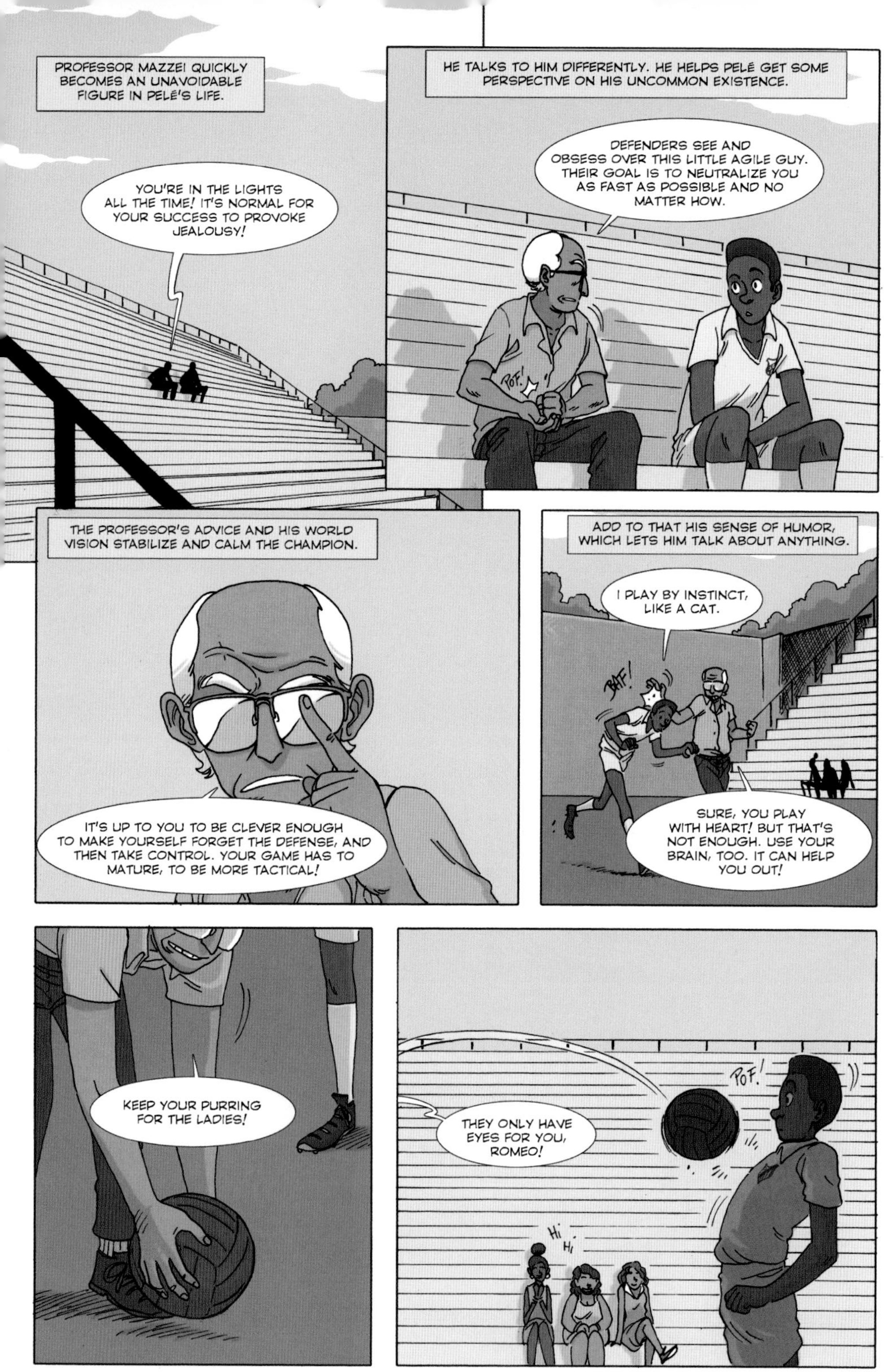
PROFESSOR MAZZEI QUICKLY BECOMES AN UNAVOIDABLE FIGURE IN PELÉ'S LIFE.
YOU'RE IN THE LIGHTS ALL THE TIME! IT'S NORMAL FOR YOUR SUCCESS TO PROVOKE JEALOUSY!
HE TALKS TO HIM DIFFERENTLY. HE HELPS PELÉ GET SOME PERSPECTIVE ON HIS UNCOMMON EXISTENCE.
DEFENDERS SEE AND OBSESS OVER THIS LITTLE AGILE GUY. THEIR GOAL IS TO NEUTRALIZE YOU AS FAST AS POSSIBLE AND NO MATTER HOW.
POF!
THE PROFESSOR'S ADVICE AND HIS WORLD VISION STABILIZE AND CALM THE CHAMPION.
IT'S UP TO YOU TO BE CLEVER ENOUGH TO MAKE YOURSELF FORGET THE DEFENSE, AND THEN TAKE CONTROL. YOUR GAME HAS TO MATURE, TO BE MORE TACTICAL!
ADD TO THAT HIS SENSE OF HUMOR, WHICH LETS HIM TALK ABOUT ANYTHING.
I PLAY BY INSTINCT, LIKE A CAT.
BAF!
SURE, YOU PLAY WITH HEART! BUT THAT'S NOT ENOUGH. USE YOUR BRAIN, TOO. IT CAN HELP YOU OUT!
KEEP YOUR PURRING FOR THE LADIES!
POF!
THEY ONLY HAVE EYES FOR YOU, ROMEO!
HI HI

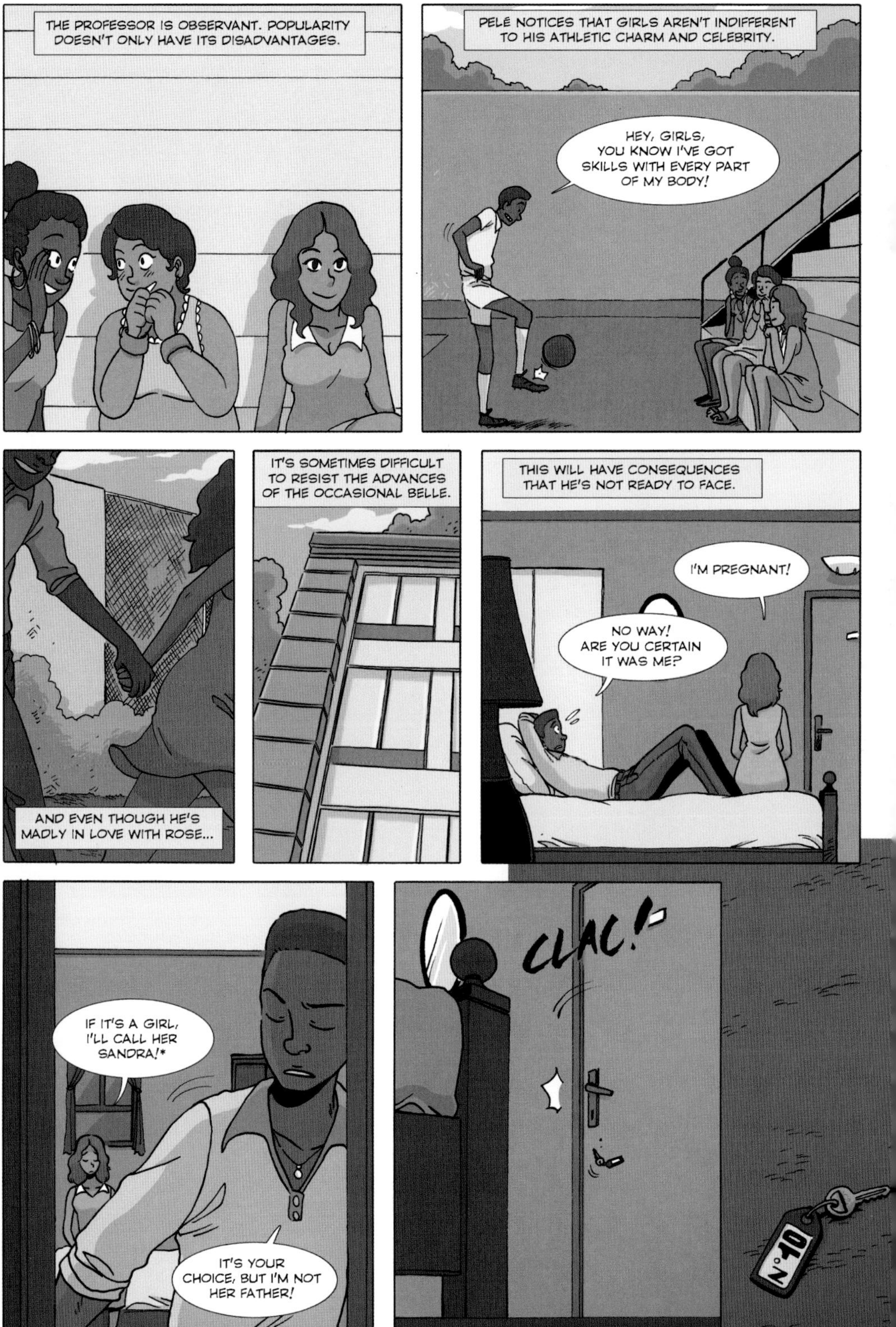
THE PROFESSOR IS OBSERVANT. POPULARITY DOESN'T ONLY HAVE ITS DISADVANTAGES.
PELÉ NOTICES THAT GIRLS AREN'T INDIFFERENT TO HIS ATHLETIC CHARM AND CELEBRITY.
HEY, GIRLS, YOU KNOW I'VE GOT SKILLS WITH EVERY PART OF MY BODY!
AND EVEN THOUGH HE'S MADLY IN LOVE WITH ROSE...
IT'S SOMETIMES DIFFICULT TO RESIST THE ADVANCES OF THE OCCASIONAL BELLE.
THIS WILL HAVE CONSEQUENCES THAT HE'S NOT READY TO FACE.
I'M PREGNANT!
NO WAY! ARE YOU CERTAIN IT WAS ME?
IF IT'S A GIRL, I'LL CALL HER SANDRA!*
IT'S YOUR CHOICE, BUT I'M NOT HER FATHER!
CLAC!

*A FEW YEARS LATER, SANDRA MACEDO WILL BE RECOGNIZED BY COURTS AS PELÉ'S ELDEST DAUGHTER. HE WILL ALWAYS REFUSE TO RECOGNIZE THIS PATERNITY.

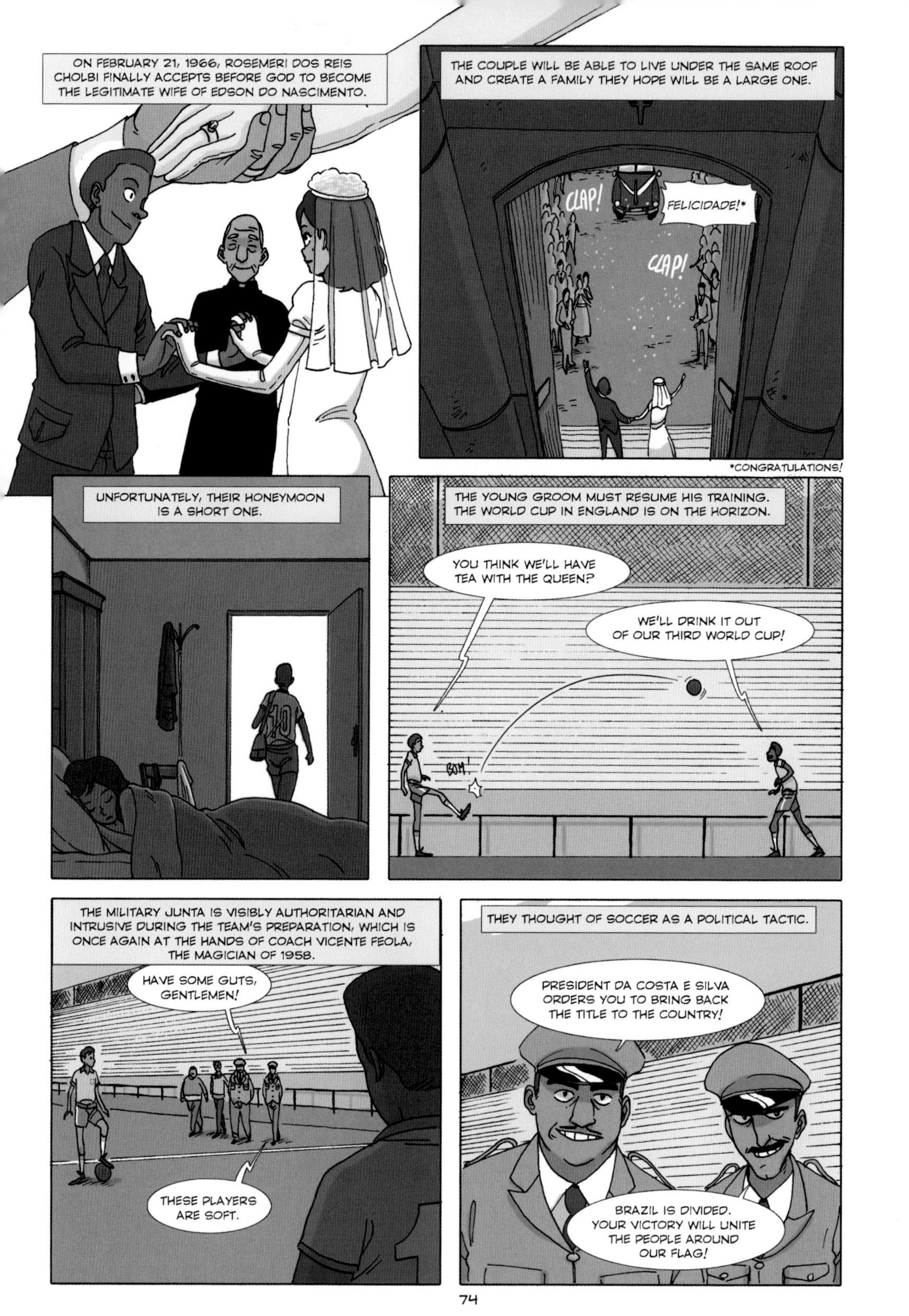
ON FEBRUARY 21, 1966, ROSEMERI DOS REIS CHOLBI FINALLY ACCEPTS BEFORE GOD TO BECOME THE LEGITIMATE WIFE OF EDSON DO NASCIMENTO.
THE COUPLE WILL BE ABLE TO LIVE UNDER THE SAME ROOF AND CREATE A FAMILY THEY HOPE WILL BE A LARGE ONE.
CLAP!
FELICIDADE!*
CLAP!
*CONGRATULATIONS!
UNFORTUNATELY, THEIR HONEYMOON IS A SHORT ONE.
THE YOUNG GROOM MUST RESUME HIS TRAINING. THE WORLD CUP IN ENGLAND IS ON THE HORIZON.
YOU THINK WE'LL HAVE TEA WITH THE QUEEN?
WE'LL DRINK IT OUT OF OUR THIRD WORLD CUP!
BOM!
THE MILITARY JUNTA IS VISIBLY AUTHORITARIAN AND INTRUSIVE DURING THE TEAM'S PREPARATION, WHICH IS ONCE AGAIN AT THE HANDS OF COACH VICENTE FEOLA, THE MAGICIAN OF 1958.
HAVE SOME GUTS, GENTLEMEN!
THESE PLAYERS ARE SOFT.
THEY THOUGHT OF SOCCER AS A POLITICAL TACTIC.
PRESIDENT DA COSTA E SILVA ORDERS YOU TO BRING BACK THE TITLE TO THE COUNTRY!
BRAZIL IS DIVIDED. YOUR VICTORY WILL UNITE THE PEOPLE AROUND OUR FLAG!

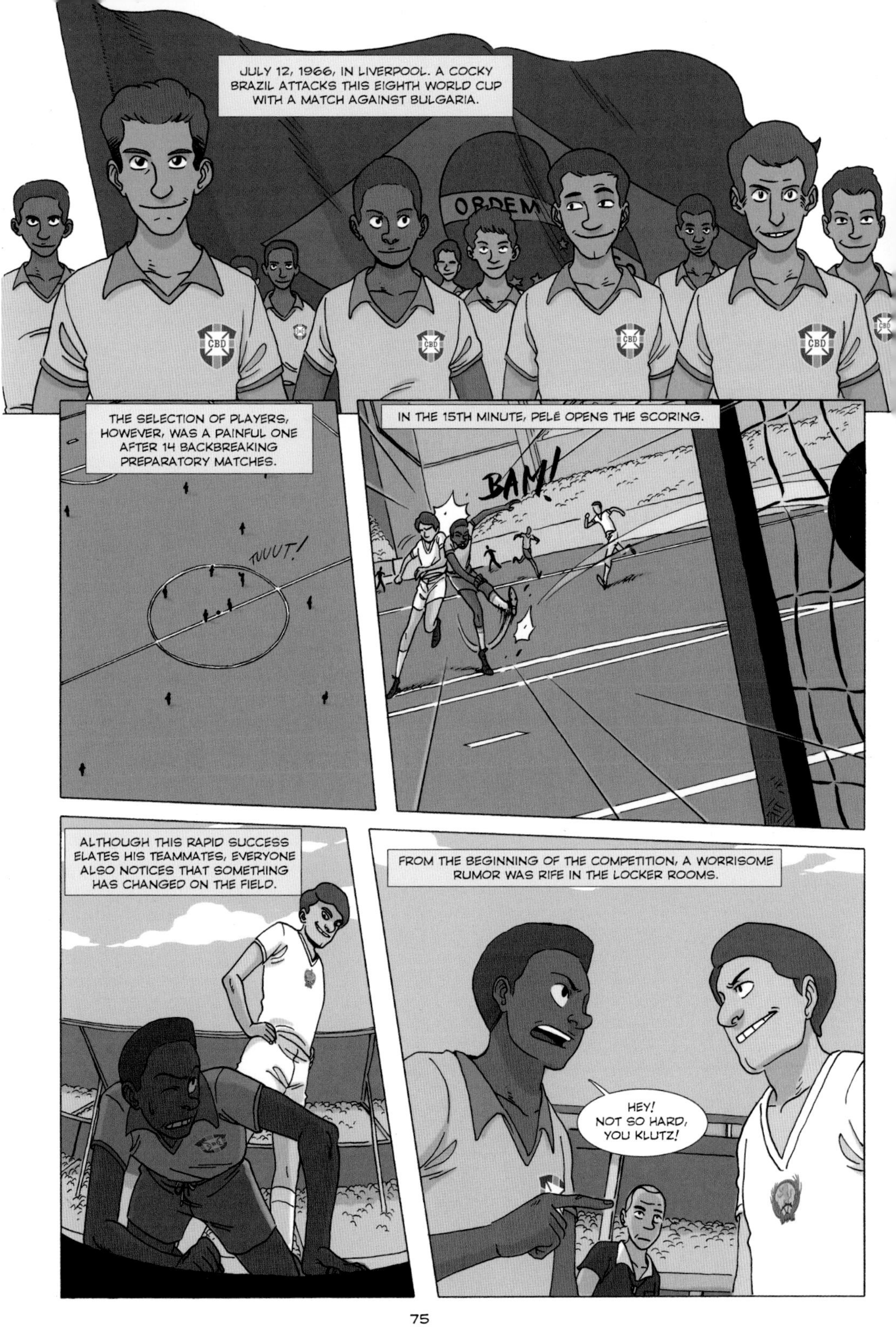
JULY 12, 1966, IN LIVERPOOL. A COCKY BRAZIL ATTACKS THIS EIGHTH WORLD CUP WITH A MATCH AGAINST BULGARIA.
ORDEM
THE SELECTION OF PLAYERS, HOWEVER, WAS A PAINFUL ONE AFTER 14 BACKBREAKING PREPARATORY MATCHES.
TUUUT!
IN THE 15TH MINUTE, PELÉ OPENS THE SCORING.
BAM!
ALTHOUGH THIS RAPID SUCCESS ELATES HIS TEAMMATES, EVERYONE ALSO NOTICES THAT SOMETHING HAS CHANGED ON THE FIELD.
FROM THE BEGINNING OF THE COMPETITION, A WORRISOME RUMOR WAS RIFE IN THE LOCKER ROOMS.
HEY! NOT SO HARD, YOU KLUTZ!

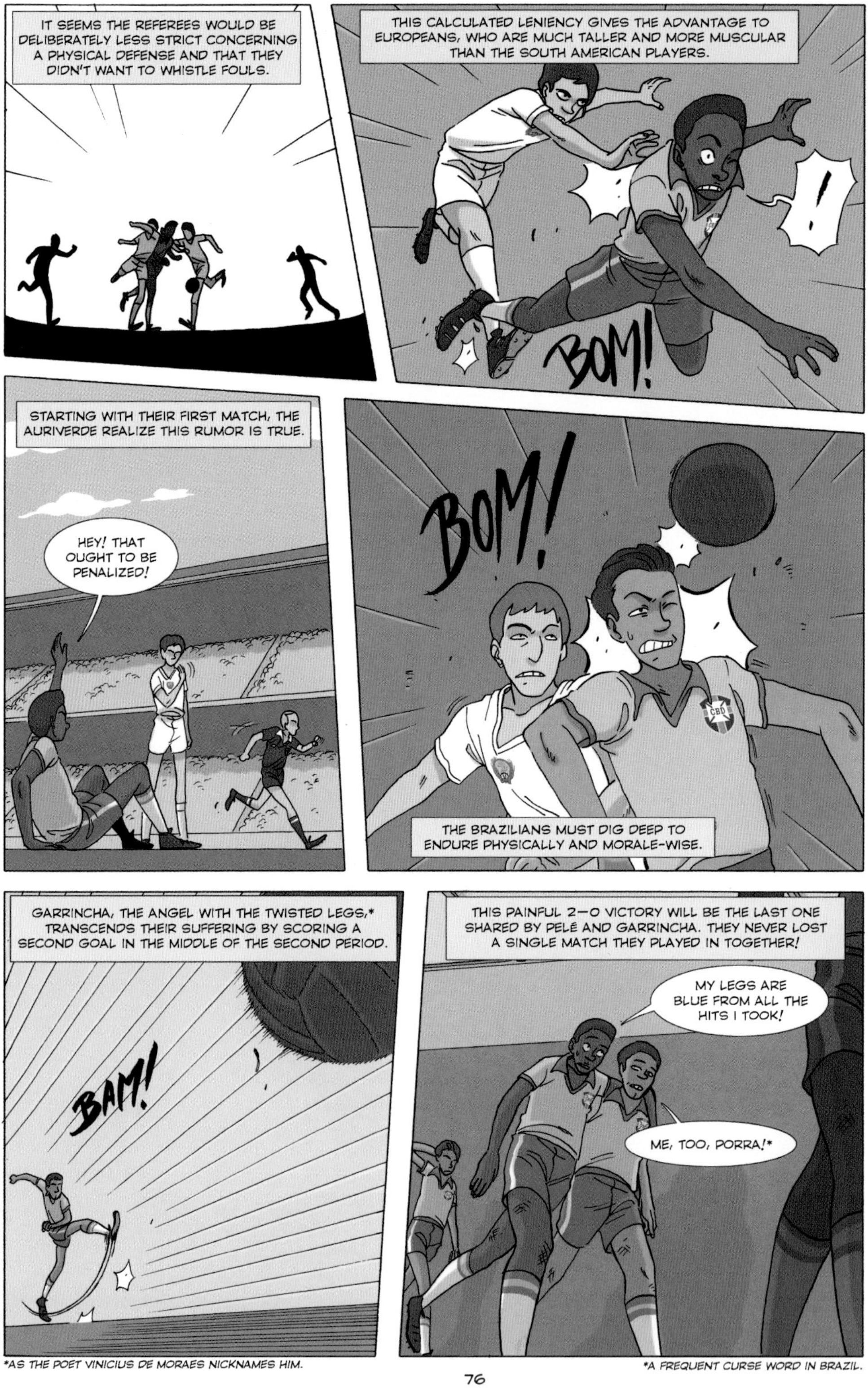
IT SEEMS THE REFEREES WOULD BE DELIBERATELY LESS STRICT CONCERNING A PHYSICAL DEFENSE AND THAT THEY DIDN'T WANT TO WHISTLE FOULS.
THIS CALCULATED LENIENCY GIVES THE ADVANTAGE TO EUROPEANS, WHO ARE MUCH TALLER AND MORE MUSCULAR THAN THE SOUTH AMERICAN PLAYERS.
!
BOM!
STARTING WITH THEIR FIRST MATCH, THE AURIVERDE REALIZE THIS RUMOR IS TRUE.
HEY! THAT OUGHT TO BE PENALIZED!
BOM!
THE BRAZILIANS MUST DIG DEEP TO ENDURE PHYSICALLY AND MORALE-WISE.
GARRINCHA, THE ANGEL WITH THE TWISTED LEGS,* TRANSCENDS THEIR SUFFERING BY SCORING A SECOND GOAL IN THE MIDDLE OF THE SECOND PERIOD.
BAM!
THIS PAINFUL 2—0 VICTORY WILL BE THE LAST ONE SHARED BY PELÉ AND GARRINCHA. THEY NEVER LOST A SINGLE MATCH THEY PLAYED IN TOGETHER!
MY LEGS ARE BLUE FROM ALL THE HITS I TOOK!
ME, TOO, PORRA!*

*AS THE POET VINICIUS DE MORAES NICKNAMES HIM.

*A FREQUENT CURSE WORD IN BRAZIL.

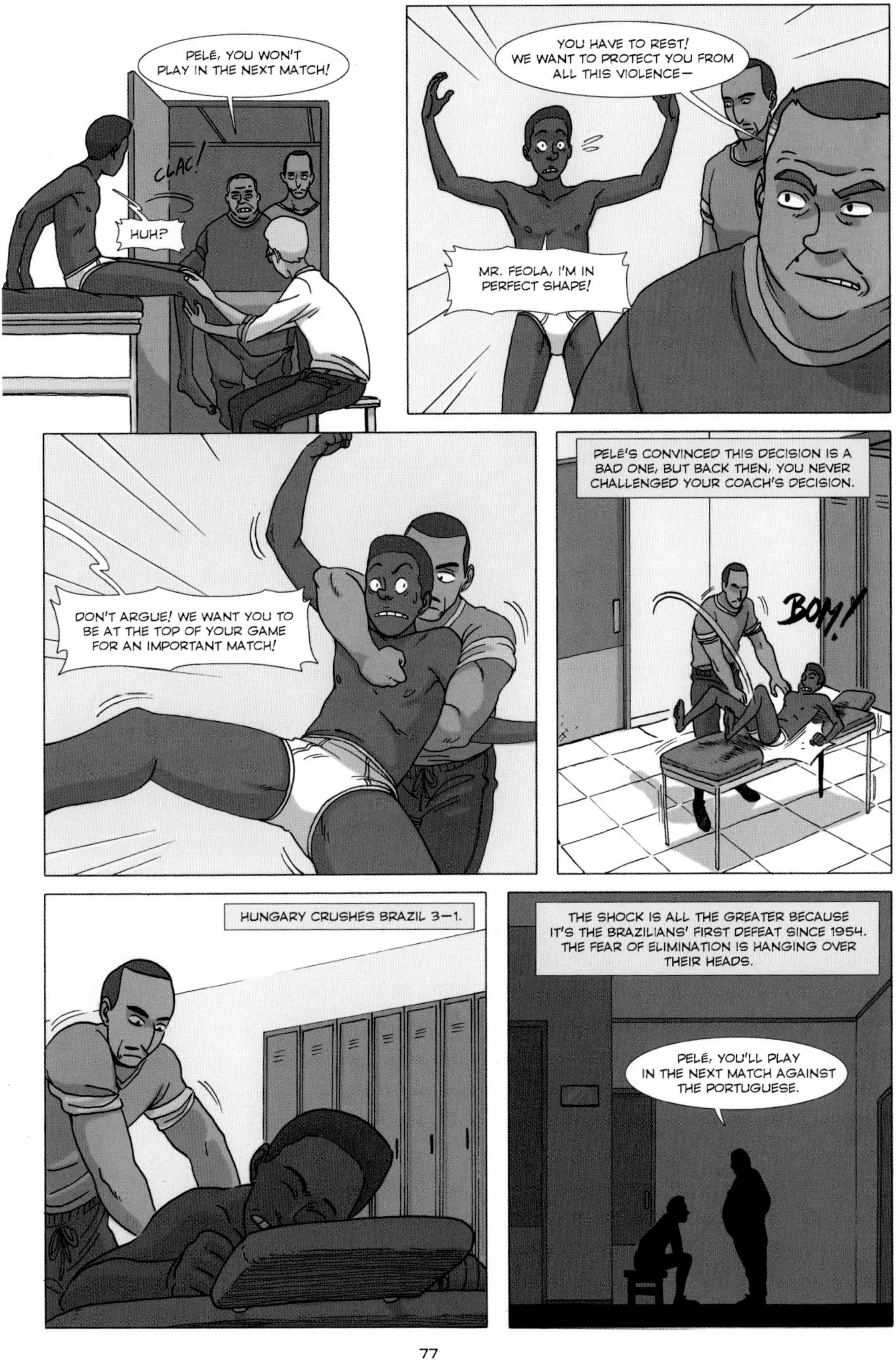
PELÉ, YOU WON'T PLAY IN THE NEXT MATCH!
CLAC!
HUH?
YOU HAVE TO REST! WE WANT TO PROTECT YOU FROM ALL THIS VIOLENCE—
MR. FEOLA, I'M IN PERFECT SHAPE!
DON'T ARGUE! WE WANT YOU TO BE AT THE TOP OF YOUR GAME FOR AN IMPORTANT MATCH!
PELÉ'S CONVINCED THIS DECISION IS A BAD ONE, BUT BACK THEN, YOU NEVER CHALLENGED YOUR COACH'S DECISION.
BOM!
HUNGARY CRUSHES BRAZIL 3—1.
THE SHOCK IS ALL THE GREATER BECAUSE IT'S THE BRAZILIANS' FIRST DEFEAT SINCE 1954. THE FEAR OF ELIMINATION IS HANGING OVER THEIR HEADS.
PELÉ, YOU'LL PLAY IN THE NEXT MATCH AGAINST THE PORTUGUESE.

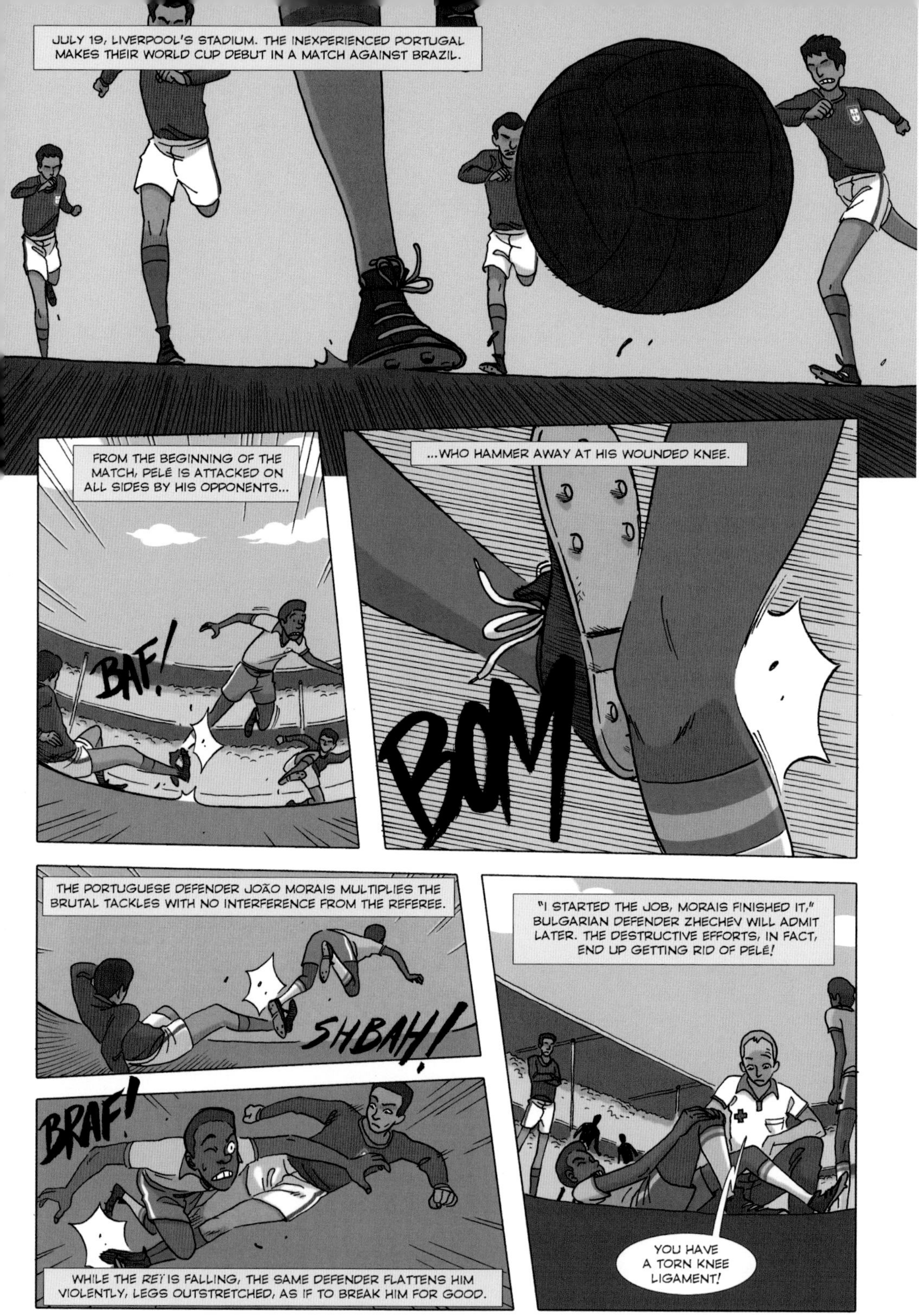
JULY 19, LIVERPOOL'S STADIUM. THE INEXPERIENCED PORTUGAL MAKES THEIR WORLD CUP DEBUT IN A MATCH AGAINST BRAZIL.
FROM THE BEGINNING OF THE MATCH, PELÉ IS ATTACKED ON ALL SIDES BY HIS OPPONENTS...
BAF!
...WHO HAMMER AWAY AT HIS WOUNDED KNEE.
BOM
THE PORTUGUESE DEFENDER JOÃO MORAIS MULTIPLIES THE BRUTAL TACKLES WITH NO INTERFERENCE FROM THE REFEREE.
SHBAH!
BRAF!
WHILE THE REI IS FALLING, THE SAME DEFENDER FLATTENS HIM VIOLENTLY, LEGS OUTSTRETCHED, AS IF TO BREAK HIM FOR GOOD.
"I STARTED THE JOB, MORAIS FINISHED IT," BULGARIAN DEFENDER ZHECHEV WILL ADMIT LATER. THE DESTRUCTIVE EFFORTS, IN FACT, END UP GETTING RID OF PELÉ!
YOU HAVE A TORN KNEE LIGAMENT!

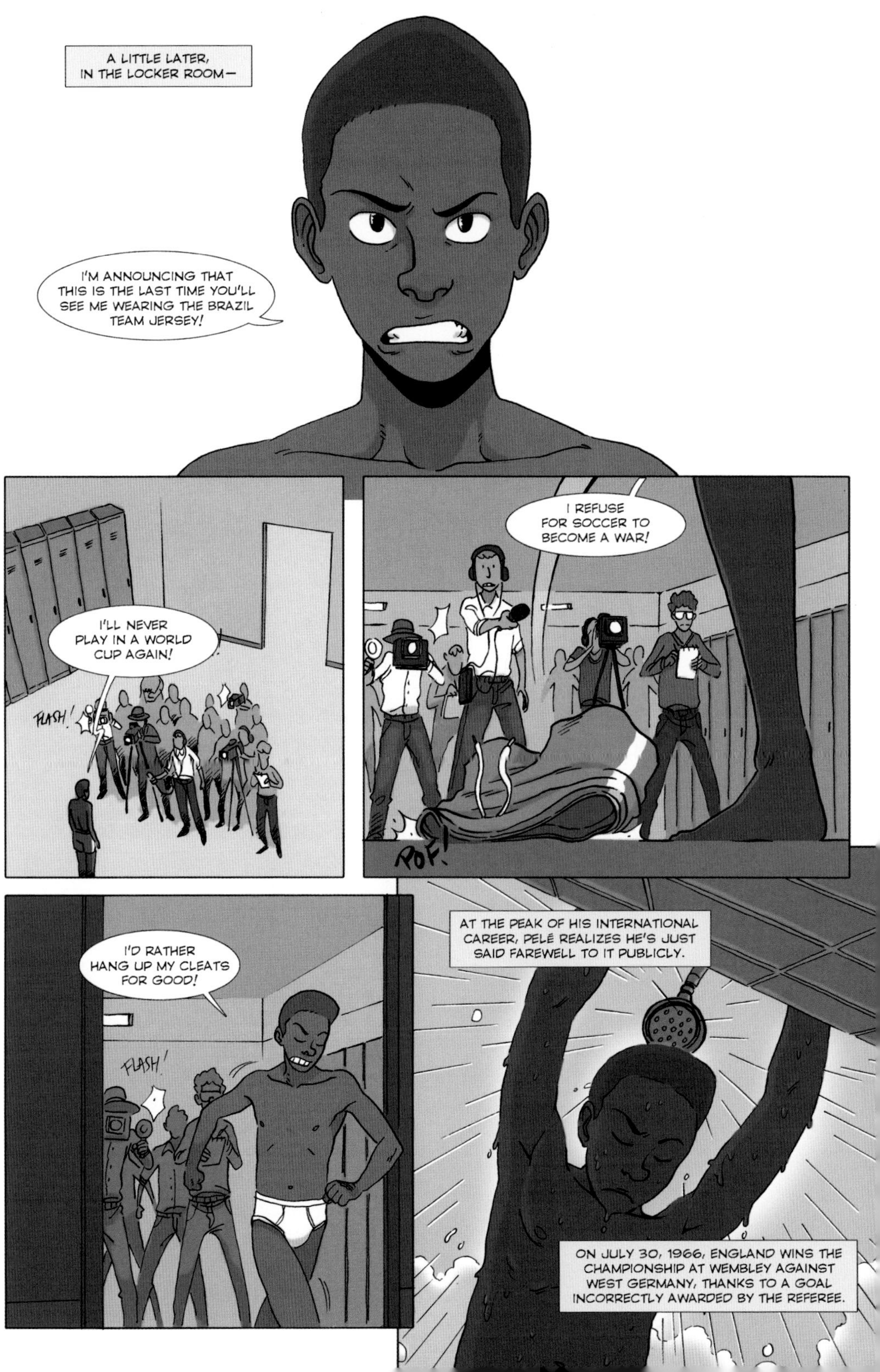
A LITTLE LATER, IN THE LOCKER ROOM—
I'M ANNOUNCING THAT THIS IS THE LAST TIME YOU'LL SEE ME WEARING THE BRAZIL TEAM JERSEY!
I'LL NEVER PLAY IN A WORLD CUP AGAIN!
FLASH!
I REFUSE FOR SOCCER TO BECOME A WAR!
POF!
I'D RATHER HANG UP MY CLEATS FOR GOOD!
FLASH!
AT THE PEAK OF HIS INTERNATIONAL CAREER, PELÉ REALIZES HE'S JUST SAID FAREWELL TO IT PUBLICLY.
ON JULY 30, 1966, ENGLAND WINS THE CHAMPIONSHIP AT WEMBLEY AGAINST WEST GERMANY, THANKS TO A GOAL INCORRECTLY AWARDED BY THE REFEREE.

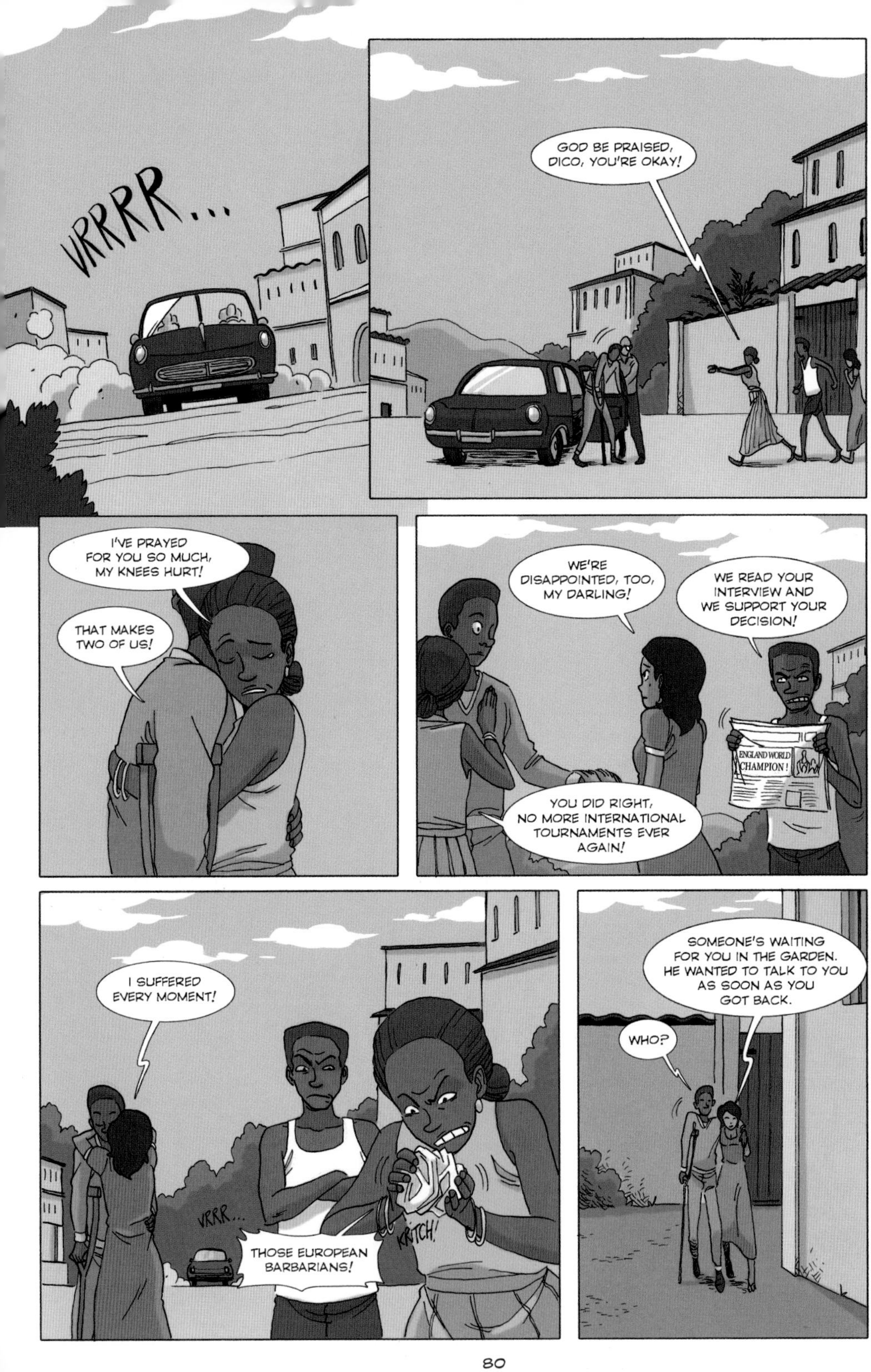
VRRRR...
GOD BE PRAISED, DICO, YOU'RE OKAY!
I'VE PRAYED FOR YOU SO MUCH, MY KNEES HURT!
THAT MAKES TWO OF US!
WE'RE DISAPPOINTED, TOO, MY DARLING!
WE READ YOUR INTERVIEW AND WE SUPPORT YOUR DECISION!
ENGLAND WORLD CHAMPION!
YOU DID RIGHT, NO MORE INTERNATIONAL TOURNAMENTS EVER AGAIN!
I SUFFERED EVERY MOMENT!
VRRR...
THOSE EUROPEAN BARBARIANS!
KRITCH!
SOMEONE'S WAITING FOR YOU IN THE GARDEN. HE WANTED TO TALK TO YOU AS SOON AS YOU GOT BACK.
WHO?

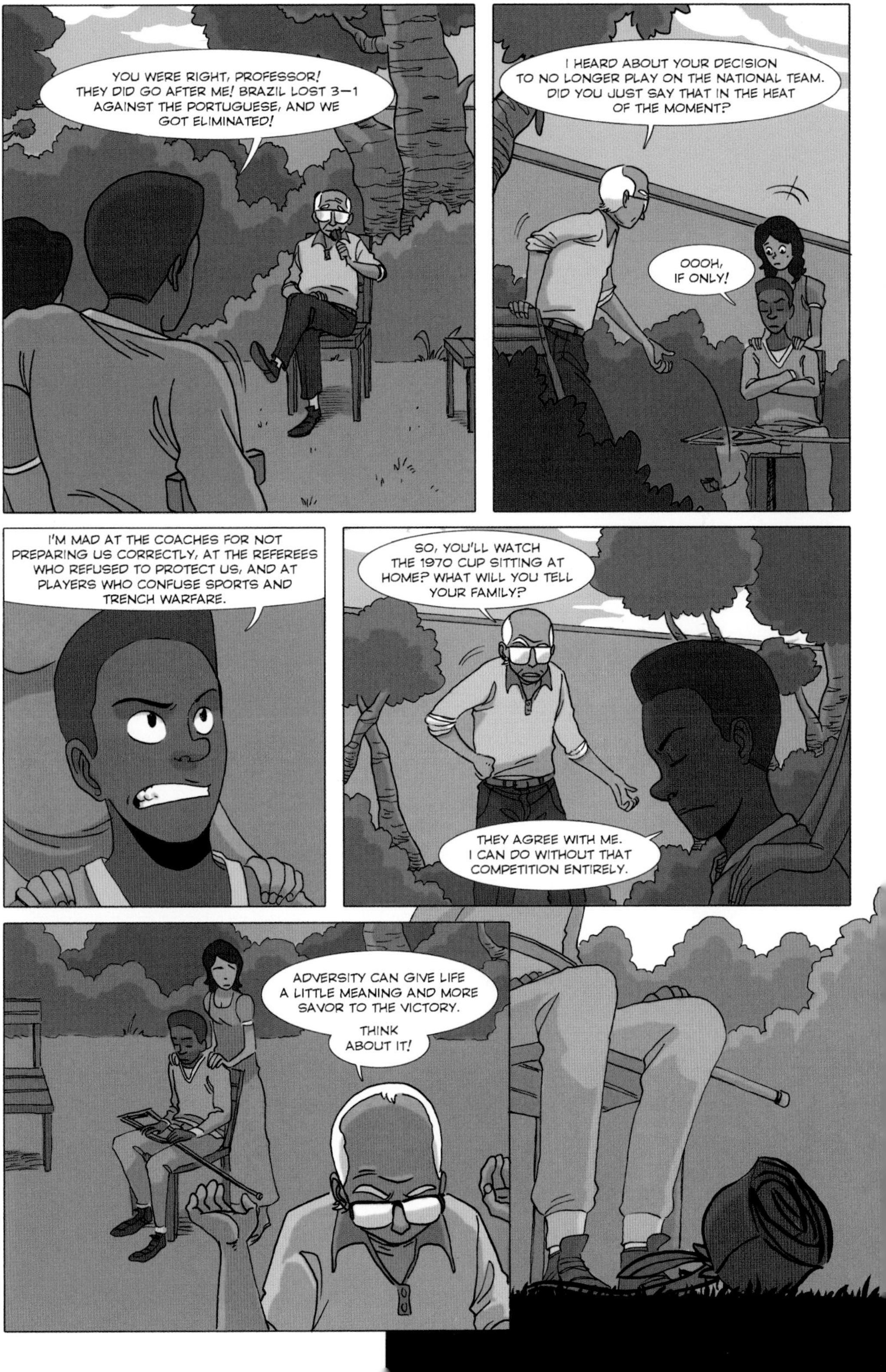
YOU WERE RIGHT, PROFESSOR! THEY DID GO AFTER ME! BRAZIL LOST 3–1 AGAINST THE PORTUGUESE, AND WE GOT ELIMINATED!
I HEARD ABOUT YOUR DECISION TO NO LONGER PLAY ON THE NATIONAL TEAM. DID YOU JUST SAY THAT IN THE HEAT OF THE MOMENT?
OOOH, IF ONLY!
I'M MAD AT THE COACHES FOR NOT PREPARING US CORRECTLY, AT THE REFEREES WHO REFUSED TO PROTECT US, AND AT PLAYERS WHO CONFUSE SPORTS AND TRENCH WARFARE.
SO, YOU'LL WATCH THE 1970 CUP SITTING AT HOME? WHAT WILL YOU TELL YOUR FAMILY?
THEY AGREE WITH ME. I CAN DO WITHOUT THAT COMPETITION ENTIRELY.
ADVERSITY CAN GIVE LIFE A LITTLE MEANING AND MORE SAVOR TO THE VICTORY.
THINK ABOUT IT!

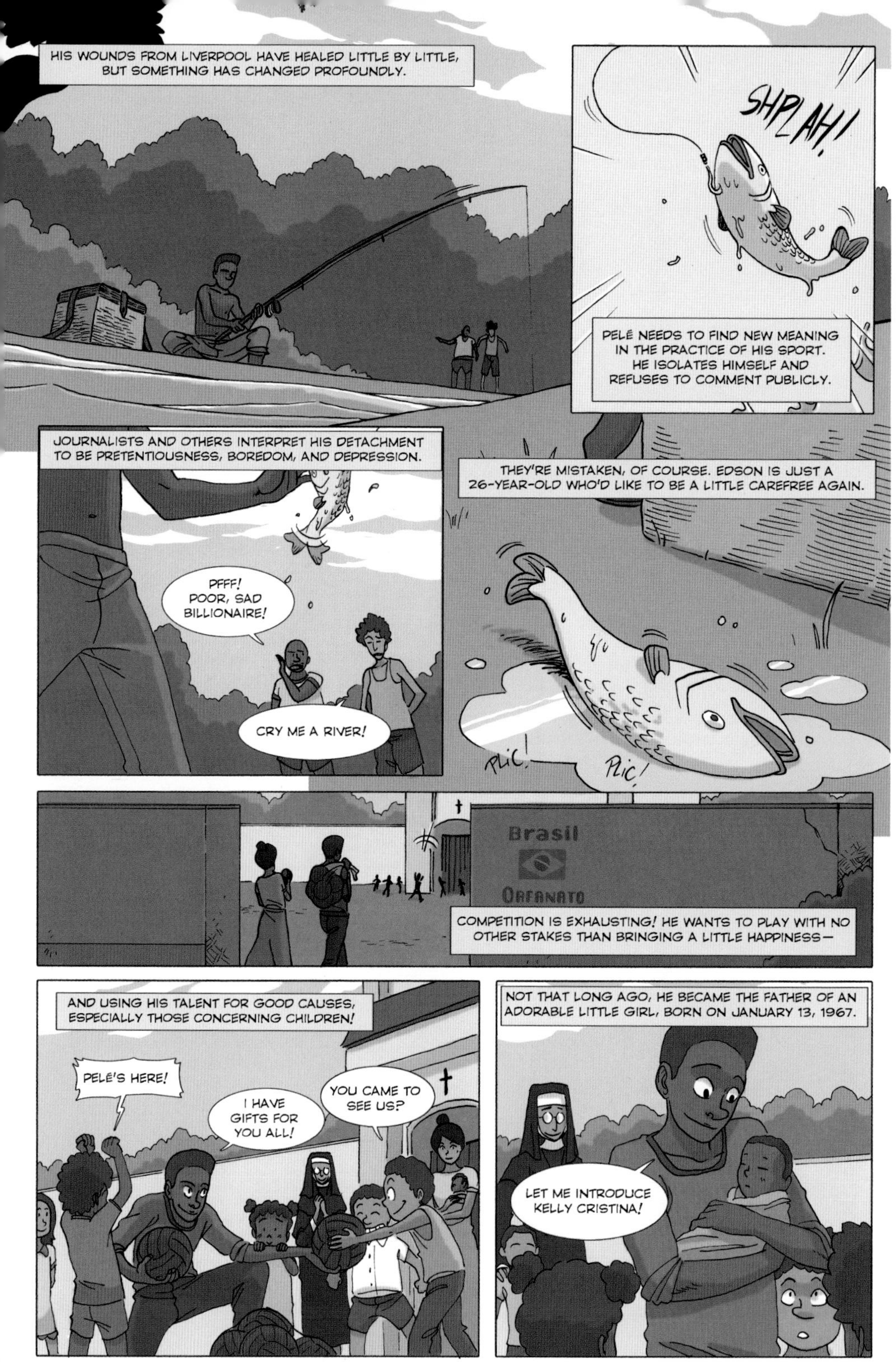
HIS WOUNDS FROM LIVERPOOL HAVE HEALED LITTLE BY LITTLE, BUT SOMETHING HAS CHANGED PROFOUNDLY.
SHPLAH!
PELÉ NEEDS TO FIND NEW MEANING IN THE PRACTICE OF HIS SPORT. HE ISOLATES HIMSELF AND REFUSES TO COMMENT PUBLICLY.
JOURNALISTS AND OTHERS INTERPRET HIS DETACHMENT TO BE PRETENTIOUSNESS, BOREDOM, AND DEPRESSION.
PFFF! POOR, SAD BILLIONAIRE!
CRY ME A RIVER!
THEY'RE MISTAKEN, OF COURSE. EDSON IS JUST A 26-YEAR-OLD WHO'D LIKE TO BE A LITTLE CAREFREE AGAIN.
PLIC!
PLIC!
Brasil
ORFANATO
COMPETITION IS EXHAUSTING! HE WANTS TO PLAY WITH NO OTHER STAKES THAN BRINGING A LITTLE HAPPINESS—
AND USING HIS TALENT FOR GOOD CAUSES, ESPECIALLY THOSE CONCERNING CHILDREN!
PELÉ'S HERE!
I HAVE GIFTS FOR YOU ALL!
YOU CAME TO SEE US?
NOT THAT LONG AGO, HE BECAME THE FATHER OF AN ADORABLE LITTLE GIRL, BORN ON JANUARY 13, 1967.
LET ME INTRODUCE KELLY CRISTINA!

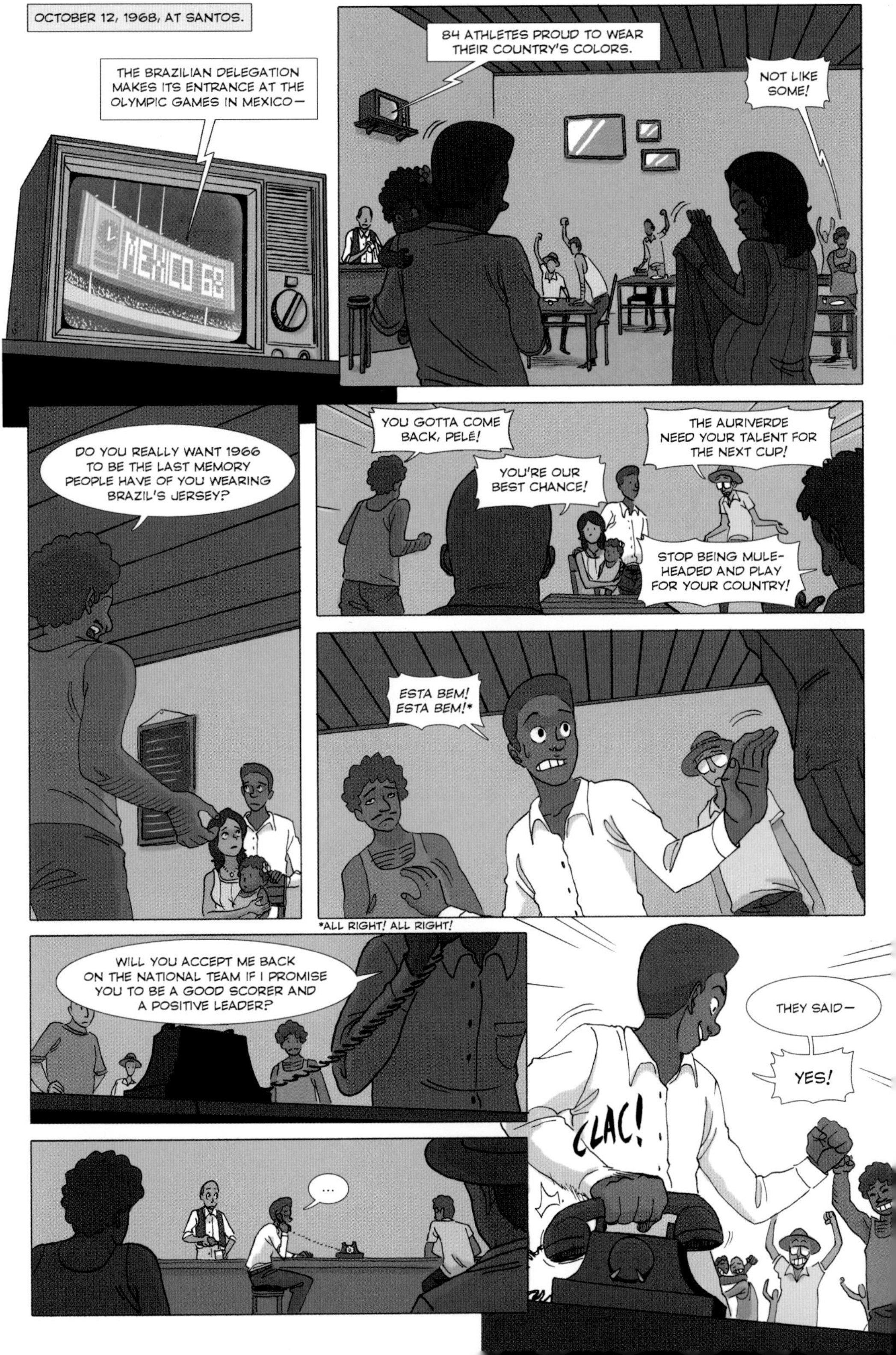

OCTOBER 12, 1968, AT SANTOS.
THE BRAZILIAN DELEGATION MAKES ITS ENTRANCE AT THE OLYMPIC GAMES IN MEXICO—
MEXICO 68
84 ATHLETES PROUD TO WEAR THEIR COUNTRY'S COLORS.
NOT LIKE SOME!
DO YOU REALLY WANT 1966 TO BE THE LAST MEMORY PEOPLE HAVE OF YOU WEARING BRAZIL'S JERSEY?
YOU GOTTA COME BACK, PELÉ!
YOU'RE OUR BEST CHANCE!
THE AURIVERDE NEED YOUR TALENT FOR THE NEXT CUP!
STOP BEING MULE-HEADED AND PLAY FOR YOUR COUNTRY!
ESTA BEM! ESTA BEM!*
*ALL RIGHT! ALL RIGHT!
WILL YOU ACCEPT ME BACK ON THE NATIONAL TEAM IF I PROMISE YOU TO BE A GOOD SCORER AND A POSITIVE LEADER?
...
THEY SAID—
YES!
CLAC!

Halftime!
The 1,000th

"Scoring one thousand goals like Pelé isn't the most difficult or most extraordinary thing. Scoring one goal like Pelé is."
—Carlos Drummond de Andrade, Brazilian poet

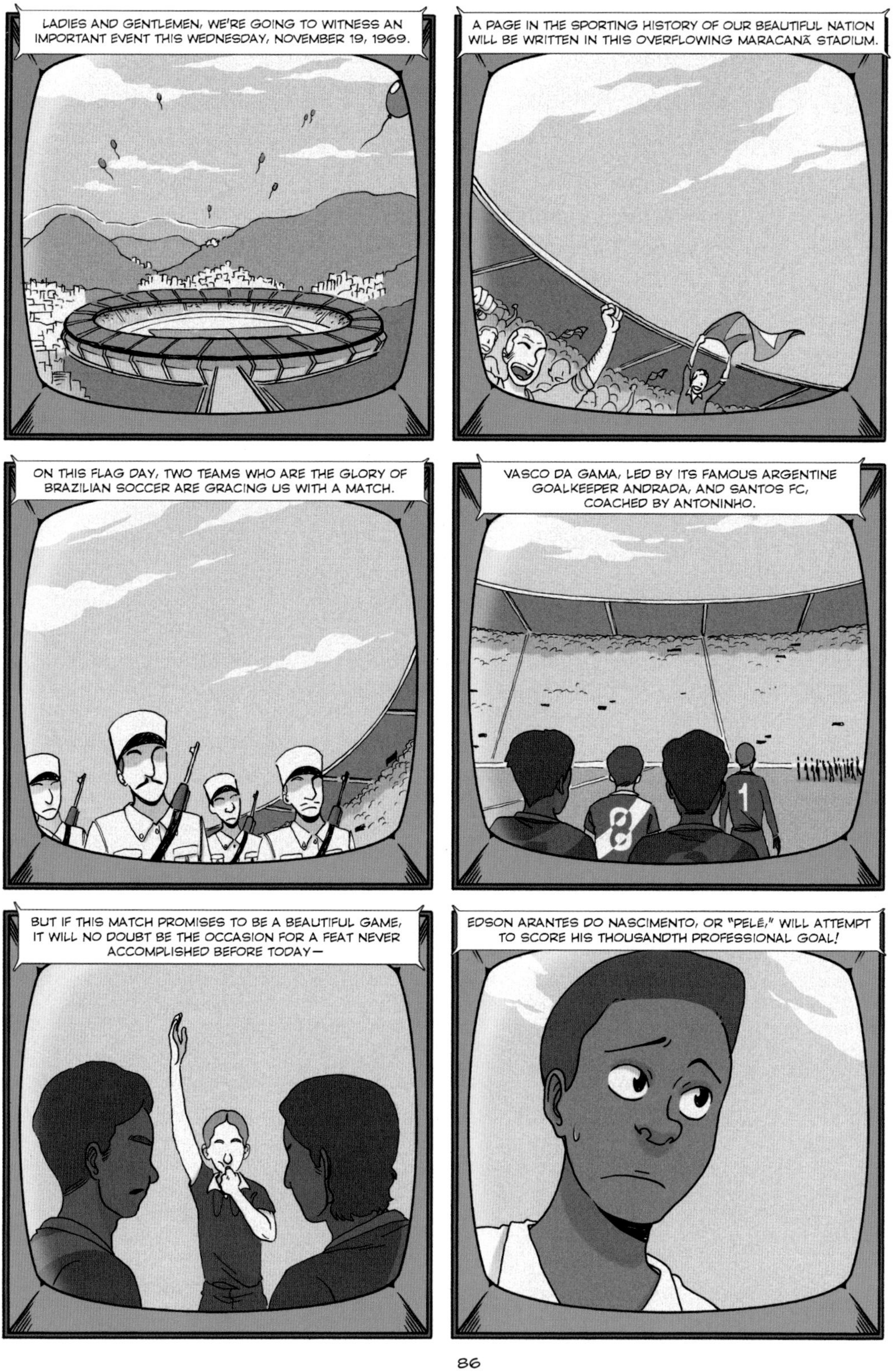
LADIES AND GENTLEMEN, WE'RE GOING TO WITNESS AN IMPORTANT EVENT THIS WEDNESDAY, NOVEMBER 19, 1969.
A PAGE IN THE SPORTING HISTORY OF OUR BEAUTIFUL NATION WILL BE WRITTEN IN THIS OVERFLOWING MARACANÃ STADIUM.
ON THIS FLAG DAY, TWO TEAMS WHO ARE THE GLORY OF BRAZILIAN SOCCER ARE GRACING US WITH A MATCH.
VASCO DA GAMA, LED BY ITS FAMOUS ARGENTINE GOALKEEPER ANDRADA, AND SANTOS FC, COACHED BY ANTONINHO.
8
1
BUT IF THIS MATCH PROMISES TO BE A BEAUTIFUL GAME, IT WILL NO DOUBT BE THE OCCASION FOR A FEAT NEVER ACCOMPLISHED BEFORE TODAY—
EDSON ARANTES DO NASCIMENTO, OR "PELÉ," WILL ATTEMPT TO SCORE HIS THOUSANDTH PROFESSIONAL GOAL!

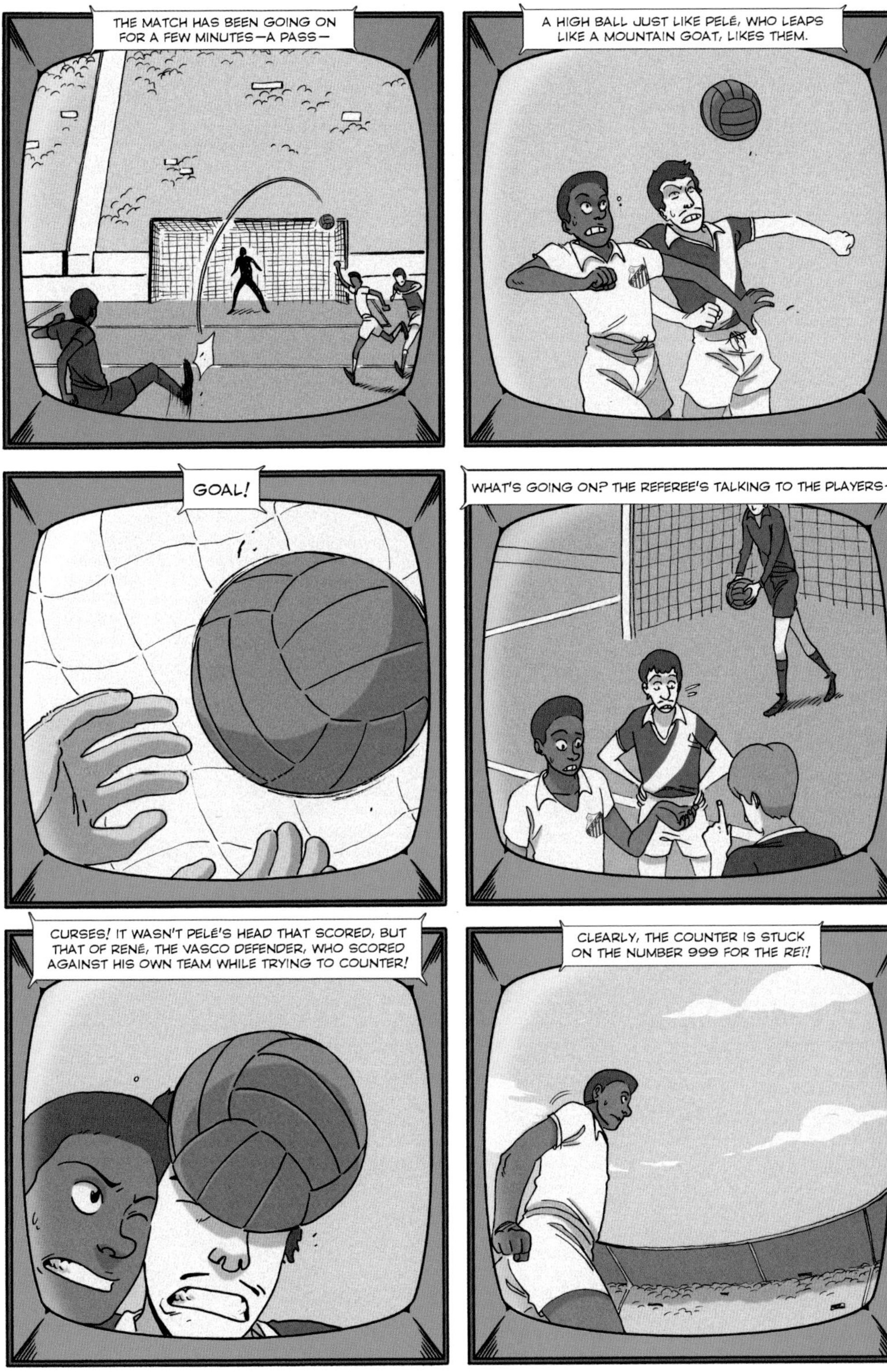
THE MATCH HAS BEEN GOING ON FOR A FEW MINUTES—A PASS—
A HIGH BALL JUST LIKE PELÉ, WHO LEAPS LIKE A MOUNTAIN GOAT, LIKES THEM.
GOAL!
WHAT'S GOING ON? THE REFEREE'S TALKING TO THE PLAYERS—
CURSES! IT WASN'T PELÉ'S HEAD THAT SCORED, BUT THAT OF RENÉ, THE VASCO DEFENDER, WHO SCORED AGAINST HIS OWN TEAM WHILE TRYING TO COUNTER!
CLEARLY, THE COUNTER IS STUCK ON THE NUMBER 999 FOR THE REI!

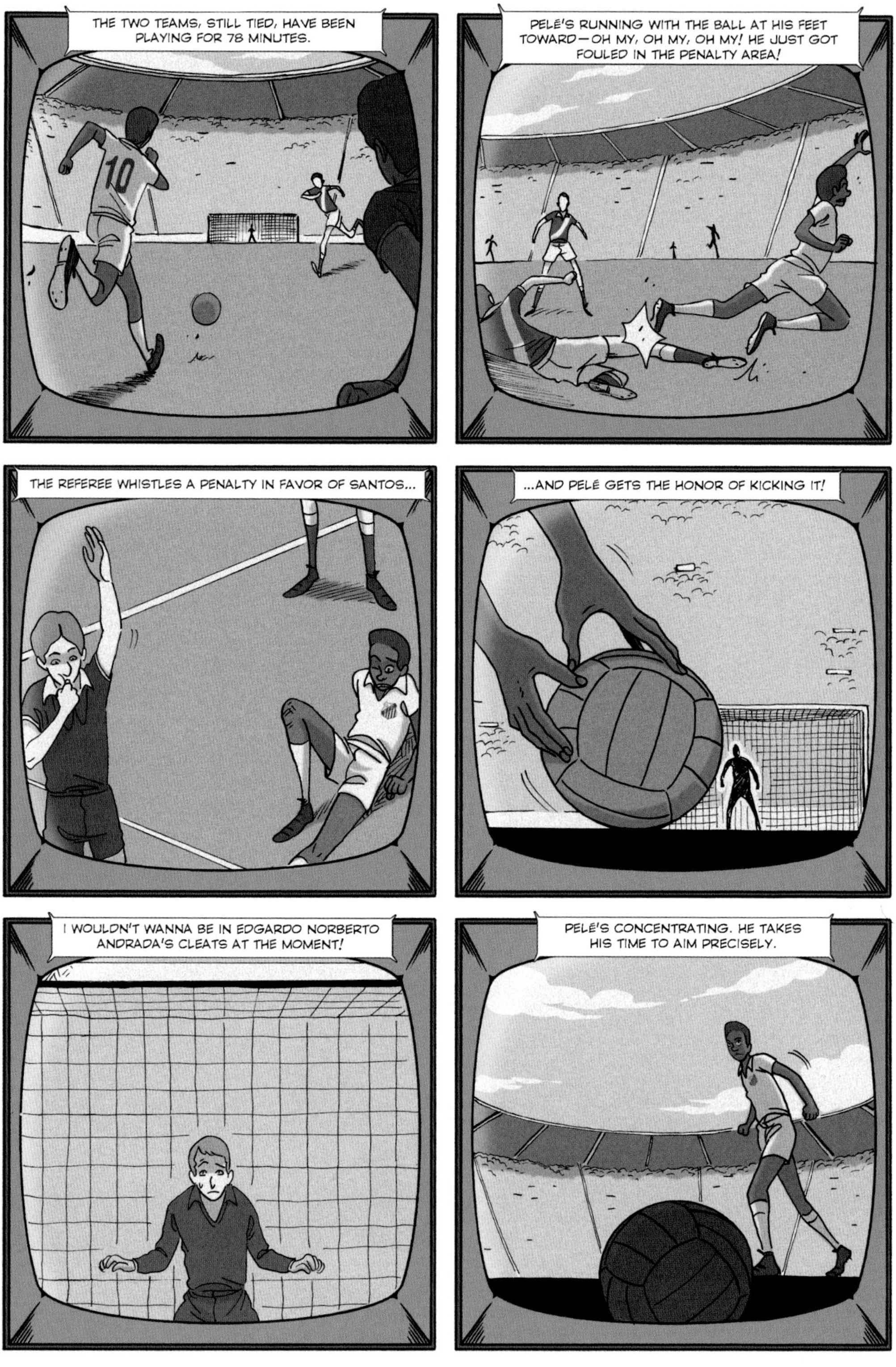
THE TWO TEAMS, STILL TIED, HAVE BEEN PLAYING FOR 78 MINUTES.
10
PELÉ'S RUNNING WITH THE BALL AT HIS FEET TOWARD—OH MY, OH MY, OH MY! HE JUST GOT FOULED IN THE PENALTY AREA!
THE REFEREE WHISTLES A PENALTY IN FAVOR OF SANTOS...
...AND PELÉ GETS THE HONOR OF KICKING IT!
I WOULDN'T WANNA BE IN EDGARDO NORBERTO ANDRADA'S CLEATS AT THE MOMENT!
PELÉ'S CONCENTRATING. HE TAKES HIS TIME TO AIM PRECISELY.

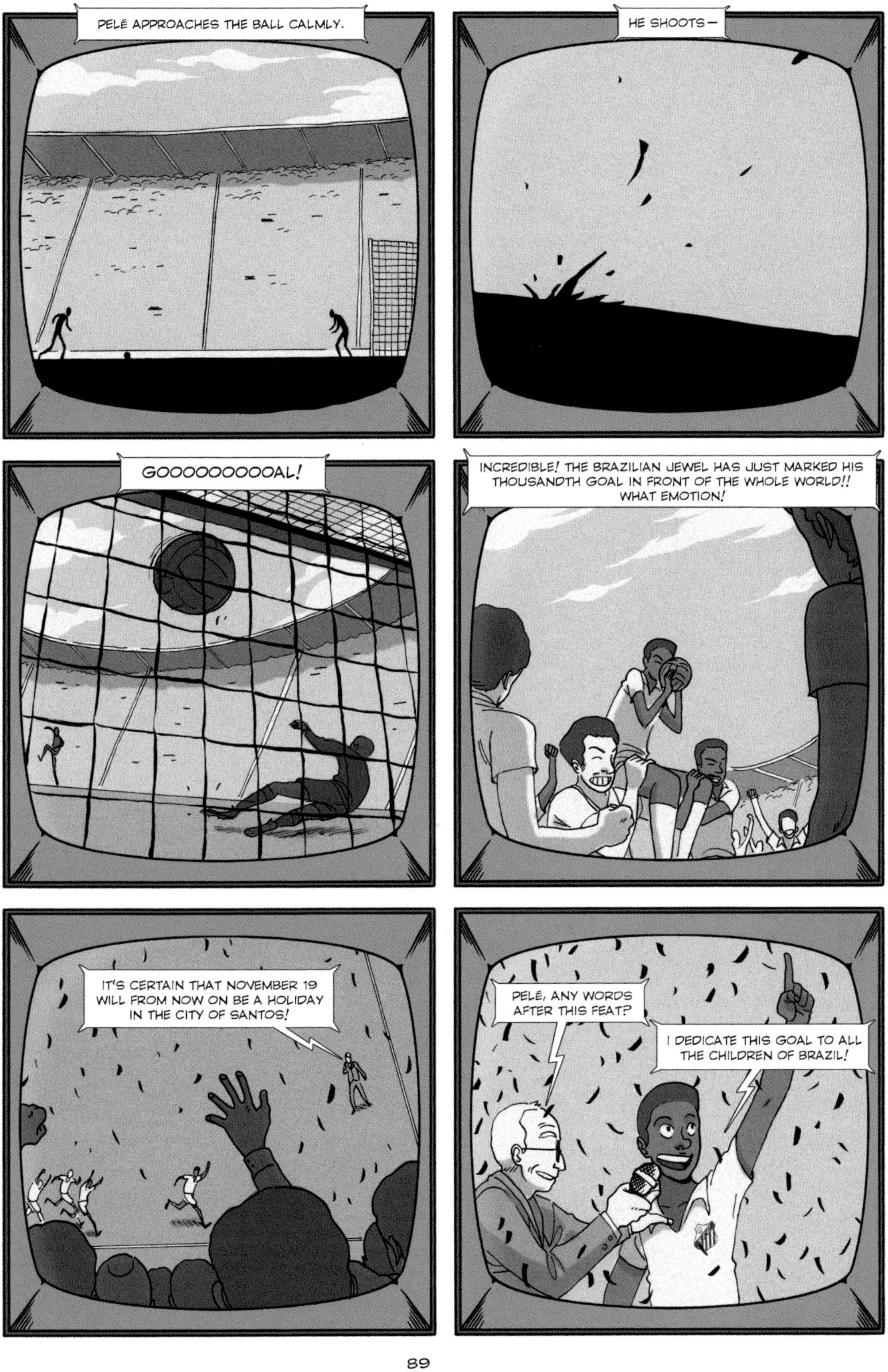
PELÉ APPROACHES THE BALL CALMLY.
HE SHOOTS—
GOOOOOOOOOAL!
INCREDIBLE! THE BRAZILIAN JEWEL HAS JUST MARKED HIS THOUSANDTH GOAL IN FRONT OF THE WHOLE WORLD!! WHAT EMOTION!
IT'S CERTAIN THAT NOVEMBER 19 WILL FROM NOW ON BE A HOLIDAY IN THE CITY OF SANTOS!
PELÉ, ANY WORDS AFTER THIS FEAT?
I DEDICATE THIS GOAL TO ALL THE CHILDREN OF BRAZIL!

Chapter 6
Never Two Without Three!

"Before the match, I told myself: he's just flesh and bones, like me.
Later I understood I was mistaken."
—Tarcisio Burgnich, defender for the Italian national team

1970. BRAZIL IS PLUNGING INTO OBSCURANTISM. THE MILITARY DICTATORSHIP, LED BY THE NEW HEAD OF GOVERNMENT EMILIO MÉDICI, HAS STRENGTHENED.

THE MEDIA, UNIVERSITIES, AND ALL INSTITUTIONS ARE SYSTEMATICALLY PURGED OF ANY INDIVIDUAL SUSPECTED OF "SUBVERSION."

THE POPULATION IS SHOCKED TO LEARN OF THE ABDUCTIONS, THE USE OF TORTURE, AND SUMMARY EXECUTIONS THAT OCCUR DAILY.

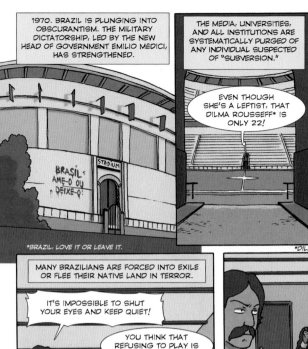

BRASIL·AME-O OU DEIXE-O!

STADIUM

*BRAZIL, LOVE IT OR LEAVE IT.

EVEN THOUGH SHE'S A LEFTIST, THAT DILMA ROUSSEFF* IS ONLY 22!

HOW SHAMEFUL!

THE SOLDIERS TORTURED HER FOR SEVERAL DAYS IN PRISON!

*DILMA ROUSSEFF WILL BECOME PRESIDENT OF BRAZIL IN 2010.

MANY BRAZILIANS ARE FORCED INTO EXILE OR FLEE THEIR NATIVE LAND IN TERROR.

IT'S IMPOSSIBLE TO SHUT YOUR EYES AND KEEP QUIET!

YOU THINK THAT REFUSING TO PLAY IS A SOLUTION?

WE'RE ATHLETES, NOT POLITICIANS!

WHAT DO YOU THINK, ZAGALLO?

PELÉ, I'M NO LONGER A PLAYER, BUT YOUR NEW COACH. MY POSITION IS FRAGILE.*

THE CUP IS STARTING IN MEXICO IN A FEW WEEKS AND...

...PRESIDENT MÉDICI ASKED ME IN PERSON TO PUT HIS FAVORITE SOCCER PLAYER ON THE TEAM!

HUH? WHO'S THIS GUY WITH CONNECTIONS?

*MÁRIO ZAGALLO WAS THE FIRST PLAYER IN HISTORY TO WIN TWO WORLD CUPS AND BECOME A NATIONAL COACH.

DARIO JOSÉ DOS SANTOS, FROM ATLÉTICO MINEIRO!

DADÁ MARAVILHA* IS A GOOD ATTACKER, BUT WE DON'T NEED HIM!

*DADÁ THE MARVEL.

I WASN'T GIVEN A CHOICE!

I'LL LET IT GO WITH THIS CUP. BUT AFTERWARD, I'LL INFORM THE AUTHORITIES IT'S NO LONGER POSSIBLE FOR ME TO COVER UP THEIR ATROCITIES BY PLAYING FOR THE FLAG!

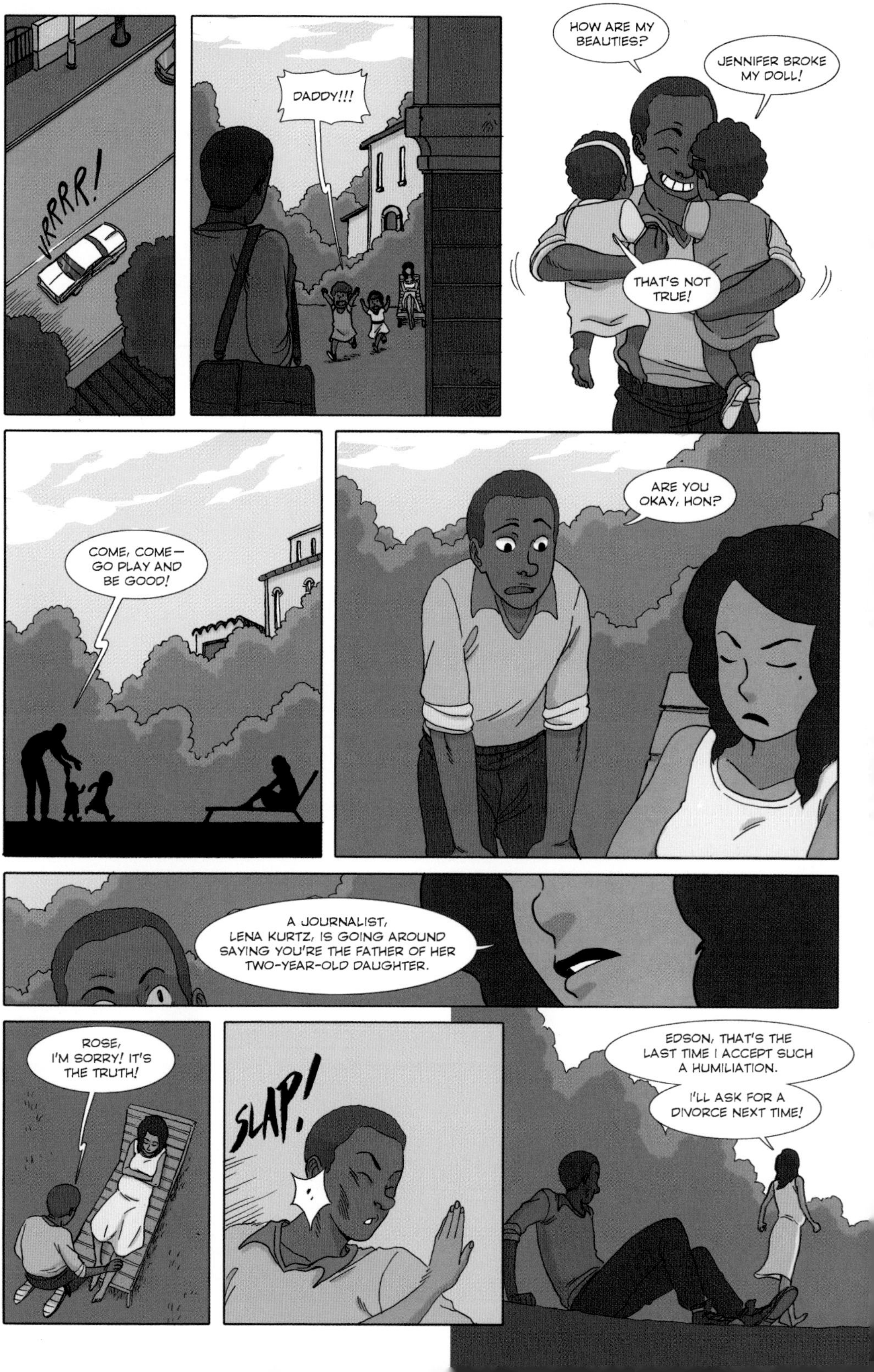
VRRRR!
DADDY!!!
HOW ARE MY BEAUTIES?
JENNIFER BROKE MY DOLL!
THAT'S NOT TRUE!
COME, COME— GO PLAY AND BE GOOD!
ARE YOU OKAY, HON?
A JOURNALIST, LENA KURTZ, IS GOING AROUND SAYING YOU'RE THE FATHER OF HER TWO-YEAR-OLD DAUGHTER.
ROSE, I'M SORRY! IT'S THE TRUTH!
SLAP!
EDSON, THAT'S THE LAST TIME I ACCEPT SUCH A HUMILIATION.
I'LL ASK FOR A DIVORCE NEXT TIME!

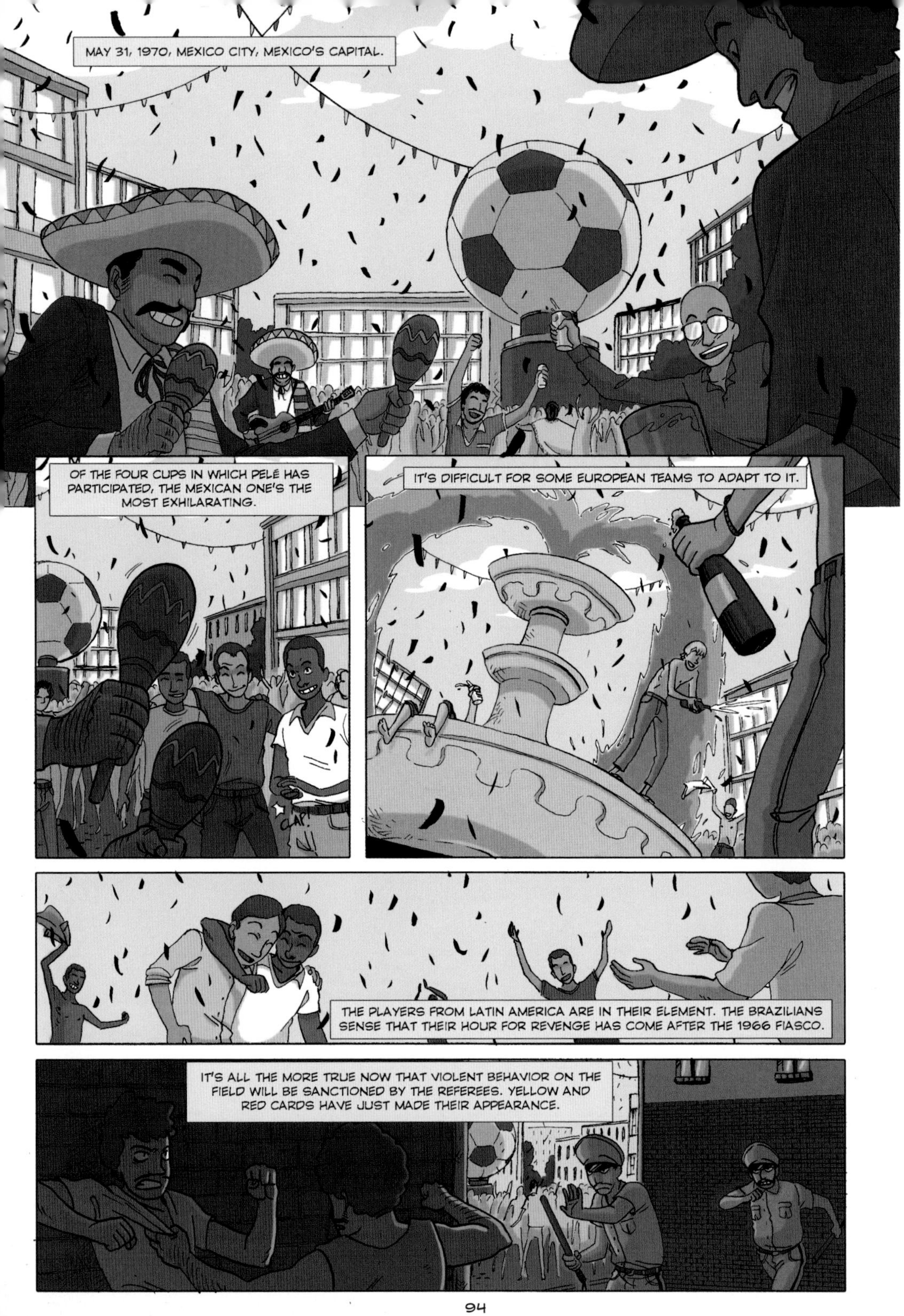
MAY 31, 1970, MEXICO CITY, MEXICO'S CAPITAL.
OF THE FOUR CUPS IN WHICH PELÉ HAS PARTICIPATED, THE MEXICAN ONE'S THE MOST EXHILARATING.
CLAP!
IT'S DIFFICULT FOR SOME EUROPEAN TEAMS TO ADAPT TO IT.
THE PLAYERS FROM LATIN AMERICA ARE IN THEIR ELEMENT. THE BRAZILIANS SENSE THAT THEIR HOUR FOR REVENGE HAS COME AFTER THE 1966 FIASCO.
IT'S ALL THE MORE TRUE NOW THAT VIOLENT BEHAVIOR ON THE FIELD WILL BE SANCTIONED BY THE REFEREES. YELLOW AND RED CARDS HAVE JUST MADE THEIR APPEARANCE.

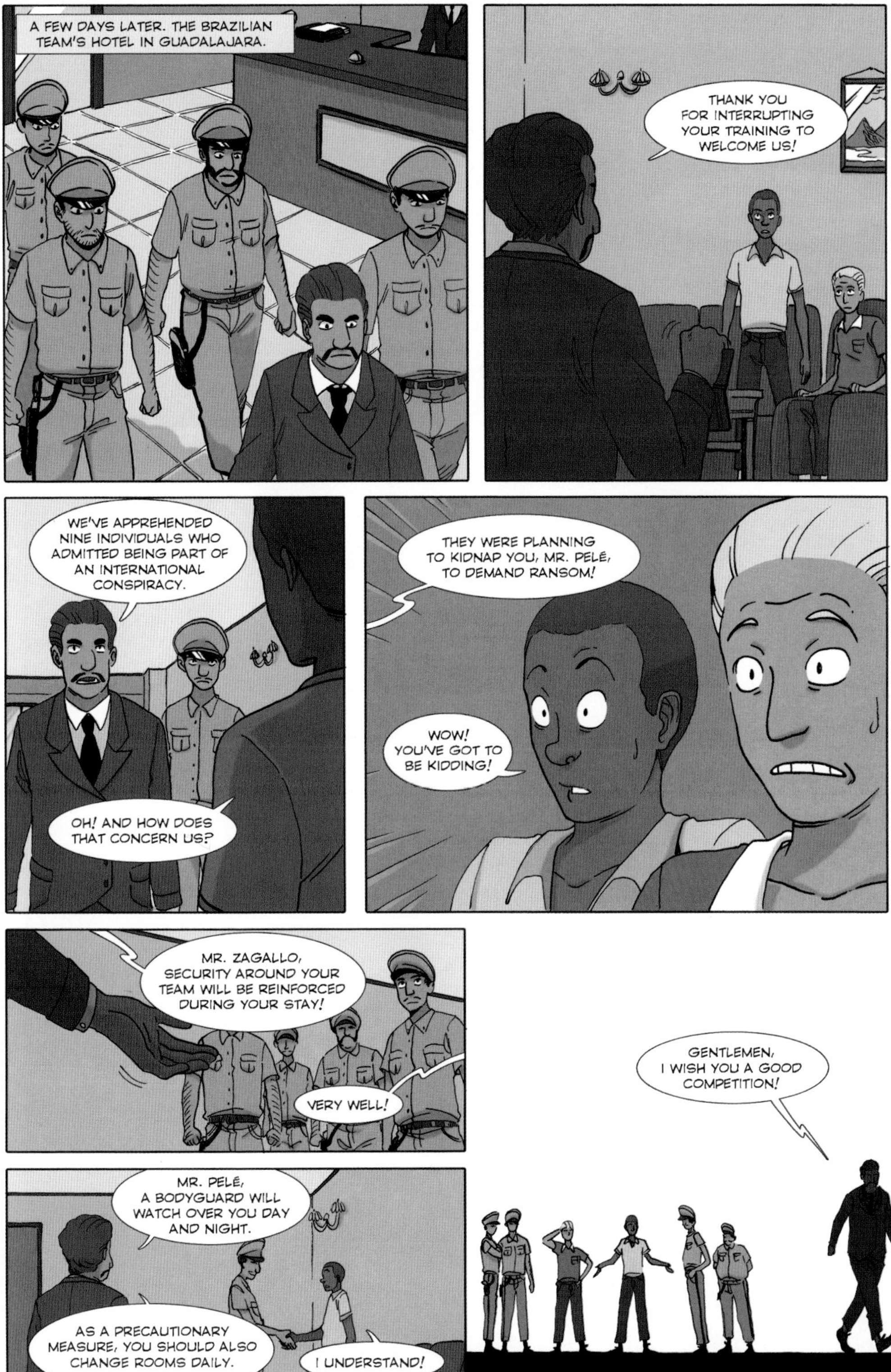
A FEW DAYS LATER. THE BRAZILIAN TEAM'S HOTEL IN GUADALAJARA.
THANK YOU FOR INTERRUPTING YOUR TRAINING TO WELCOME US!
WE'VE APPREHENDED NINE INDIVIDUALS WHO ADMITTED BEING PART OF AN INTERNATIONAL CONSPIRACY.
OH! AND HOW DOES THAT CONCERN US?
THEY WERE PLANNING TO KIDNAP YOU, MR. PELÉ, TO DEMAND RANSOM!
WOW! YOU'VE GOT TO BE KIDDING!
MR. ZAGALLO, SECURITY AROUND YOUR TEAM WILL BE REINFORCED DURING YOUR STAY!
VERY WELL!
MR. PELÉ, A BODYGUARD WILL WATCH OVER YOU DAY AND NIGHT.
AS A PRECAUTIONARY MEASURE, YOU SHOULD ALSO CHANGE ROOMS DAILY.
I UNDERSTAND!
GENTLEMEN, I WISH YOU A GOOD COMPETITION!

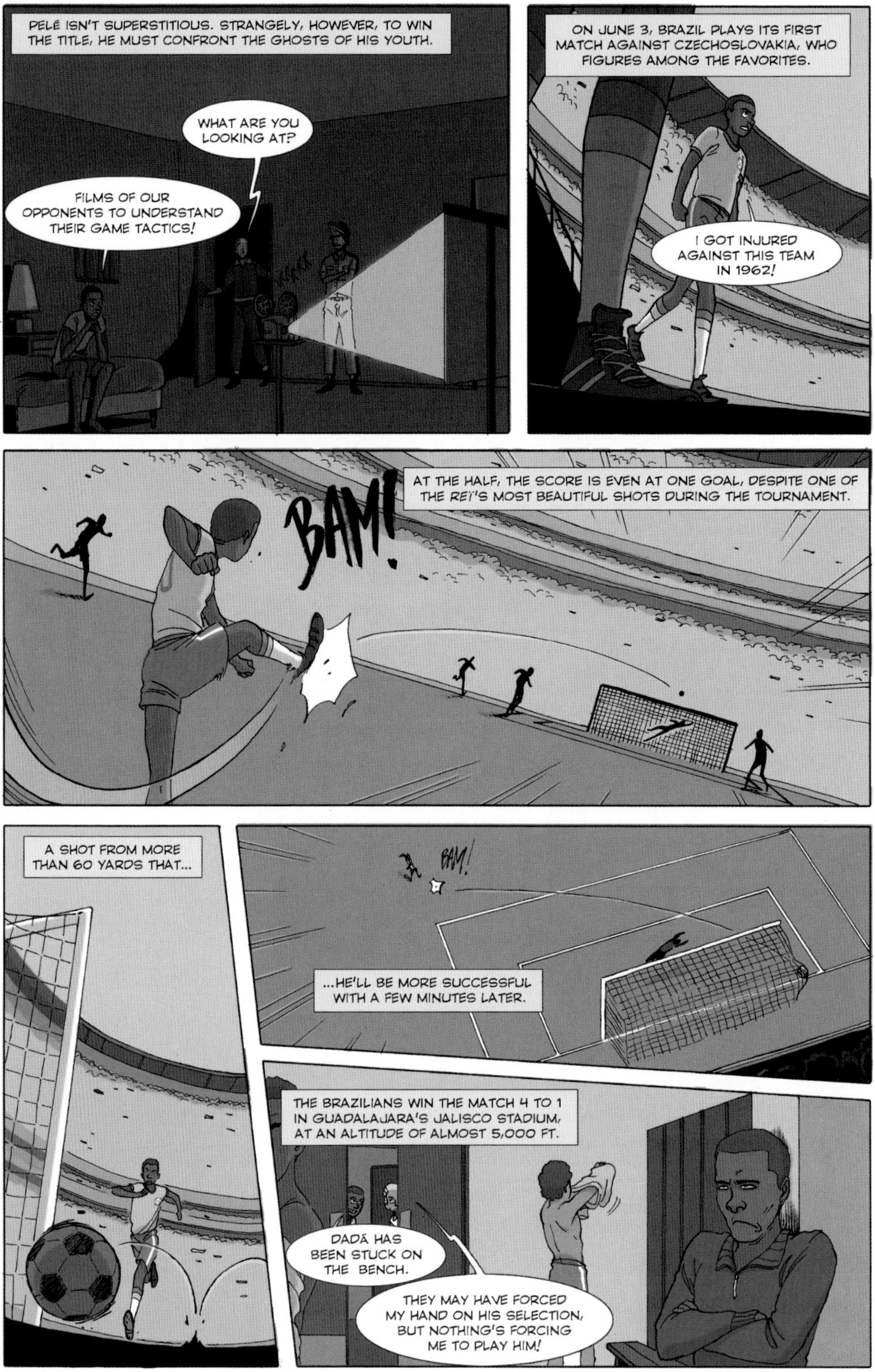
PELÉ ISN'T SUPERSTITIOUS. STRANGELY, HOWEVER, TO WIN THE TITLE, HE MUST CONFRONT THE GHOSTS OF HIS YOUTH.
WHAT ARE YOU LOOKING AT?
FILMS OF OUR OPPONENTS TO UNDERSTAND THEIR GAME TACTICS!
ON JUNE 3, BRAZIL PLAYS ITS FIRST MATCH AGAINST CZECHOSLOVAKIA, WHO FIGURES AMONG THE FAVORITES.
I GOT INJURED AGAINST THIS TEAM IN 1962!
AT THE HALF, THE SCORE IS EVEN AT ONE GOAL, DESPITE ONE OF THE *REI*'S MOST BEAUTIFUL SHOTS DURING THE TOURNAMENT.
BAM!
A SHOT FROM MORE THAN 60 YARDS THAT...
BAM!
...HE'LL BE MORE SUCCESSFUL WITH A FEW MINUTES LATER.
THE BRAZILIANS WIN THE MATCH 4 TO 1 IN GUADALAJARA'S JALISCO STADIUM, AT AN ALTITUDE OF ALMOST 5,000 FT.
DADÁ HAS BEEN STUCK ON THE BENCH.
THEY MAY HAVE FORCED MY HAND ON HIS SELECTION, BUT NOTHING'S FORCING ME TO PLAY HIM!

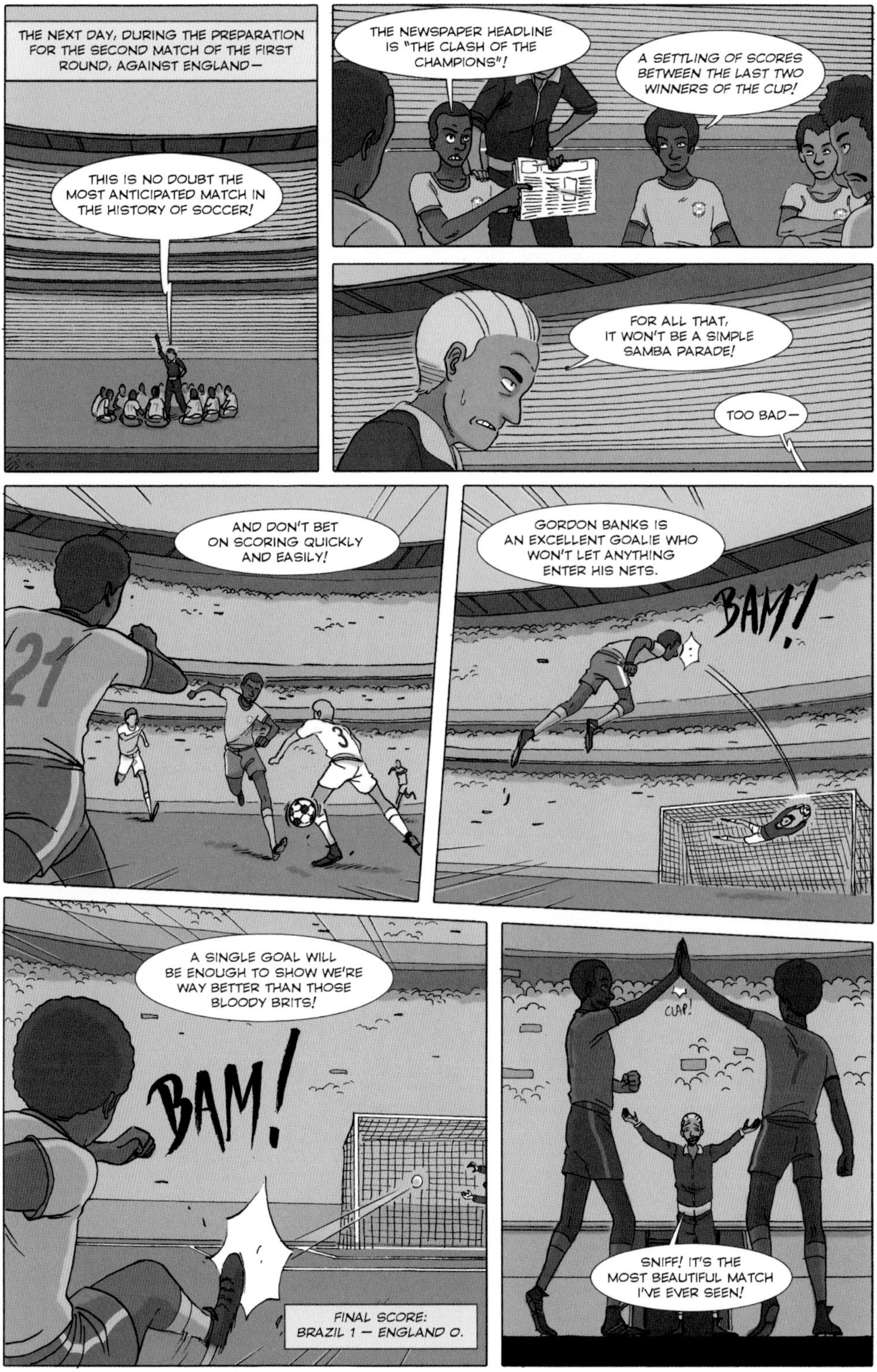
THE NEXT DAY, DURING THE PREPARATION FOR THE SECOND MATCH OF THE FIRST ROUND, AGAINST ENGLAND—
THIS IS NO DOUBT THE MOST ANTICIPATED MATCH IN THE HISTORY OF SOCCER!
THE NEWSPAPER HEADLINE IS "THE CLASH OF THE CHAMPIONS"!
A SETTLING OF SCORES BETWEEN THE LAST TWO WINNERS OF THE CUP!
FOR ALL THAT, IT WON'T BE A SIMPLE SAMBA PARADE!
TOO BAD—
AND DON'T BET ON SCORING QUICKLY AND EASILY!
GORDON BANKS IS AN EXCELLENT GOALIE WHO WON'T LET ANYTHING ENTER HIS NETS.
BAM!
A SINGLE GOAL WILL BE ENOUGH TO SHOW WE'RE WAY BETTER THAN THOSE BLOODY BRITS!
BAM!
FINAL SCORE: BRAZIL 1 — ENGLAND 0.
CLAP!
SNIFF! IT'S THE MOST BEAUTIFUL MATCH I'VE EVER SEEN!

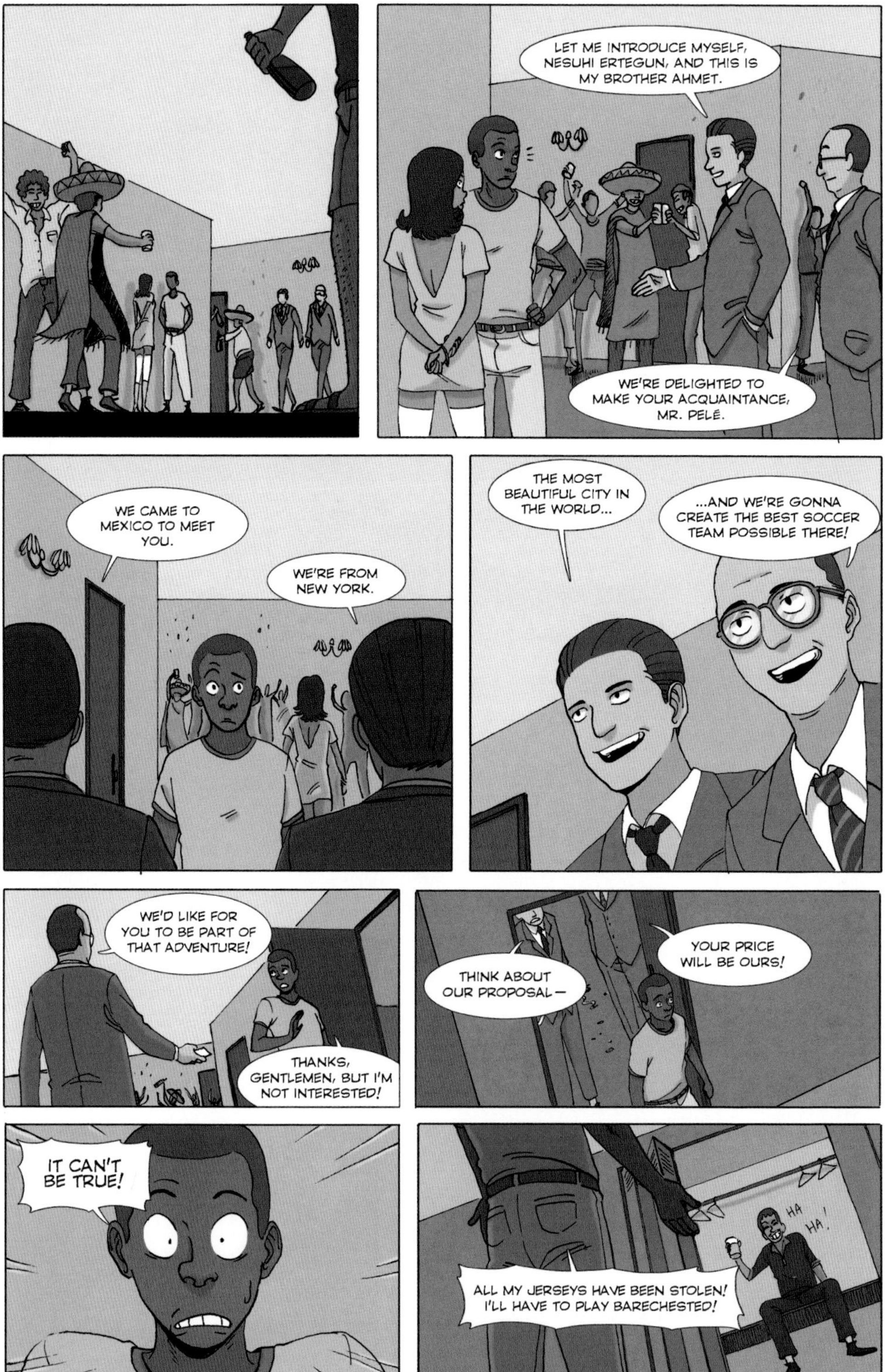
LET ME INTRODUCE MYSELF, NESUHI ERTEGUN, AND THIS IS MY BROTHER AHMET.
WE'RE DELIGHTED TO MAKE YOUR ACQUAINTANCE, MR. PELÉ.
WE CAME TO MEXICO TO MEET YOU.
WE'RE FROM NEW YORK.
THE MOST BEAUTIFUL CITY IN THE WORLD...
...AND WE'RE GONNA CREATE THE BEST SOCCER TEAM POSSIBLE THERE!
WE'D LIKE FOR YOU TO BE PART OF THAT ADVENTURE!
THANKS, GENTLEMEN, BUT I'M NOT INTERESTED!
THINK ABOUT OUR PROPOSAL—
YOUR PRICE WILL BE OURS!
IT CAN'T BE TRUE!
ALL MY JERSEYS HAVE BEEN STOLEN! I'LL HAVE TO PLAY BARECHESTED!
HA HA!

THOUGH, ON PAPER, THE BRAZILIAN TEAM DOESN'T SEEM TO HAVE THE FLAIR OF ITS 1958 AND 1962 ELDERS, IT PROVES TO BE TALENTED AND COURAGEOUS IN THE COURSE OF ITS MATCHES.

WE'VE BEEN NICKNAMED "THE BEAUTIFUL TEAM."

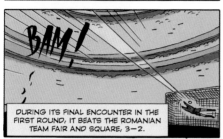

BAM!

DURING ITS FINAL ENCOUNTER IN THE FIRST ROUND, IT BEATS THE ROMANIAN TEAM FAIR AND SQUARE, 3–2.

THE QUARTERFINALS PITS THE AURIVERDE AGAINST PERU, WHOSE COACH IS AN OLD ACQUAINTANCE.

DEAR OLD DIDI, I NEVER WOULD'VE IMAGINED IN SWEDEN THAT, 12 YEARS LATER, YOU'D HAVE GONE OVER TO THE ENEMY!

HEH-HEH! I KNOW ALL YOUR WEAK POINTS, AND MY PLAYERS DO, TOO!

DESPITE THE PERUVIANS' OFFENSIVE GAME, CAPTAIN CARLOS ALBERTO'S TEAM OVERWHELMS THEM WITH 4 GOALS TO 2.

SORRY, BROTHER!

WE'RE BROADCASTING THE MATCH THAT WILL DECIDE THE TEAM...

...THAT WILL GO AGAINST THE BRAZILIANS IN THE SEMIFINALS.

WELL?!

GÉRSON, SHHHHHH!

ESPARRAGO HAS JUST SCORED THE QUALIFYING GOAL FOR URUGUAY!

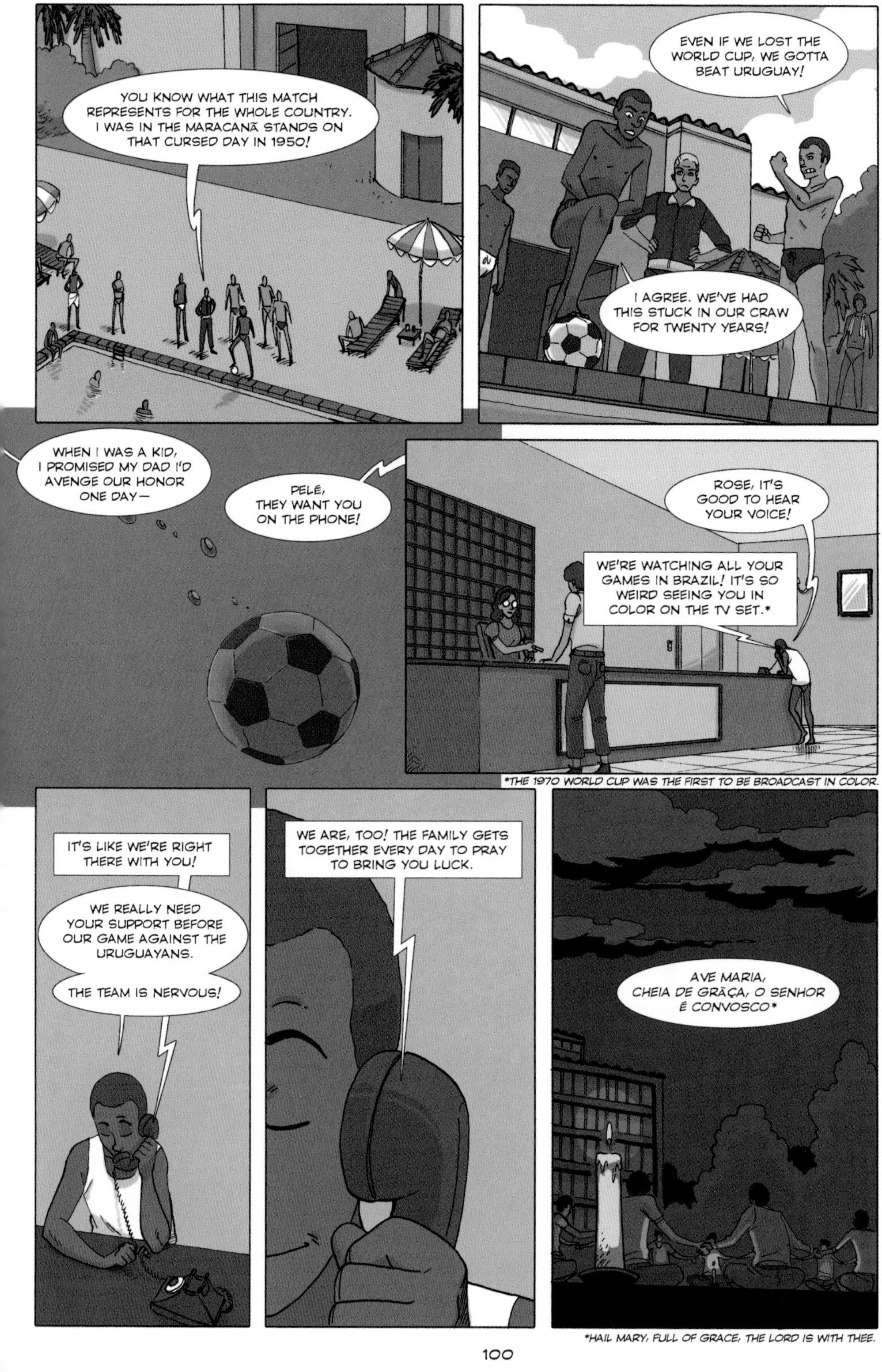
YOU KNOW WHAT THIS MATCH REPRESENTS FOR THE WHOLE COUNTRY. I WAS IN THE MARACANÃ STANDS ON THAT CURSED DAY IN 1950!
EVEN IF WE LOST THE WORLD CUP, WE GOTTA BEAT URUGUAY!
I AGREE. WE'VE HAD THIS STUCK IN OUR CRAW FOR TWENTY YEARS!
WHEN I WAS A KID, I PROMISED MY DAD I'D AVENGE OUR HONOR ONE DAY—
PELÉ, THEY WANT YOU ON THE PHONE!
ROSE, IT'S GOOD TO HEAR YOUR VOICE!
WE'RE WATCHING ALL YOUR GAMES IN BRAZIL! IT'S SO WEIRD SEEING YOU IN COLOR ON THE TV SET.*
*THE 1970 WORLD CUP WAS THE FIRST TO BE BROADCAST IN COLOR.
IT'S LIKE WE'RE RIGHT THERE WITH YOU!
WE REALLY NEED YOUR SUPPORT BEFORE OUR GAME AGAINST THE URUGUAYANS.
THE TEAM IS NERVOUS!
WE ARE, TOO! THE FAMILY GETS TOGETHER EVERY DAY TO PRAY TO BRING YOU LUCK.
AVE MARIA, CHEIA DE GRAÇA, O SENHOR É CONVOSCO*
*HAIL MARY, FULL OF GRACE, THE LORD IS WITH THEE.

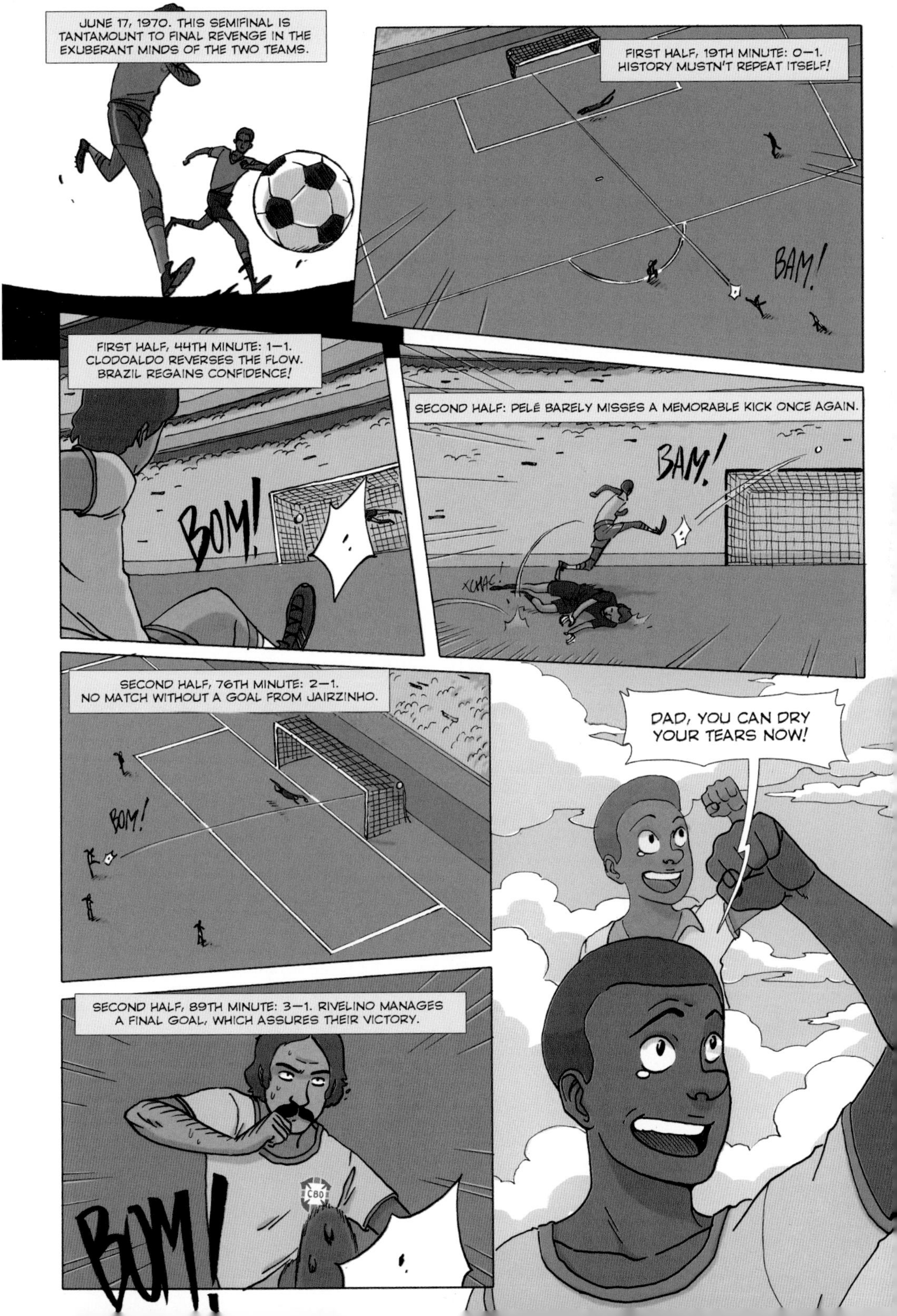
JUNE 17, 1970. THIS SEMIFINAL IS TANTAMOUNT TO FINAL REVENGE IN THE EXUBERANT MINDS OF THE TWO TEAMS.
FIRST HALF, 19TH MINUTE: 0—1. HISTORY MUSTN'T REPEAT ITSELF!
BAM!
FIRST HALF, 44TH MINUTE: 1—1. CLODOALDO REVERSES THE FLOW. BRAZIL REGAINS CONFIDENCE!
BOM!
SECOND HALF: PELÉ BARELY MISSES A MEMORABLE KICK ONCE AGAIN.
BAM!
SECOND HALF, 76TH MINUTE: 2—1. NO MATCH WITHOUT A GOAL FROM JAIRZINHO.
BOM!
SECOND HALF, 89TH MINUTE: 3—1. RIVELINO MANAGES A FINAL GOAL, WHICH ASSURES THEIR VICTORY.
CBD
BOM!
DAD, YOU CAN DRY YOUR TEARS NOW!

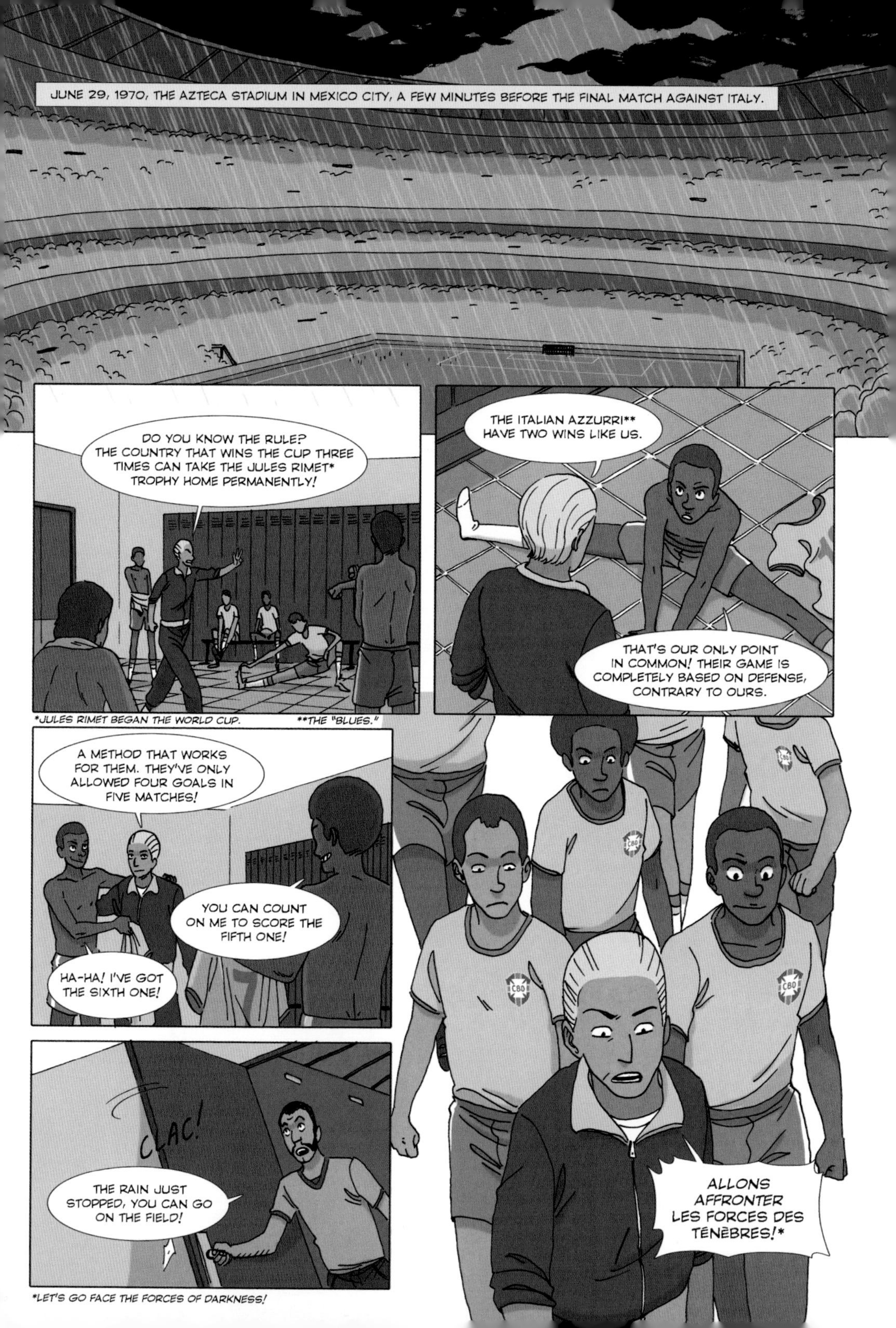
JUNE 29, 1970, THE AZTECA STADIUM IN MEXICO CITY, A FEW MINUTES BEFORE THE FINAL MATCH AGAINST ITALY.
DO YOU KNOW THE RULE? THE COUNTRY THAT WINS THE CUP THREE TIMES CAN TAKE THE JULES RIMET* TROPHY HOME PERMANENTLY!
THE ITALIAN AZZURRI** HAVE TWO WINS LIKE US.
THAT'S OUR ONLY POINT IN COMMON! THEIR GAME IS COMPLETELY BASED ON DEFENSE, CONTRARY TO OURS.
*JULES RIMET BEGAN THE WORLD CUP.
**THE "BLUES."
A METHOD THAT WORKS FOR THEM. THEY'VE ONLY ALLOWED FOUR GOALS IN FIVE MATCHES!
YOU CAN COUNT ON ME TO SCORE THE FIFTH ONE!
HA-HA! I'VE GOT THE SIXTH ONE!
CLAC!
THE RAIN JUST STOPPED, YOU CAN GO ON THE FIELD!
ALLONS AFFRONTER LES FORCES DES TÉNÈBRES!*
*LET'S GO FACE THE FORCES OF DARKNESS!

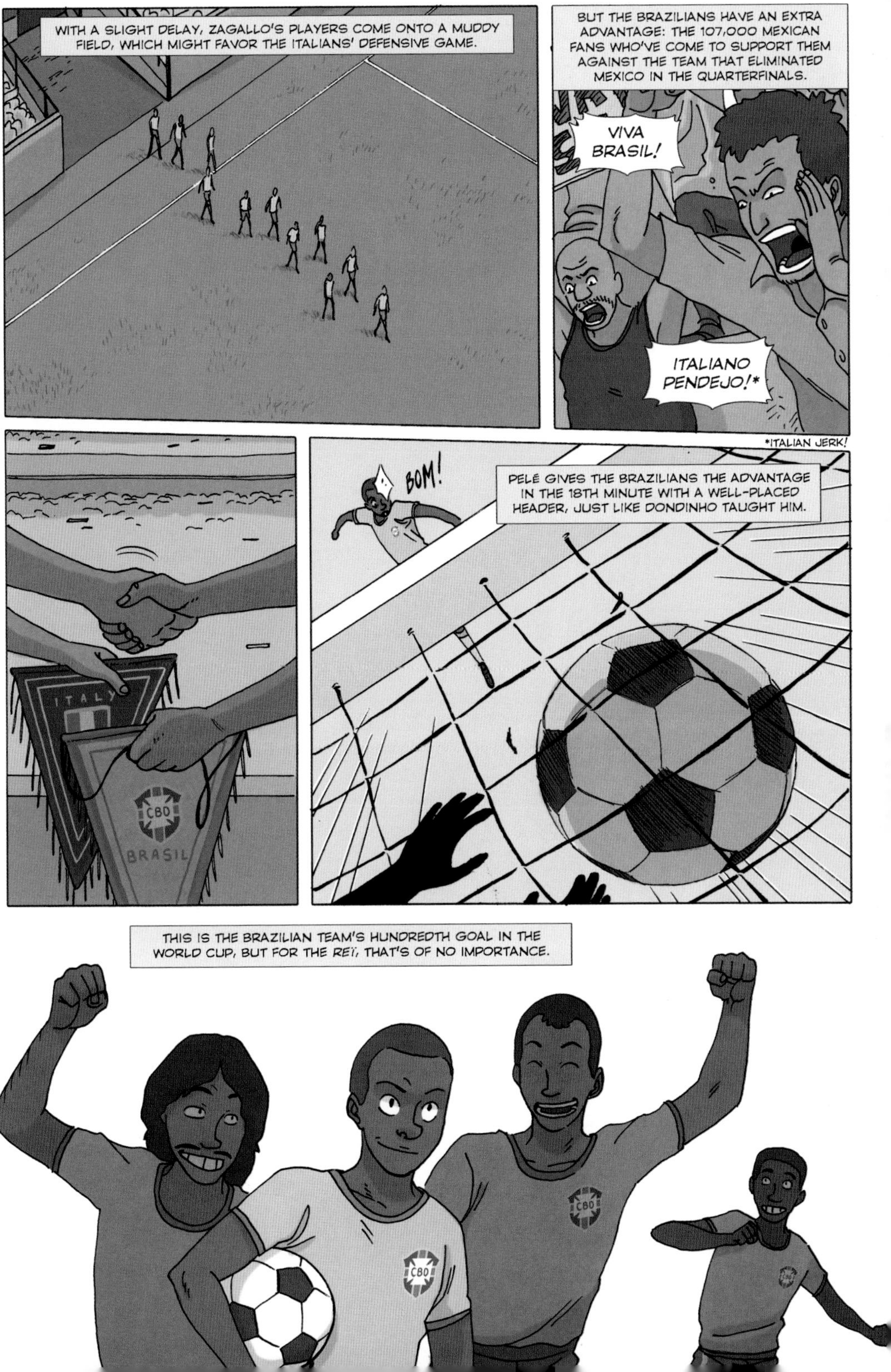
WITH A SLIGHT DELAY, ZAGALLO'S PLAYERS COME ONTO A MUDDY FIELD, WHICH MIGHT FAVOR THE ITALIANS' DEFENSIVE GAME.
BUT THE BRAZILIANS HAVE AN EXTRA ADVANTAGE: THE 107,000 MEXICAN FANS WHO'VE COME TO SUPPORT THEM AGAINST THE TEAM THAT ELIMINATED MEXICO IN THE QUARTERFINALS.
VIVA BRASIL!
ITALIANO PENDEJO!*
*ITALIAN JERK!
ITALY
CBD
BRASIL
BOM!
PELÉ GIVES THE BRAZILIANS THE ADVANTAGE IN THE 18TH MINUTE WITH A WELL-PLACED HEADER, JUST LIKE DONDINHO TAUGHT HIM.
THIS IS THE BRAZILIAN TEAM'S HUNDREDTH GOAL IN THE WORLD CUP, BUT FOR THE *REI*, THAT'S OF NO IMPORTANCE.
CBD
CBD

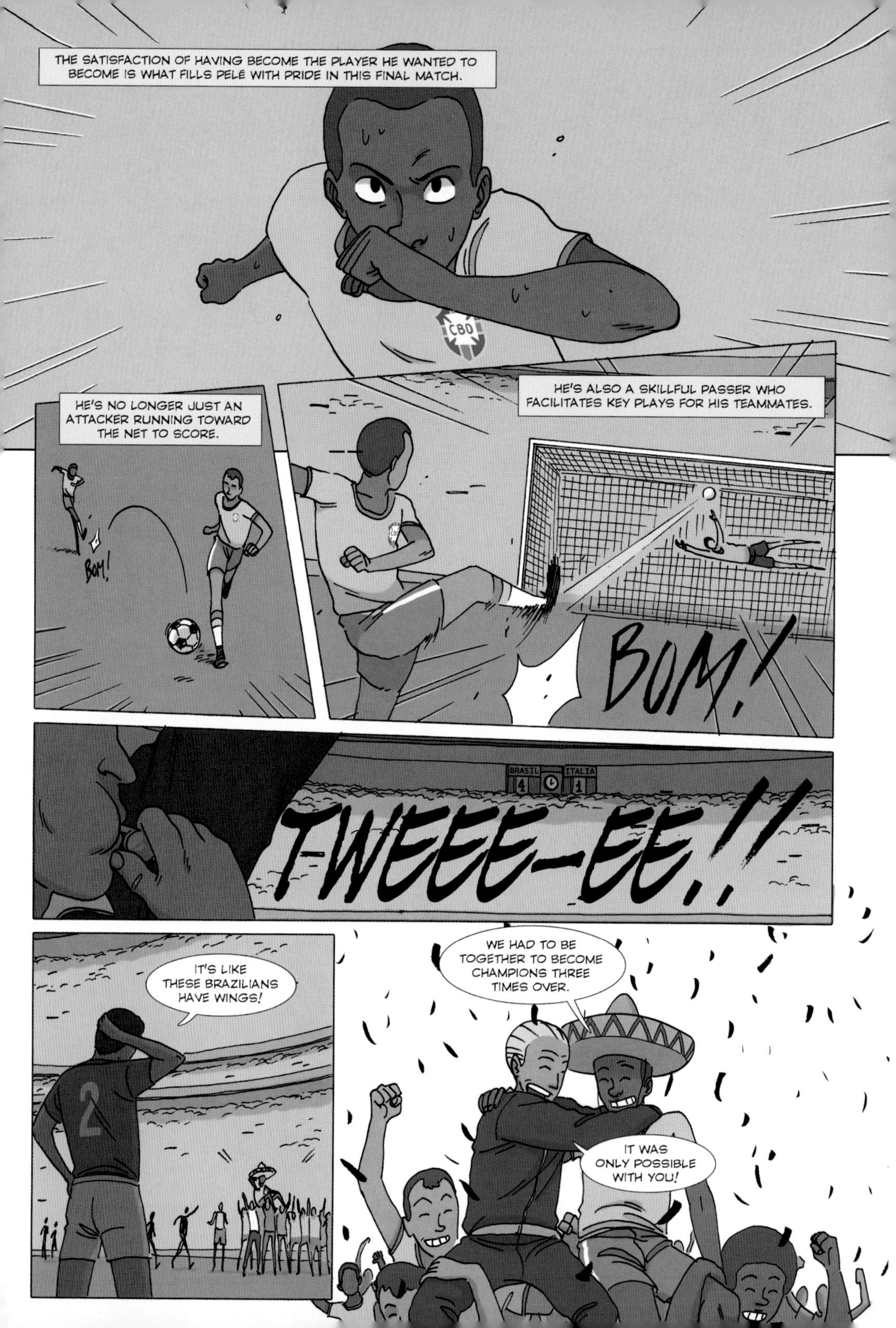
THE SATISFACTION OF HAVING BECOME THE PLAYER HE WANTED TO BECOME IS WHAT FILLS PELÉ WITH PRIDE IN THIS FINAL MATCH.
CBD
HE'S NO LONGER JUST AN ATTACKER RUNNING TOWARD THE NET TO SCORE.
BOM!
HE'S ALSO A SKILLFUL PASSER WHO FACILITATES KEY PLAYS FOR HIS TEAMMATES.
BOM!
BRASIL 4 ITALIA 1
TWEEE-EE!!
IT'S LIKE THESE BRAZILIANS HAVE WINGS!
2
WE HAD TO BE TOGETHER TO BECOME CHAMPIONS THREE TIMES OVER.
IT WAS ONLY POSSIBLE WITH YOU!

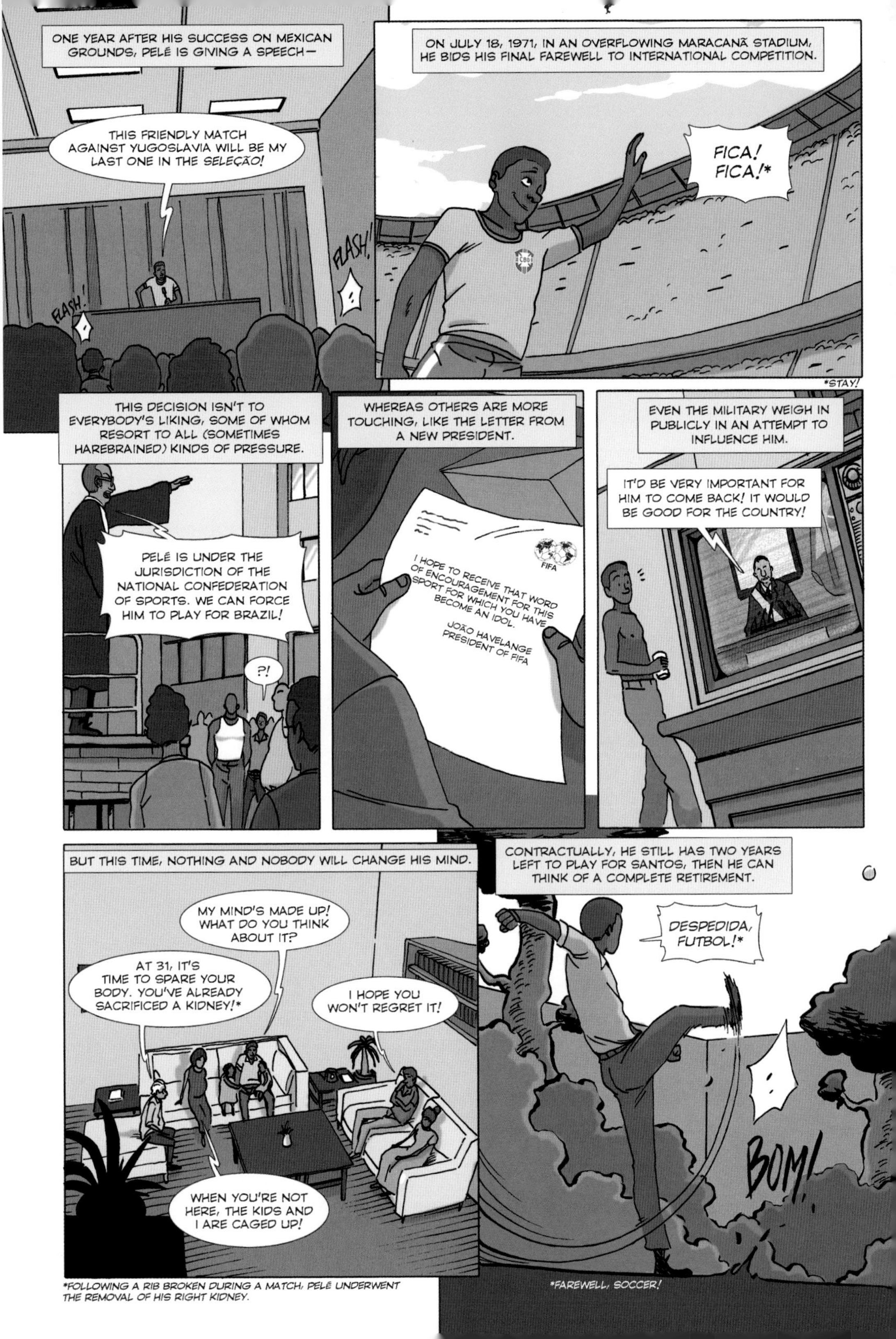
ONE YEAR AFTER HIS SUCCESS ON MEXICAN GROUNDS, PELÉ IS GIVING A SPEECH—
THIS FRIENDLY MATCH AGAINST YUGOSLAVIA WILL BE MY LAST ONE IN THE SELEÇÃO!
FLASH!
FLASH!
ON JULY 18, 1971, IN AN OVERFLOWING MARACANÃ STADIUM, HE BIDS HIS FINAL FAREWELL TO INTERNATIONAL COMPETITION.
FICA! FICA!*
*STAY!
THIS DECISION ISN'T TO EVERYBODY'S LIKING, SOME OF WHOM RESORT TO ALL (SOMETIMES HAREBRAINED) KINDS OF PRESSURE.
PELÉ IS UNDER THE JURISDICTION OF THE NATIONAL CONFEDERATION OF SPORTS. WE CAN FORCE HIM TO PLAY FOR BRAZIL!
?!
WHEREAS OTHERS ARE MORE TOUCHING, LIKE THE LETTER FROM A NEW PRESIDENT.
FIFA
I HOPE TO RECEIVE THAT WORD OF ENCOURAGEMENT FOR THIS SPORT FOR WHICH YOU HAVE BECOME AN IDOL.
JOÃO HAVELANGE
PRESIDENT OF FIFA
EVEN THE MILITARY WEIGH IN PUBLICLY IN AN ATTEMPT TO INFLUENCE HIM.
IT'D BE VERY IMPORTANT FOR HIM TO COME BACK! IT WOULD BE GOOD FOR THE COUNTRY!
BUT THIS TIME, NOTHING AND NOBODY WILL CHANGE HIS MIND.
MY MIND'S MADE UP! WHAT DO YOU THINK ABOUT IT?
AT 31, IT'S TIME TO SPARE YOUR BODY. YOU'VE ALREADY SACRIFICED A KIDNEY!*
I HOPE YOU WON'T REGRET IT!
WHEN YOU'RE NOT HERE, THE KIDS AND I ARE CAGED UP!
*FOLLOWING A RIB BROKEN DURING A MATCH, PELÉ UNDERWENT THE REMOVAL OF HIS RIGHT KIDNEY.
CONTRACTUALLY, HE STILL HAS TWO YEARS LEFT TO PLAY FOR SANTOS, THEN HE CAN THINK OF A COMPLETE RETIREMENT.
DESPEDIDA, FUTBOL!*
BOM!
*FAREWELL, SOCCER!

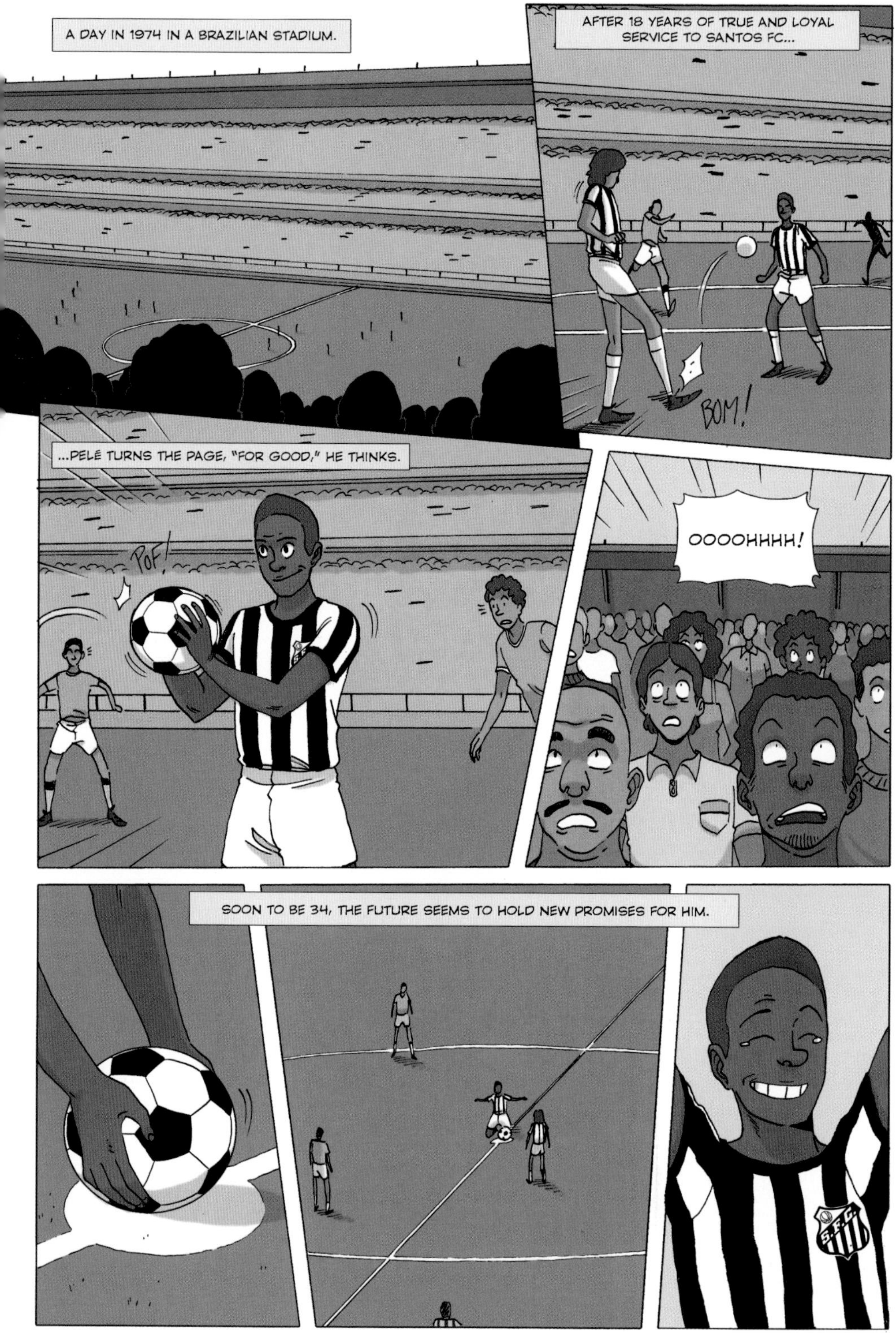
A DAY IN 1974 IN A BRAZILIAN STADIUM.
AFTER 18 YEARS OF TRUE AND LOYAL SERVICE TO SANTOS FC...
BOM!
...PELÉ TURNS THE PAGE, "FOR GOOD," HE THINKS.
POF!
OOOOHHHH!
SOON TO BE 34, THE FUTURE SEEMS TO HOLD NEW PROMISES FOR HIM.

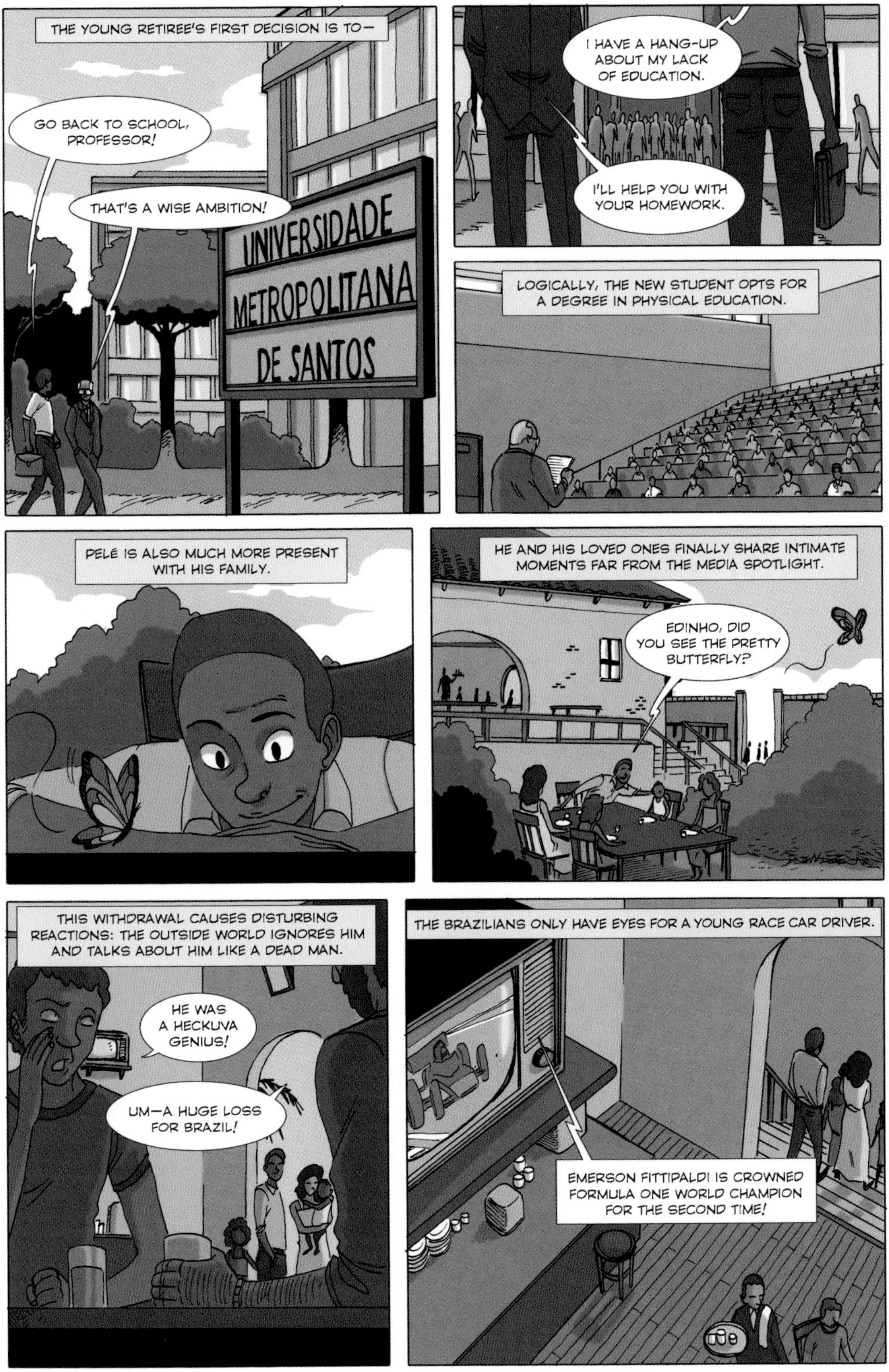
THE YOUNG RETIREE'S FIRST DECISION IS TO—
GO BACK TO SCHOOL, PROFESSOR!
THAT'S A WISE AMBITION!
UNIVERSIDADE METROPOLITANA DE SANTOS
I HAVE A HANG-UP ABOUT MY LACK OF EDUCATION.
I'LL HELP YOU WITH YOUR HOMEWORK.
LOGICALLY, THE NEW STUDENT OPTS FOR A DEGREE IN PHYSICAL EDUCATION.
PELÉ IS ALSO MUCH MORE PRESENT WITH HIS FAMILY.
HE AND HIS LOVED ONES FINALLY SHARE INTIMATE MOMENTS FAR FROM THE MEDIA SPOTLIGHT.
EDINHO, DID YOU SEE THE PRETTY BUTTERFLY?
THIS WITHDRAWAL CAUSES DISTURBING REACTIONS: THE OUTSIDE WORLD IGNORES HIM AND TALKS ABOUT HIM LIKE A DEAD MAN.
HE WAS A HECKUVA GENIUS!
UM—A HUGE LOSS FOR BRAZIL!
THE BRAZILIANS ONLY HAVE EYES FOR A YOUNG RACE CAR DRIVER.
EMERSON FITTIPALDI IS CROWNED FORMULA ONE WORLD CHAMPION FOR THE SECOND TIME!

FANTASTIC!

I GOT MY DIPLOMA!

CONGRATULATIONS, EDSON!

HURRAY, DADDY!

WE HAVE TO CELEBRATE THIS—

THE ACCOUNTANT WANTS TO SEE YOU ABOUT THE AUDIT ON YOUR MONEY!

SO, HOW MANY MILLIONS DO WE HAVE?

CLAC!

IT'S COMPLICATED—

MEANING?

THE FIOLAX COMPANY OF WHICH YOU'RE A STOCKHOLDER HAS BECOME INSOLVENT. THEY'RE SEVERAL MILLION DOLLARS IN DEBT. THE BANK IS ASKING YOU TO HONOR THAT DEBT—

WHAT? I'M RUINED?!

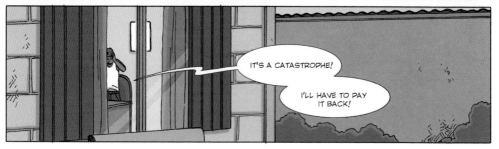

IT'S A CATASTROPHE!

I'LL HAVE TO PAY IT BACK!

108

Chapter 7
The American Dream

"We had superstars in the United States, but nothing at the level of Pelé. Everyone wanted to touch him, shake his hand, get a photo with him."
—John O'Reilly, spokesperson for the New York Cosmos

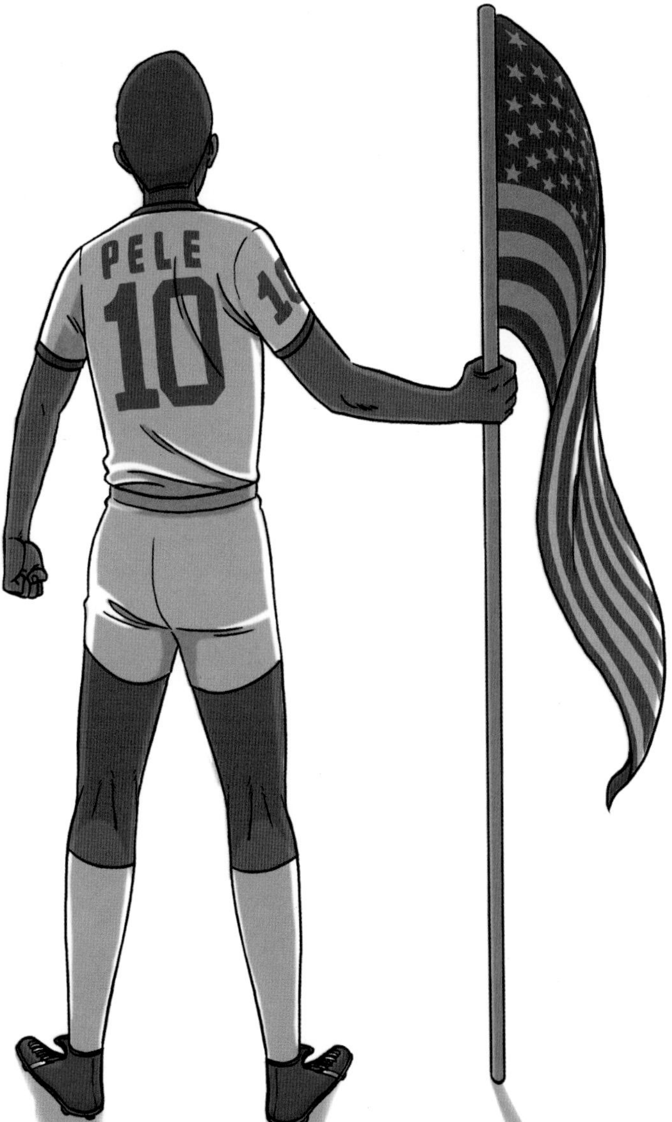
PELE
10

FEBRUARY 1975, THE 21 CLUB IN NEW YORK.

WE'D LIKE YOU TO PARTICIPATE IN THE DEVELOPMENT OF SOCCER IN THE UNITED STATES.

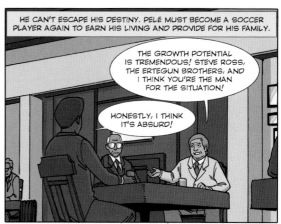

HE CAN'T ESCAPE HIS DESTINY. PELÉ MUST BECOME A SOCCER PLAYER AGAIN TO EARN HIS LIVING AND PROVIDE FOR HIS FAMILY.

THE GROWTH POTENTIAL IS TREMENDOUS! STEVE ROSS, THE ERTEGUN BROTHERS, AND I THINK YOU'RE THE MAN FOR THE SITUATION!

HONESTLY, I THINK IT'S ABSURD!

HE COULD SIGN WITH A EUROPEAN CLUB, BUT THE SCHEDULE OF MATCHES WOULD BE AS INTENSE AS IN BRAZIL. HE NO LONGER WANTS THAT!

IF YOU PLAY WITH THE COSMOS IN NEW YORK, YOU COULD WIN OVER THE WHOLE COUNTRY!

KRRR

THE AMERICANS GUARANTEE HIM A COMFORTABLE SALARY THAT WILL LET HIM PAY BACK HIS DEBTS WHILE ASSURING HIM AN ACCEPTABLE PLAYING RHYTHM.

I DON'T KNOW—

COME ON, PELÉ, JUST THREE SHORT YEARS!

EDSON, THE MANAGER'S OFFER SEEMS LEGIT TO ME!

COSMOS NY

ALL

MR. TOYE, YOU CAN PREPARE YOUR CONTRACT.

THE KING OF SOCCER IS GOING TO CONQUER THE LAND OF QUARTERBACKS!

7 4 MILLIONS $ PER YEAR

Pelé

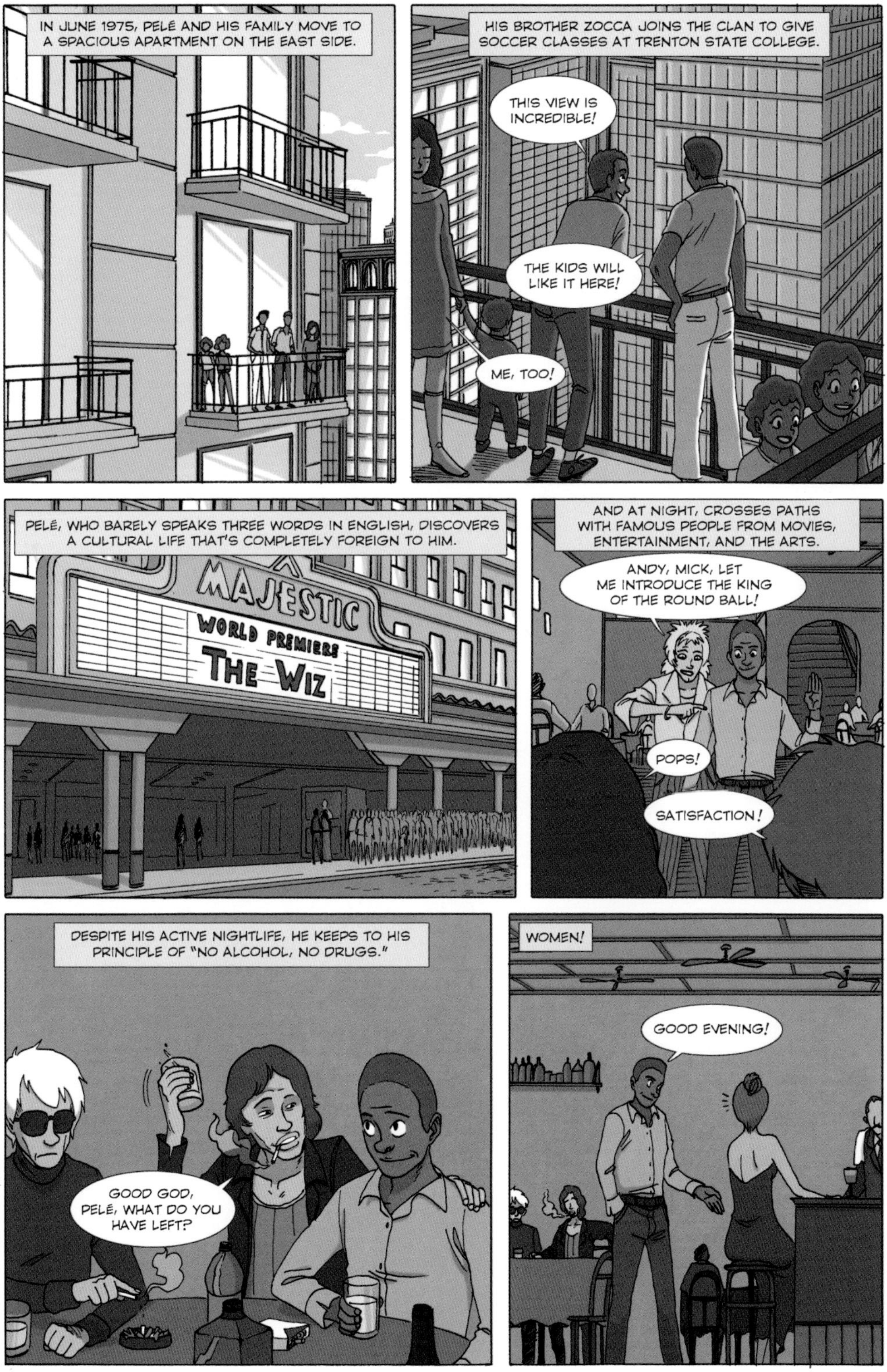
IN JUNE 1975, PELÉ AND HIS FAMILY MOVE TO A SPACIOUS APARTMENT ON THE EAST SIDE.
HIS BROTHER ZOCCA JOINS THE CLAN TO GIVE SOCCER CLASSES AT TRENTON STATE COLLEGE.
THIS VIEW IS INCREDIBLE!
THE KIDS WILL LIKE IT HERE!
ME, TOO!
PELÉ, WHO BARELY SPEAKS THREE WORDS IN ENGLISH, DISCOVERS A CULTURAL LIFE THAT'S COMPLETELY FOREIGN TO HIM.
MAJESTIC
WORLD PREMIERE
THE WIZ
AND AT NIGHT, CROSSES PATHS WITH FAMOUS PEOPLE FROM MOVIES, ENTERTAINMENT, AND THE ARTS.
ANDY, MICK, LET ME INTRODUCE THE KING OF THE ROUND BALL!
POPS!
SATISFACTION!
DESPITE HIS ACTIVE NIGHTLIFE, HE KEEPS TO HIS PRINCIPLE OF "NO ALCOHOL, NO DRUGS."
GOOD GOD, PELÉ, WHAT DO YOU HAVE LEFT?
WOMEN!
GOOD EVENING!

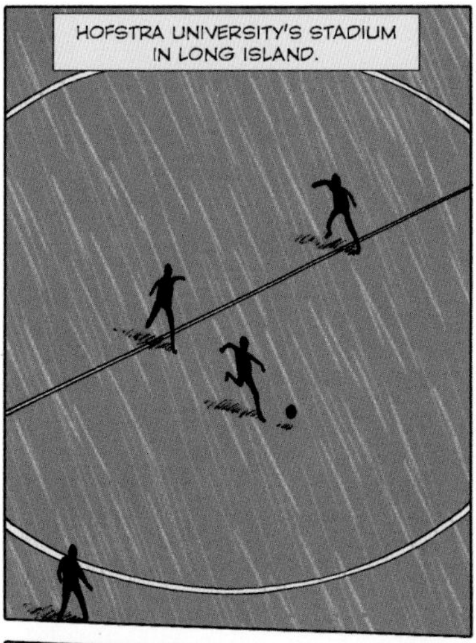
HOFSTRA UNIVERSITY'S STADIUM IN LONG ISLAND.

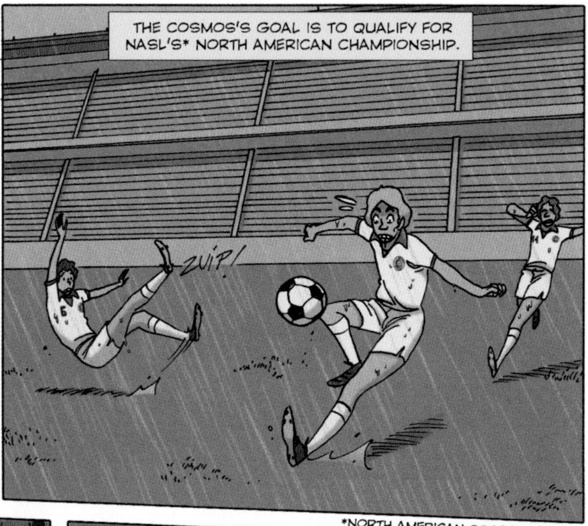
THE COSMOS'S GOAL IS TO QUALIFY FOR NASL'S* NORTH AMERICAN CHAMPIONSHIP.
ZUIP!

*NORTH AMERICAN SOCCER LEAGUE.

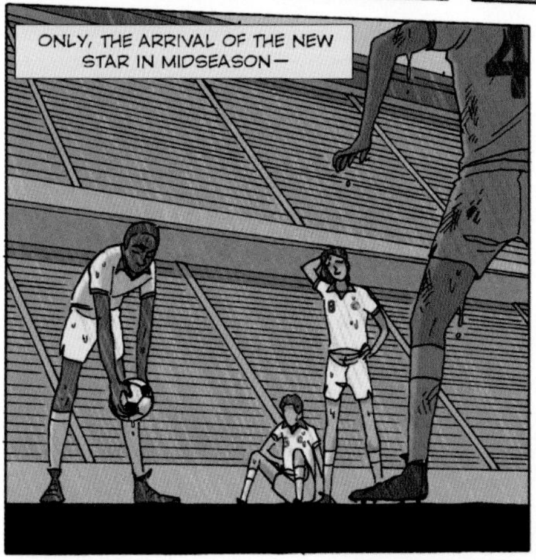
ONLY, THE ARRIVAL OF THE NEW STAR IN MIDSEASON—

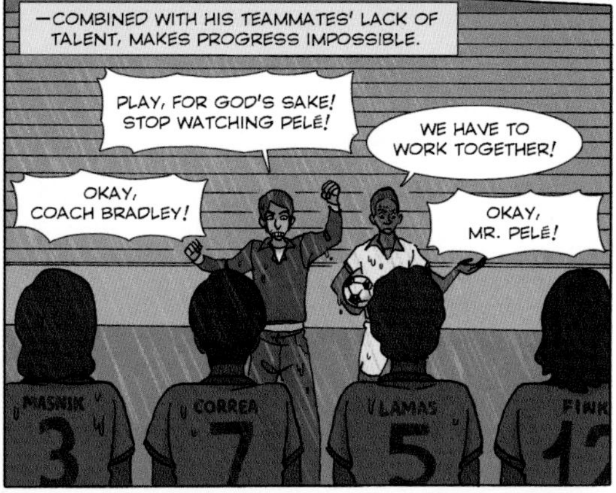
—COMBINED WITH HIS TEAMMATES' LACK OF TALENT, MAKES PROGRESS IMPOSSIBLE.
PLAY, FOR GOD'S SAKE! STOP WATCHING PELÉ!
WE HAVE TO WORK TOGETHER!
OKAY, COACH BRADLEY!
OKAY, MR. PELÉ!
MASNIK
3
CORREA
7
LAMAS
5
FINK

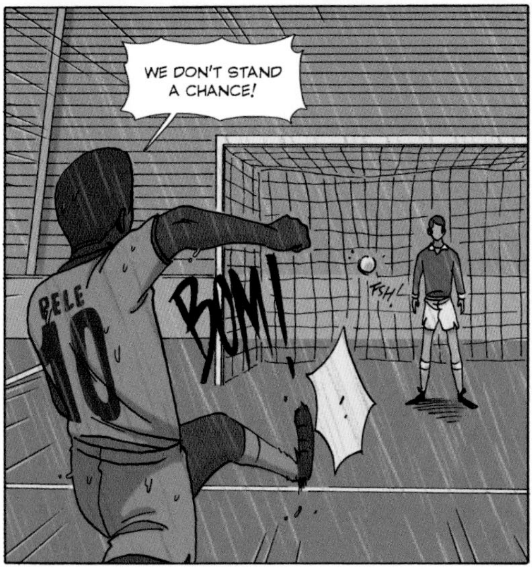
WE DON'T STAND A CHANCE!
PELE
10
BOM!
FSH!

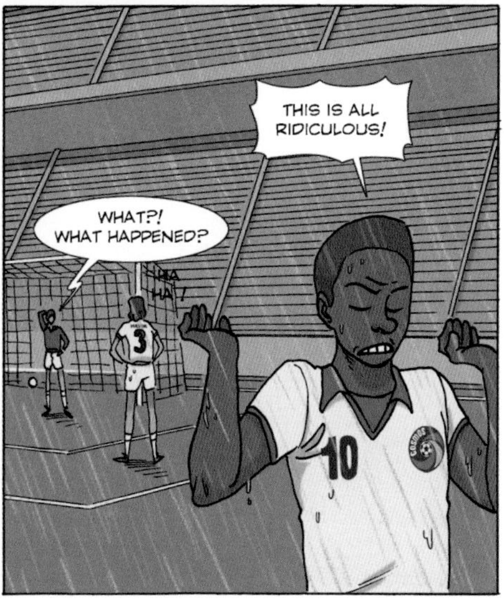
THIS IS ALL RIDICULOUS!
WHAT?! WHAT HAPPENED?
HA HA!
3
10

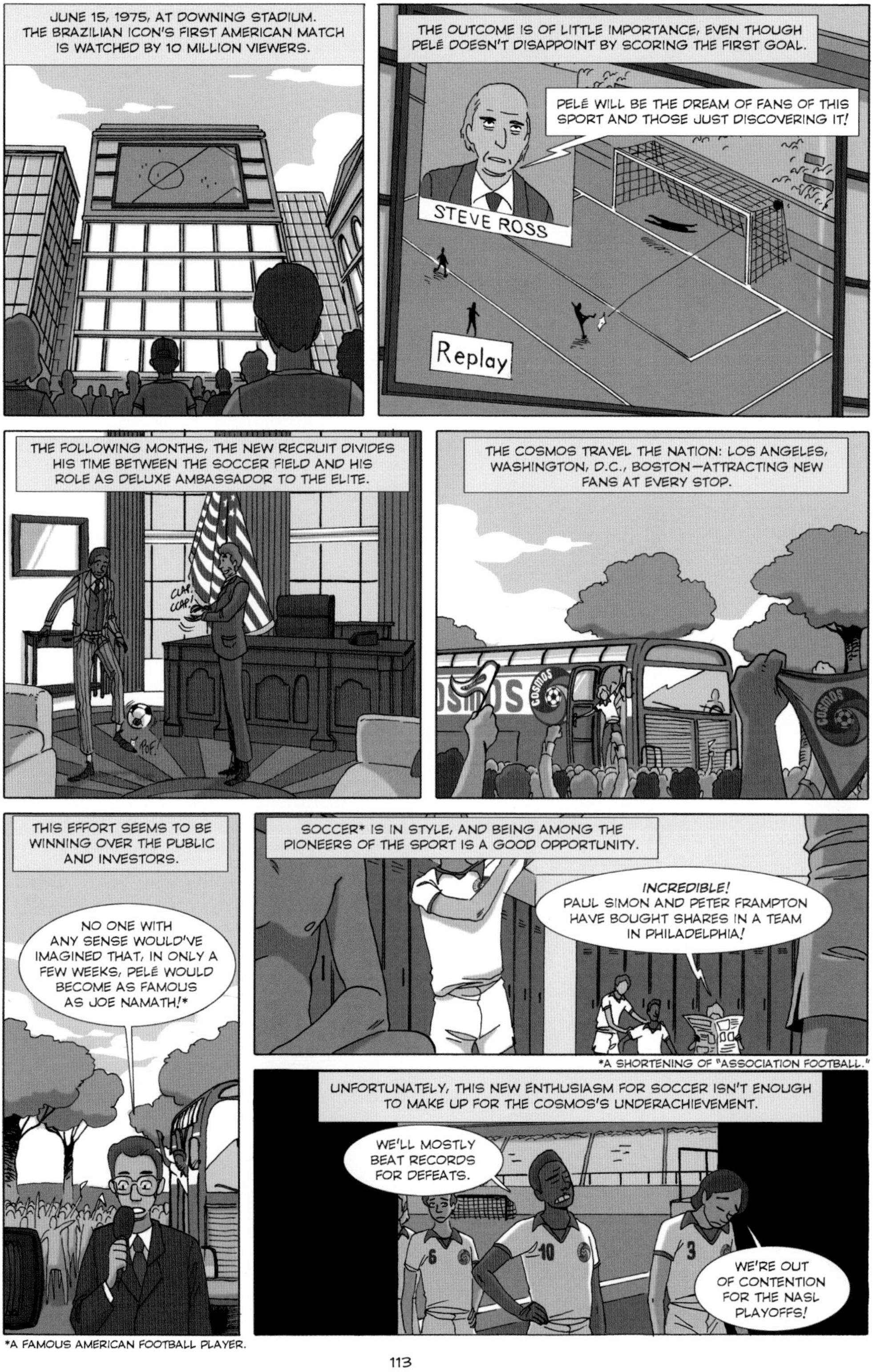
JUNE 15, 1975, AT DOWNING STADIUM. THE BRAZILIAN ICON'S FIRST AMERICAN MATCH IS WATCHED BY 10 MILLION VIEWERS.
THE OUTCOME IS OF LITTLE IMPORTANCE, EVEN THOUGH PELÉ DOESN'T DISAPPOINT BY SCORING THE FIRST GOAL.
PELÉ WILL BE THE DREAM OF FANS OF THIS SPORT AND THOSE JUST DISCOVERING IT!
STEVE ROSS
Replay
THE FOLLOWING MONTHS, THE NEW RECRUIT DIVIDES HIS TIME BETWEEN THE SOCCER FIELD AND HIS ROLE AS DELUXE AMBASSADOR TO THE ELITE.
CLAP! CLAP!
POF!
THE COSMOS TRAVEL THE NATION: LOS ANGELES, WASHINGTON, D.C., BOSTON—ATTRACTING NEW FANS AT EVERY STOP.
COSMOS
THIS EFFORT SEEMS TO BE WINNING OVER THE PUBLIC AND INVESTORS.
NO ONE WITH ANY SENSE WOULD'VE IMAGINED THAT, IN ONLY A FEW WEEKS, PELÉ WOULD BECOME AS FAMOUS AS JOE NAMATH!*
SOCCER* IS IN STYLE, AND BEING AMONG THE PIONEERS OF THE SPORT IS A GOOD OPPORTUNITY.
INCREDIBLE! PAUL SIMON AND PETER FRAMPTON HAVE BOUGHT SHARES IN A TEAM IN PHILADELPHIA!
*A SHORTENING OF "ASSOCIATION FOOTBALL."
UNFORTUNATELY, THIS NEW ENTHUSIASM FOR SOCCER ISN'T ENOUGH TO MAKE UP FOR THE COSMOS'S UNDERACHIEVEMENT.
WE'LL MOSTLY BEAT RECORDS FOR DEFEATS.
WE'RE OUT OF CONTENTION FOR THE NASL PLAYOFFS!

*A FAMOUS AMERICAN FOOTBALL PLAYER.

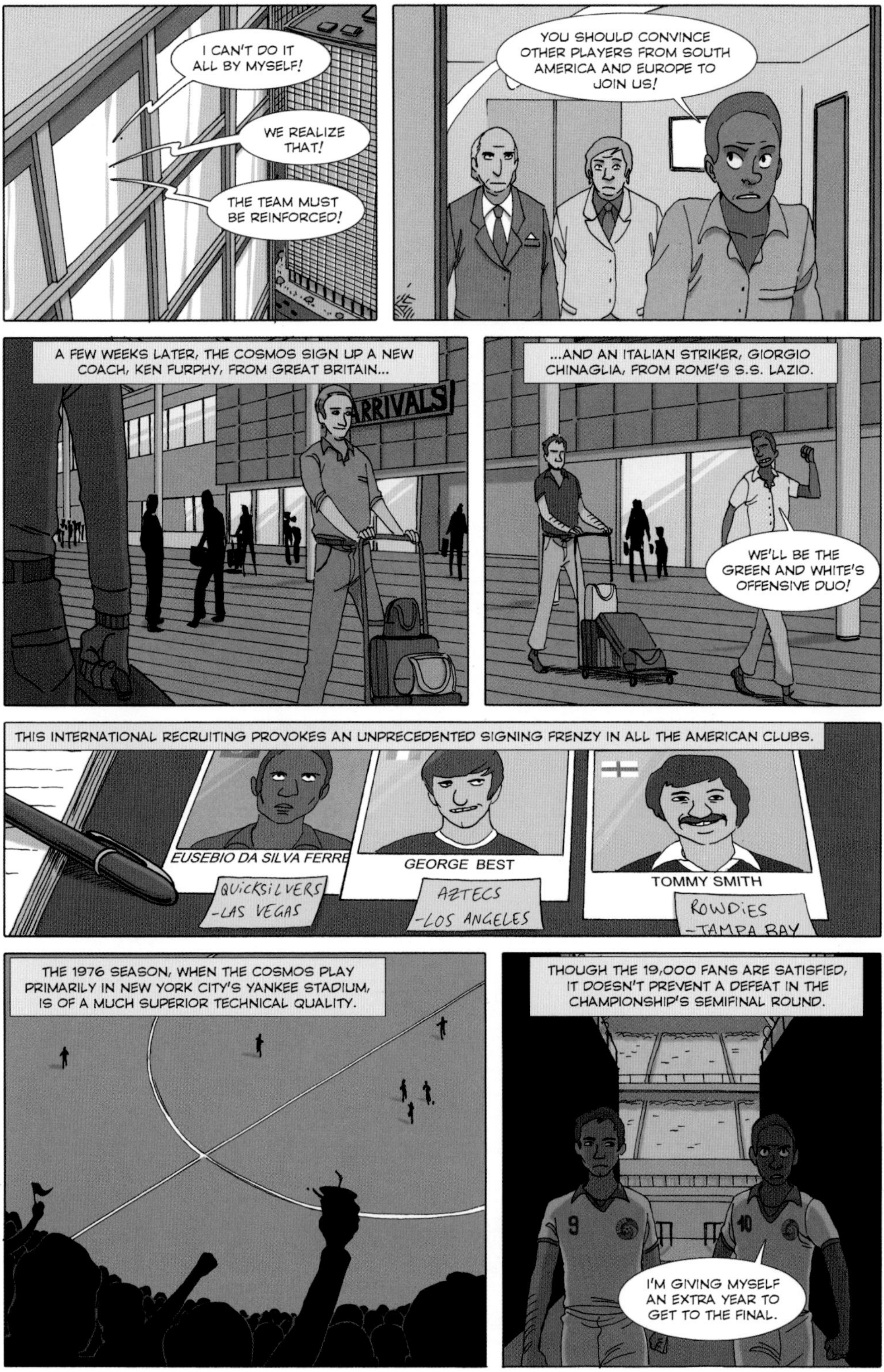
I CAN'T DO IT ALL BY MYSELF!
WE REALIZE THAT!
THE TEAM MUST BE REINFORCED!
YOU SHOULD CONVINCE OTHER PLAYERS FROM SOUTH AMERICA AND EUROPE TO JOIN US!
A FEW WEEKS LATER, THE COSMOS SIGN UP A NEW COACH, KEN FURPHY, FROM GREAT BRITAIN...
ARRIVALS
...AND AN ITALIAN STRIKER, GIORGIO CHINAGLIA, FROM ROME'S S.S. LAZIO.
WE'LL BE THE GREEN AND WHITE'S OFFENSIVE DUO!
THIS INTERNATIONAL RECRUITING PROVOKES AN UNPRECEDENTED SIGNING FRENZY IN ALL THE AMERICAN CLUBS.
EUSEBIO DA SILVA FERRE
QUICKSILVERS -LAS VEGAS
GEORGE BEST
AZTECS -LOS ANGELES
TOMMY SMITH
ROWDIES -TAMPA BAY
THE 1976 SEASON, WHEN THE COSMOS PLAY PRIMARILY IN NEW YORK CITY'S YANKEE STADIUM, IS OF A MUCH SUPERIOR TECHNICAL QUALITY.
THOUGH THE 19,000 FANS ARE SATISFIED, IT DOESN'T PREVENT A DEFEAT IN THE CHAMPIONSHIP'S SEMIFINAL ROUND.
I'M GIVING MYSELF AN EXTRA YEAR TO GET TO THE FINAL.

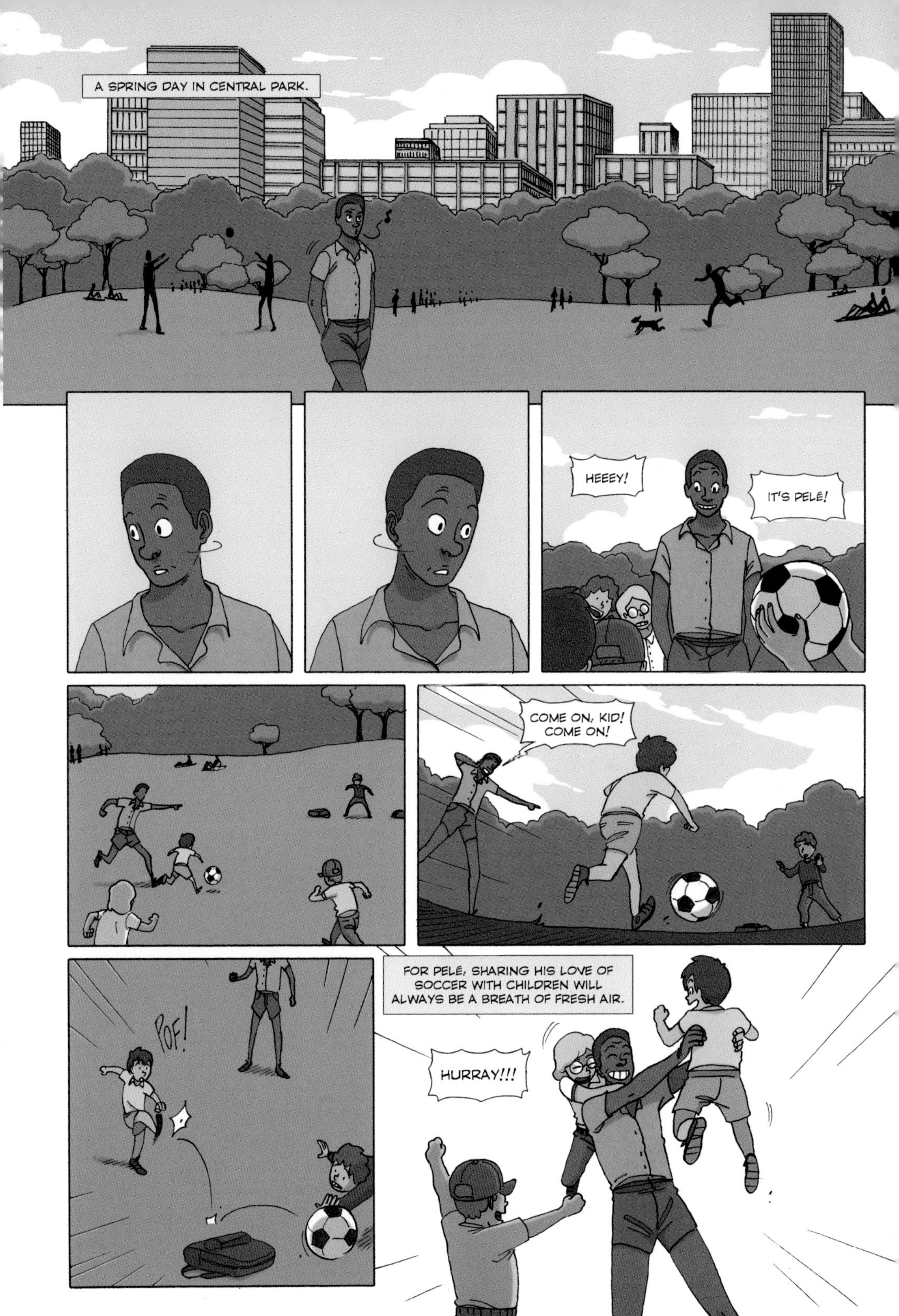
A SPRING DAY IN CENTRAL PARK.
HEEEY!
IT'S PELÉ!
COME ON, KID! COME ON!
POF!
FOR PELÉ, SHARING HIS LOVE OF SOCCER WITH CHILDREN WILL ALWAYS BE A BREATH OF FRESH AIR.
HURRAY!!!

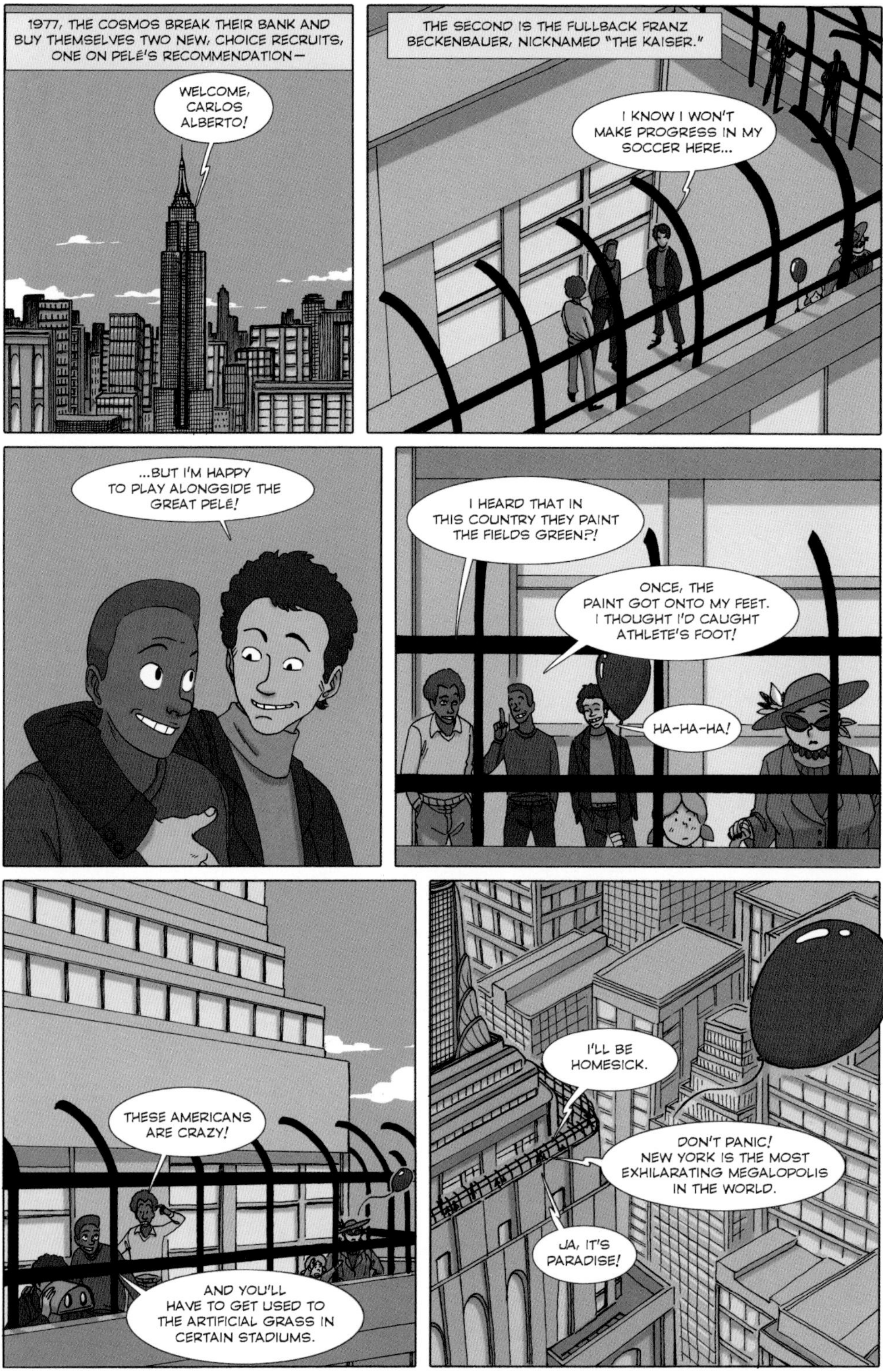
1977, THE COSMOS BREAK THEIR BANK AND BUY THEMSELVES TWO NEW, CHOICE RECRUITS, ONE ON PELÉ'S RECOMMENDATION—
WELCOME, CARLOS ALBERTO!
THE SECOND IS THE FULLBACK FRANZ BECKENBAUER, NICKNAMED "THE KAISER."
I KNOW I WON'T MAKE PROGRESS IN MY SOCCER HERE...
...BUT I'M HAPPY TO PLAY ALONGSIDE THE GREAT PELÉ!
I HEARD THAT IN THIS COUNTRY THEY PAINT THE FIELDS GREEN?!
ONCE, THE PAINT GOT ONTO MY FEET. I THOUGHT I'D CAUGHT ATHLETE'S FOOT!
HA-HA-HA!
THESE AMERICANS ARE CRAZY!
AND YOU'LL HAVE TO GET USED TO THE ARTIFICIAL GRASS IN CERTAIN STADIUMS.
I'LL BE HOMESICK.
DON'T PANIC! NEW YORK IS THE MOST EXHILARATING MEGALOPOLIS IN THE WORLD.
JA, IT'S PARADISE!

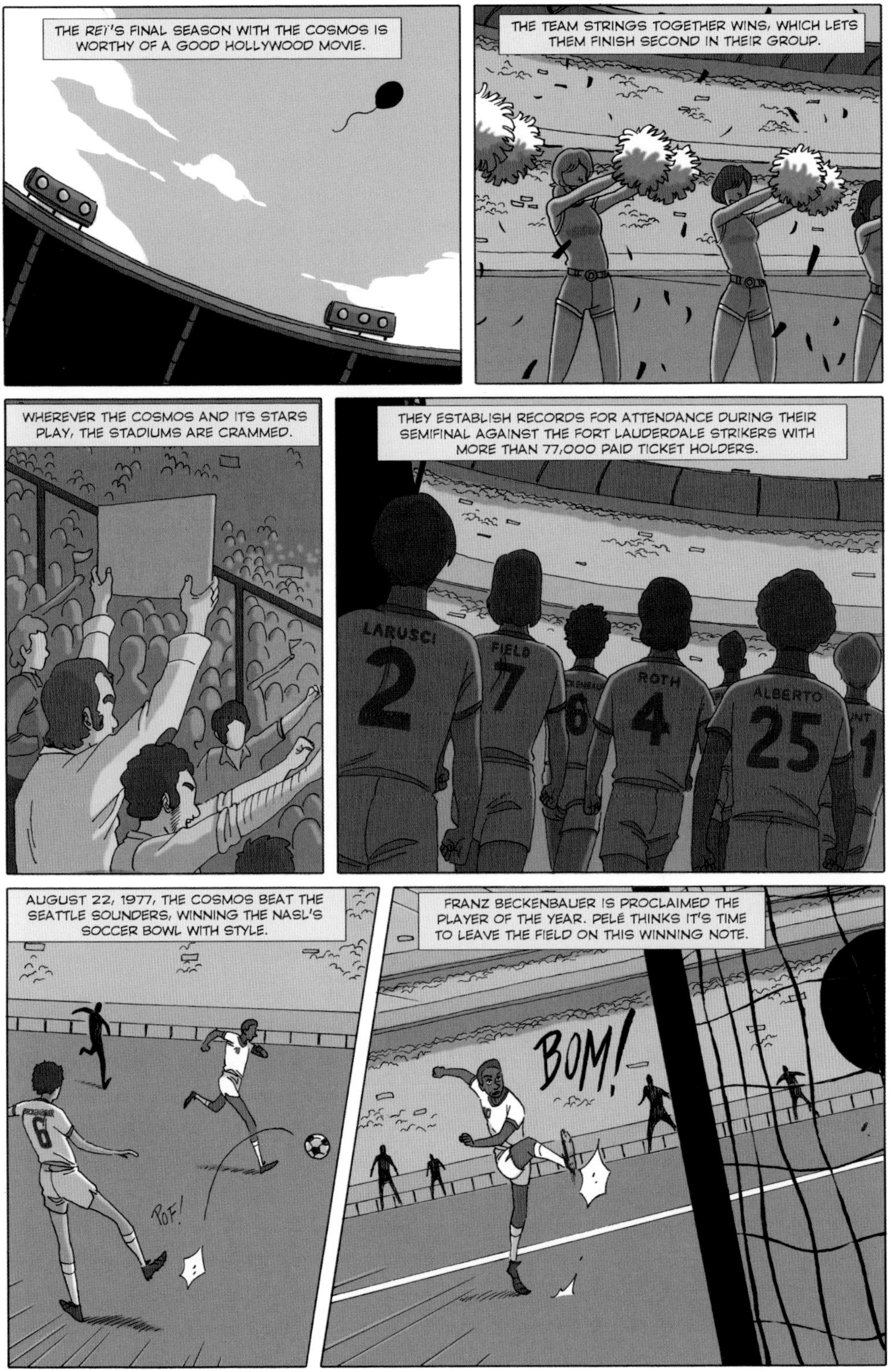
THE REI'S FINAL SEASON WITH THE COSMOS IS WORTHY OF A GOOD HOLLYWOOD MOVIE.
THE TEAM STRINGS TOGETHER WINS, WHICH LETS THEM FINISH SECOND IN THEIR GROUP.
WHEREVER THE COSMOS AND ITS STARS PLAY, THE STADIUMS ARE CRAMMED.
THEY ESTABLISH RECORDS FOR ATTENDANCE DURING THEIR SEMIFINAL AGAINST THE FORT LAUDERDALE STRIKERS WITH MORE THAN 77,000 PAID TICKET HOLDERS.
LARUSCI 2
FIELD 7
ROTH 4
ALBERTO 25
AUGUST 22, 1977, THE COSMOS BEAT THE SEATTLE SOUNDERS, WINNING THE NASL'S SOCCER BOWL WITH STYLE.
POF!
FRANZ BECKENBAUER IS PROCLAIMED THE PLAYER OF THE YEAR. PELÉ THINKS IT'S TIME TO LEAVE THE FIELD ON THIS WINNING NOTE.
BOM!

WHAT NOBODY KNOWS YET IS THAT THIS FLAMBOYANT YEAR IS THE BEGINNING OF SOCCER'S DECLINE IN THE UNITED STATES.

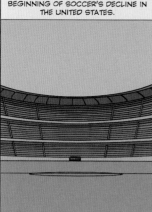

THE THUNDEROUS SUCCESS OF THIS SPORT LED TO EXTRAVAGANT EXPENDITURES, WHICH INDEBTED THE CLUBS.

AND AGAINST ALL EXPECTATIONS, THE PUBLIC WILL QUICKLY LOSE INTEREST IN SOCCER. A FEW SPECIALISTS ARE ALREADY EXPRESSING A HYPOTHESIS.

WHAT FUTURE IS THERE FOR SOCCER HERE IN THE U.S. WITHOUT THE CHARISMATIC PELÉ?

NONE, I'M VERY AFRAID!

ON OCTOBER 1, 1977, A VERY SYMBOLIC FAREWELL MATCH.

I'M PLAYING THE FIRST HALF WITH THE COSMOS—

THEN THE SECOND WITH THE SANTOS!

PELÉ SCORES HIS FINAL PROFESSIONAL GOAL* WITH HIS FATHER WATCHING FROM THE VIP STANDS.

BOM!

PELÉ IS 37. HE'S CONQUERED THE ENTIRE EARTH, AND FREE FROM WANT, HE CAN FINALLY STOP FOR GOOD.

LOVE! LOVE! LOVE!

THE KING

PELE

*ACCORDING TO THE GUINNESS WORLD RECORDS, HIS TOTAL IS 1,274 GOALS IN PROFESSIONAL MATCHES BETWEEN SEPTEMBER 7, 1956, AND OCTOBER 1, 1977.

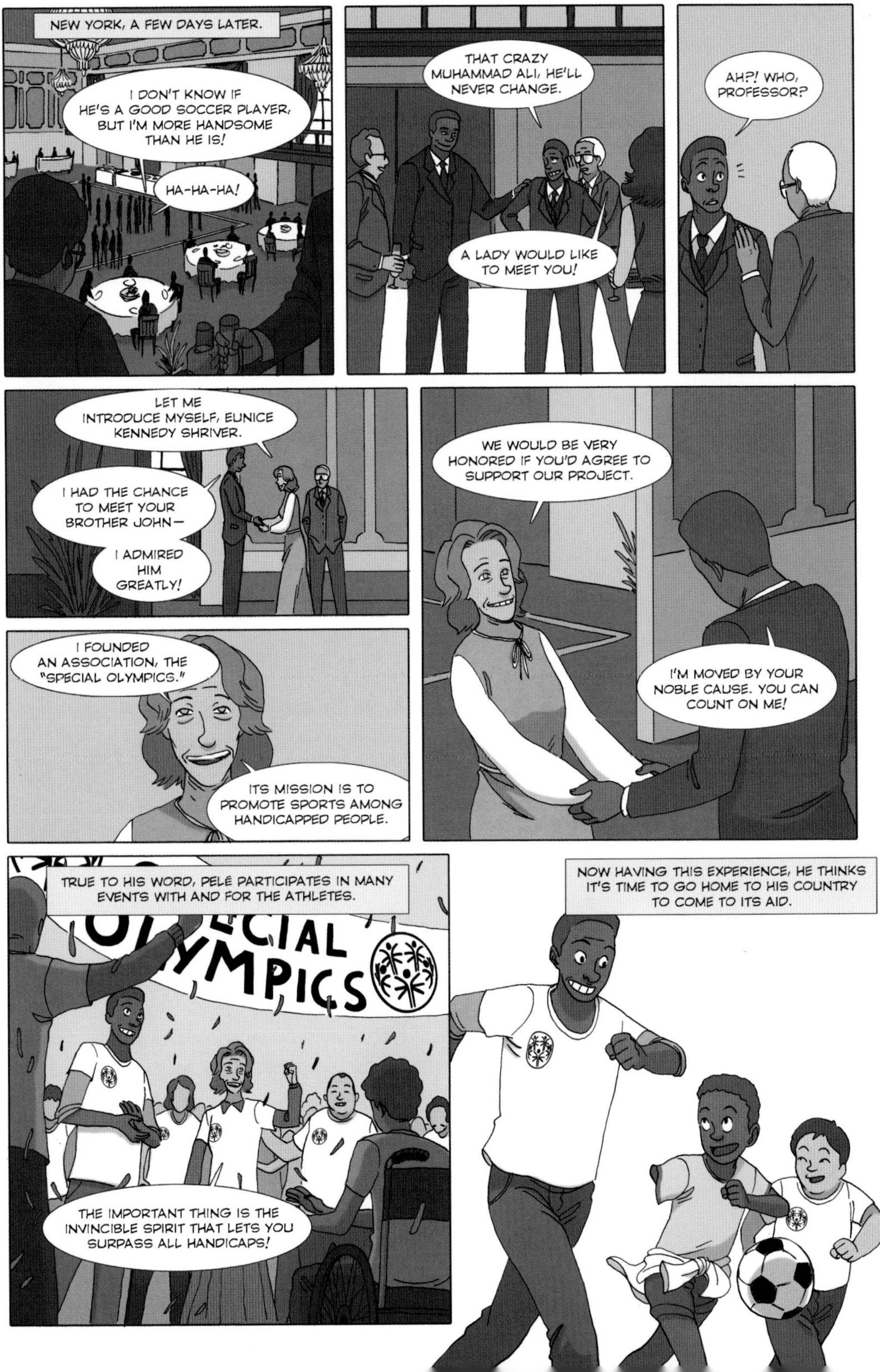

NEW YORK, A FEW DAYS LATER.
I DON'T KNOW IF HE'S A GOOD SOCCER PLAYER, BUT I'M MORE HANDSOME THAN HE IS!
HA-HA-HA!
THAT CRAZY MUHAMMAD ALI, HE'LL NEVER CHANGE.
A LADY WOULD LIKE TO MEET YOU!
AH?! WHO, PROFESSOR?
LET ME INTRODUCE MYSELF, EUNICE KENNEDY SHRIVER.
I HAD THE CHANCE TO MEET YOUR BROTHER JOHN—
I ADMIRED HIM GREATLY!
WE WOULD BE VERY HONORED IF YOU'D AGREE TO SUPPORT OUR PROJECT.
I'M MOVED BY YOUR NOBLE CAUSE. YOU CAN COUNT ON ME!
I FOUNDED AN ASSOCIATION, THE "SPECIAL OLYMPICS."
ITS MISSION IS TO PROMOTE SPORTS AMONG HANDICAPPED PEOPLE.
TRUE TO HIS WORD, PELÉ PARTICIPATES IN MANY EVENTS WITH AND FOR THE ATHLETES.
ECIAL YMPICS
THE IMPORTANT THING IS THE INVINCIBLE SPIRIT THAT LETS YOU SURPASS ALL HANDICAPS!
NOW HAVING THIS EXPERIENCE, HE THINKS IT'S TIME TO GO HOME TO HIS COUNTRY TO COME TO ITS AID.

Chapter 8
World Ambassador

"Pelé played soccer for twenty-two years, and during that time, he did more for friendship and brotherhood than any other ambassador."
—J. B. Pinheiro, Brazilian ambassador to the United Nations

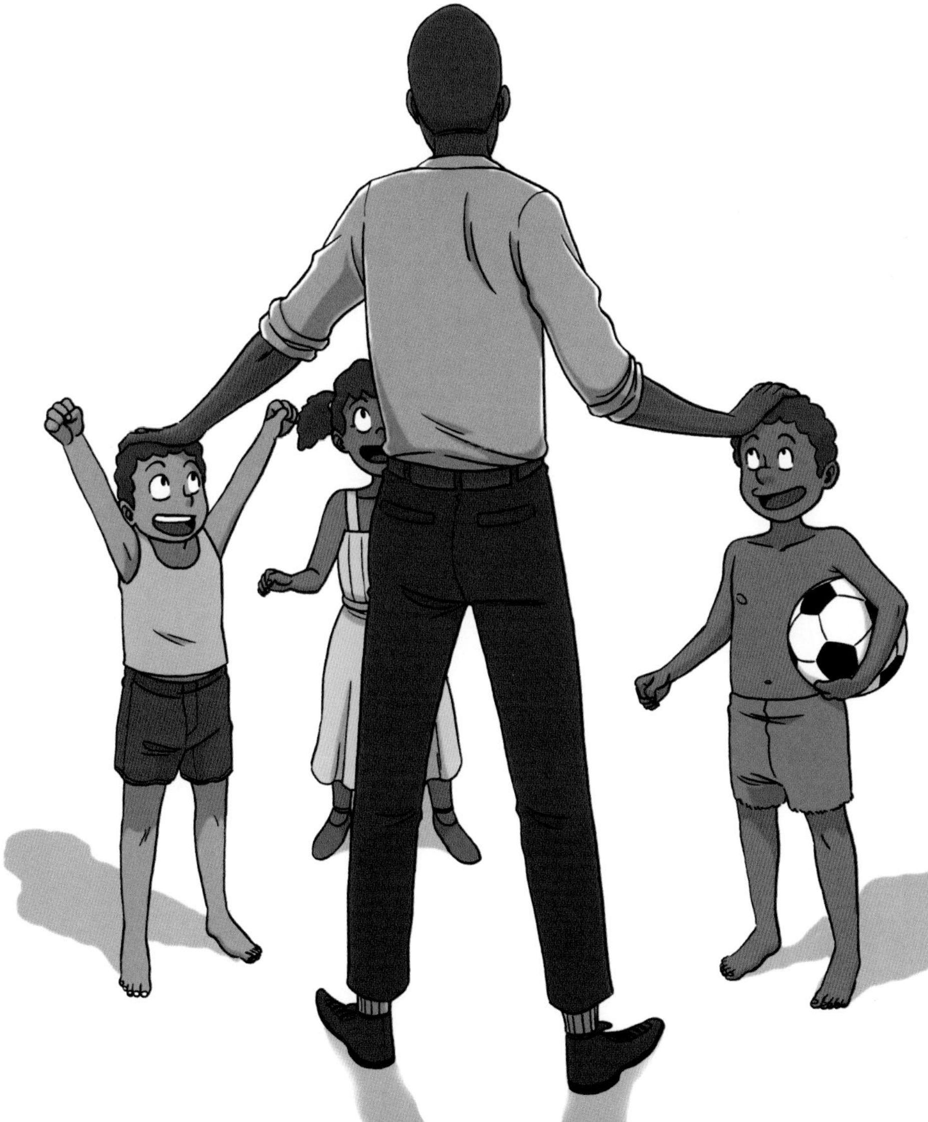

BEGINNING IN 1977, PELÉ IS A "WORLD CITIZEN." THE UNITED NATIONS HAS ACCORDED HIM THIS HONORARY TITLE FOR HIS GENEROSITY IN SHARING HIS SPORT.

I'M PLANNING TO GIVE MEANING TO IT!

HE COMMITS HIMSELF TO UNESCO AND UNICEF AS A GOODWILL AMBASSADOR.

HE TRAVELS AND COLLECTS FUNDS TO COME TO THE AID OF DISADVANTAGED CHILDREN.

THERE IS MISERY HERE IN BRAZIL, TOO!

IN BRAZIL, THE POLITICAL SITUATION HAS HARDLY EVOLVED. THE MILITARY JUNTA CONTINUES TO IMPOSE ITS DIKTAT.

THE DOPS* HAS BEEN SPYING ON ME FOR A LONG TIME!

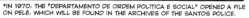

*IN 1970, THE "DEPARTAMENTO DE ORDEM POLÍTICA E SOCIAL" OPENED A FILE ON PELÉ, WHICH WILL BE FOUND IN THE ARCHIVES OF THE SANTOS POLICE.

WHY DIDN'T YOU USE YOUR FAME TO DENOUNCE ALL THIS?

BOM!

I FEARED LOSING EVERYTHING AND PUTTING MY FAMILY IN DANGER.

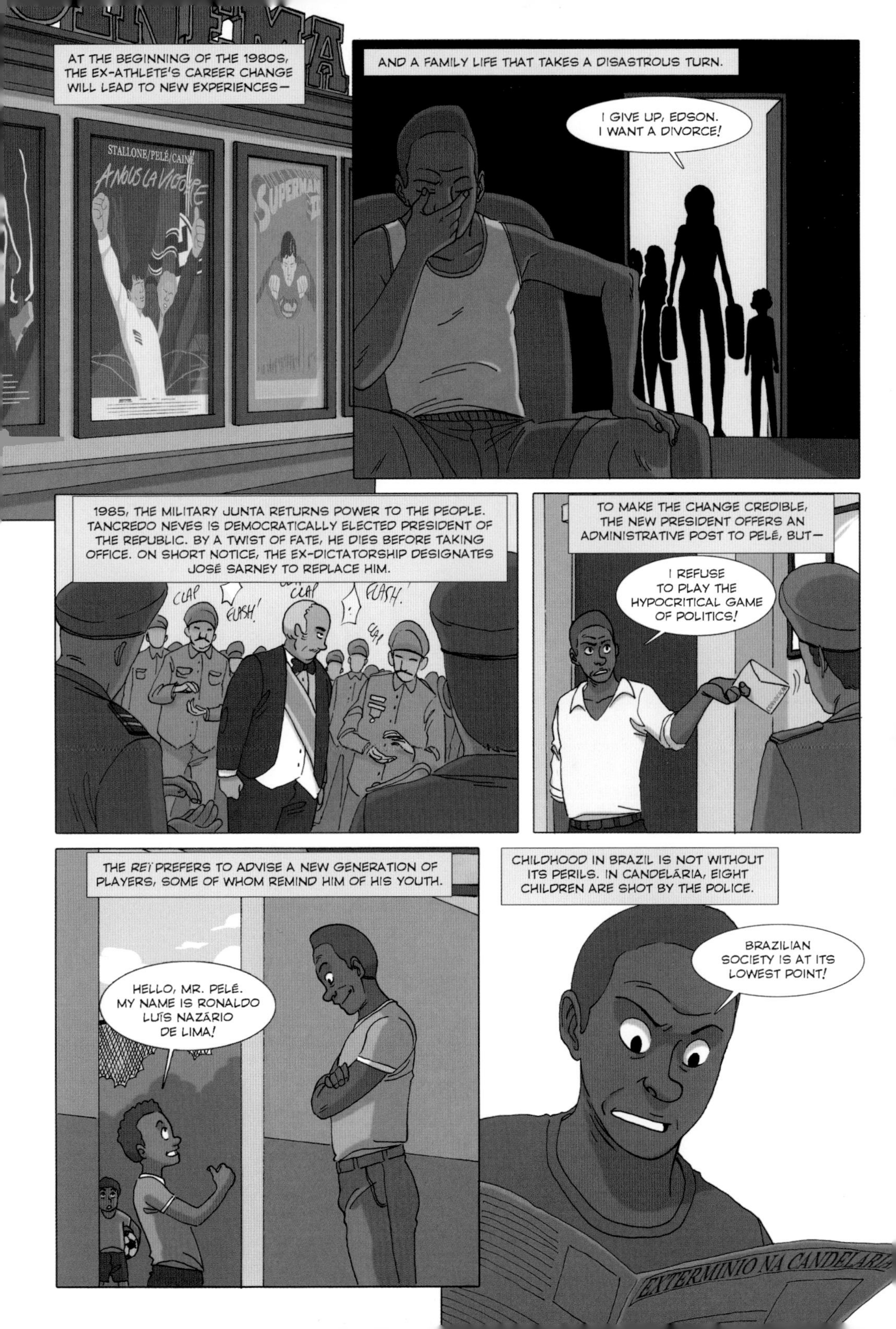
AT THE BEGINNING OF THE 1980S, THE EX-ATHLETE'S CAREER CHANGE WILL LEAD TO NEW EXPERIENCES—
STALLONE/PELÉ/CAINE
A NOUS LA VICTOIRE
SUPERMAN
AND A FAMILY LIFE THAT TAKES A DISASTROUS TURN.
I GIVE UP, EDSON. I WANT A DIVORCE!
1985, THE MILITARY JUNTA RETURNS POWER TO THE PEOPLE. TANCREDO NEVES IS DEMOCRATICALLY ELECTED PRESIDENT OF THE REPUBLIC. BY A TWIST OF FATE, HE DIES BEFORE TAKING OFFICE. ON SHORT NOTICE, THE EX-DICTATORSHIP DESIGNATES JOSÉ SARNEY TO REPLACE HIM.
CLAP
FLASH!
CLAP
FLASH.
TO MAKE THE CHANGE CREDIBLE, THE NEW PRESIDENT OFFERS AN ADMINISTRATIVE POST TO PELÉ, BUT—
I REFUSE TO PLAY THE HYPOCRITICAL GAME OF POLITICS!
THE *REI* PREFERS TO ADVISE A NEW GENERATION OF PLAYERS, SOME OF WHOM REMIND HIM OF HIS YOUTH.
HELLO, MR. PELÉ. MY NAME IS RONALDO LUÍS NAZÁRIO DE LIMA!
CHILDHOOD IN BRAZIL IS NOT WITHOUT ITS PERILS. IN CANDELÁRIA, EIGHT CHILDREN ARE SHOT BY THE POLICE.
BRAZILIAN SOCIETY IS AT ITS LOWEST POINT!
EXTERMINIO NA CANDELARIA

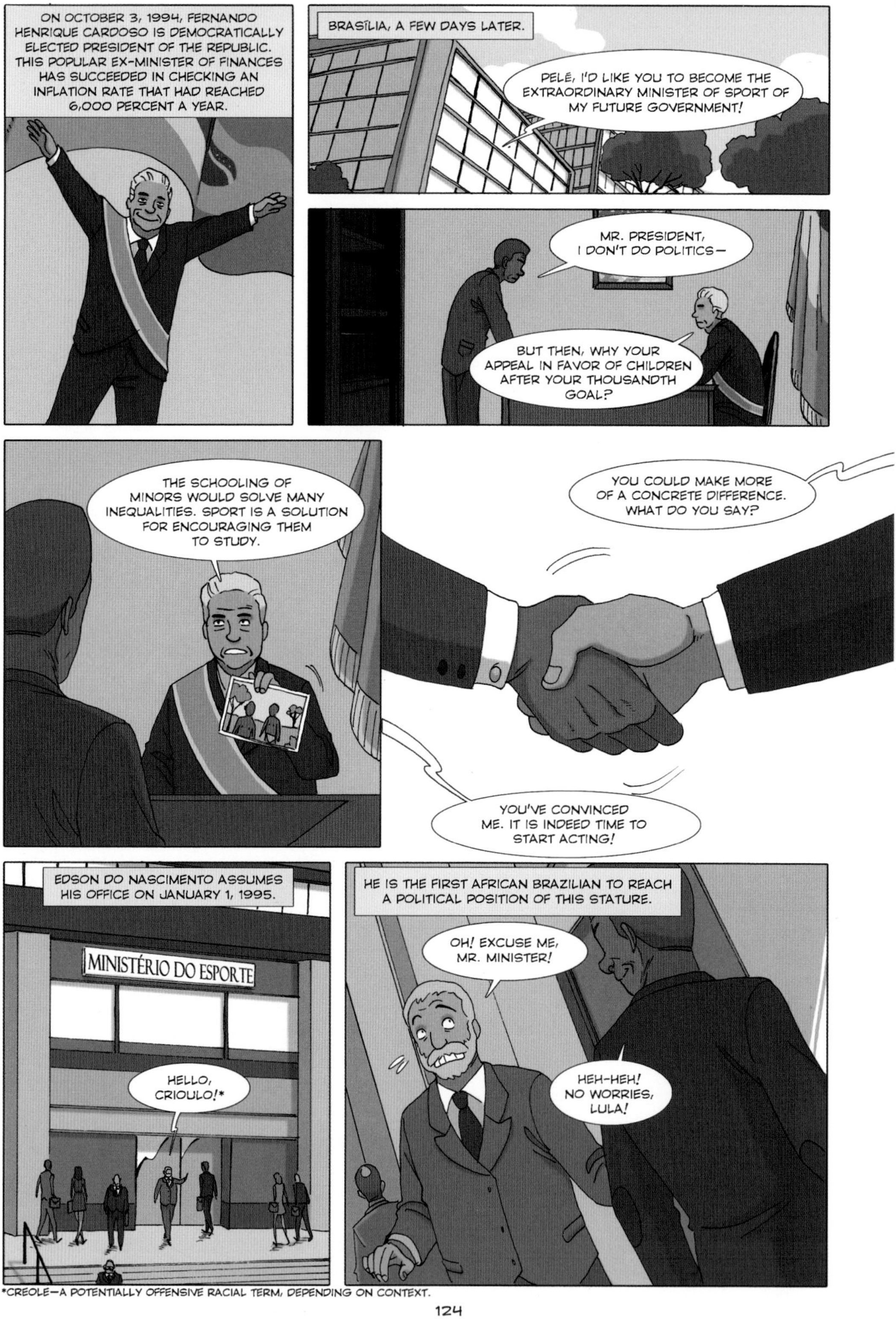
ON OCTOBER 3, 1994, FERNANDO HENRIQUE CARDOSO IS DEMOCRATICALLY ELECTED PRESIDENT OF THE REPUBLIC. THIS POPULAR EX-MINISTER OF FINANCES HAS SUCCEEDED IN CHECKING AN INFLATION RATE THAT HAD REACHED 6,000 PERCENT A YEAR.
BRASÍLIA, A FEW DAYS LATER.
PELÉ, I'D LIKE YOU TO BECOME THE EXTRAORDINARY MINISTER OF SPORT OF MY FUTURE GOVERNMENT!
MR. PRESIDENT, I DON'T DO POLITICS—
BUT THEN, WHY YOUR APPEAL IN FAVOR OF CHILDREN AFTER YOUR THOUSANDTH GOAL?
THE SCHOOLING OF MINORS WOULD SOLVE MANY INEQUALITIES. SPORT IS A SOLUTION FOR ENCOURAGING THEM TO STUDY.
YOU COULD MAKE MORE OF A CONCRETE DIFFERENCE. WHAT DO YOU SAY?
YOU'VE CONVINCED ME. IT IS INDEED TIME TO START ACTING!
EDSON DO NASCIMENTO ASSUMES HIS OFFICE ON JANUARY 1, 1995.
MINISTÉRIO DO ESPORTE
HELLO, CRIOULO!*
HE IS THE FIRST AFRICAN BRAZILIAN TO REACH A POLITICAL POSITION OF THIS STATURE.
OH! EXCUSE ME, MR. MINISTER!
HEH-HEH! NO WORRIES, LULA!

*CREOLE—A POTENTIALLY OFFENSIVE RACIAL TERM, DEPENDING ON CONTEXT.

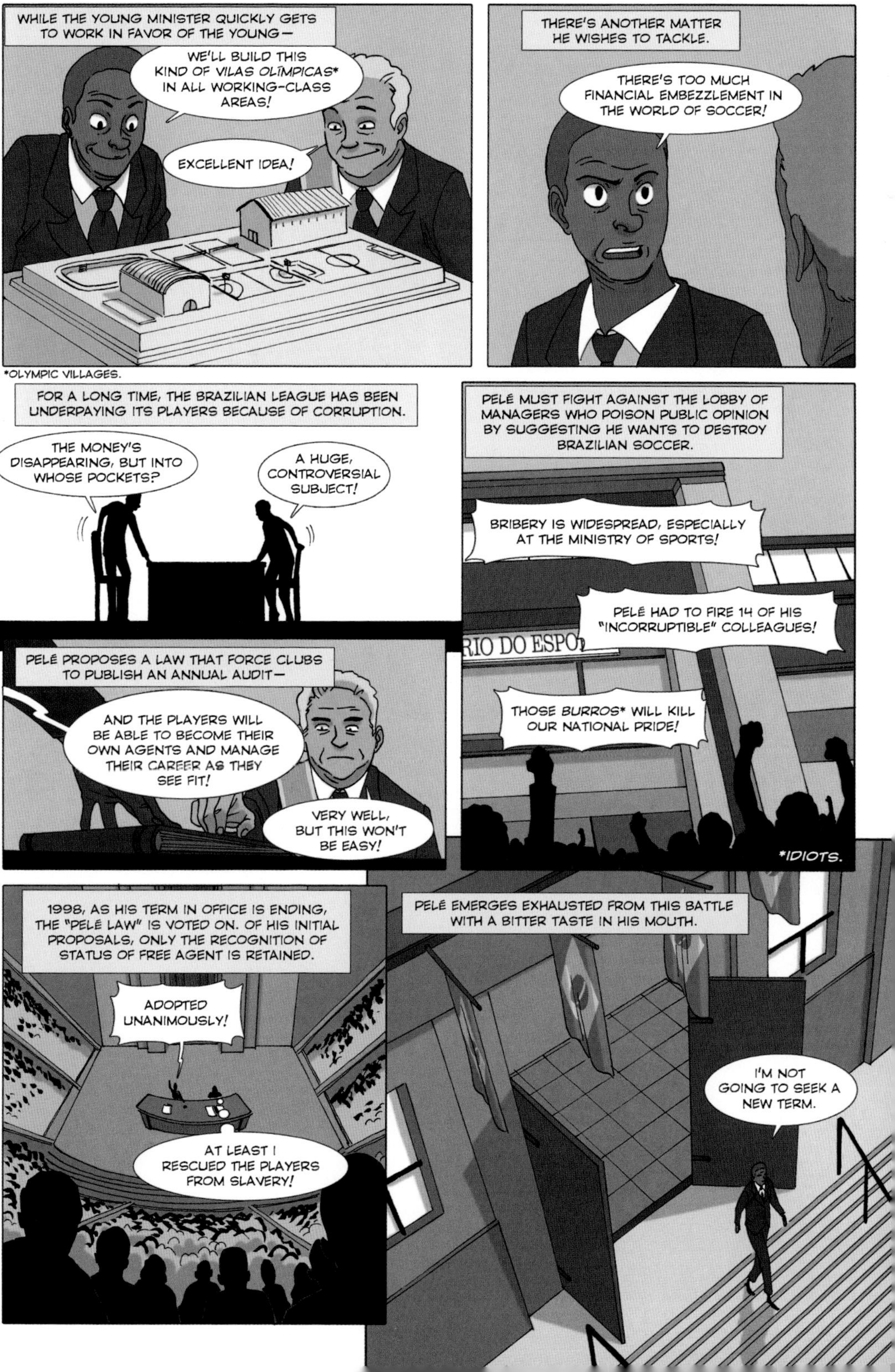
WHILE THE YOUNG MINISTER QUICKLY GETS TO WORK IN FAVOR OF THE YOUNG—
WE'LL BUILD THIS KIND OF *VILAS OLÍMPICAS** IN ALL WORKING-CLASS AREAS!
EXCELLENT IDEA!
THERE'S ANOTHER MATTER HE WISHES TO TACKLE.
THERE'S TOO MUCH FINANCIAL EMBEZZLEMENT IN THE WORLD OF SOCCER!
*OLYMPIC VILLAGES.
FOR A LONG TIME, THE BRAZILIAN LEAGUE HAS BEEN UNDERPAYING ITS PLAYERS BECAUSE OF CORRUPTION.
THE MONEY'S DISAPPEARING, BUT INTO WHOSE POCKETS?
A HUGE, CONTROVERSIAL SUBJECT!
PELÉ PROPOSES A LAW THAT FORCE CLUBS TO PUBLISH AN ANNUAL AUDIT—
AND THE PLAYERS WILL BE ABLE TO BECOME THEIR OWN AGENTS AND MANAGE THEIR CAREER AS THEY SEE FIT!
VERY WELL, BUT THIS WON'T BE EASY!
PELÉ MUST FIGHT AGAINST THE LOBBY OF MANAGERS WHO POISON PUBLIC OPINION BY SUGGESTING HE WANTS TO DESTROY BRAZILIAN SOCCER.
BRIBERY IS WIDESPREAD, ESPECIALLY AT THE MINISTRY OF SPORTS!
PELÉ HAD TO FIRE 14 OF HIS "INCORRUPTIBLE" COLLEAGUES!
RIO DO ESPO
THOSE *BURROS** WILL KILL OUR NATIONAL PRIDE!
*IDIOTS.
1998, AS HIS TERM IN OFFICE IS ENDING, THE "PELÉ LAW" IS VOTED ON. OF HIS INITIAL PROPOSALS, ONLY THE RECOGNITION OF STATUS OF FREE AGENT IS RETAINED.
ADOPTED UNANIMOUSLY!
AT LEAST I RESCUED THE PLAYERS FROM SLAVERY!
PELÉ EMERGES EXHAUSTED FROM THIS BATTLE WITH A BITTER TASTE IN HIS MOUTH.
I'M NOT GOING TO SEEK A NEW TERM.

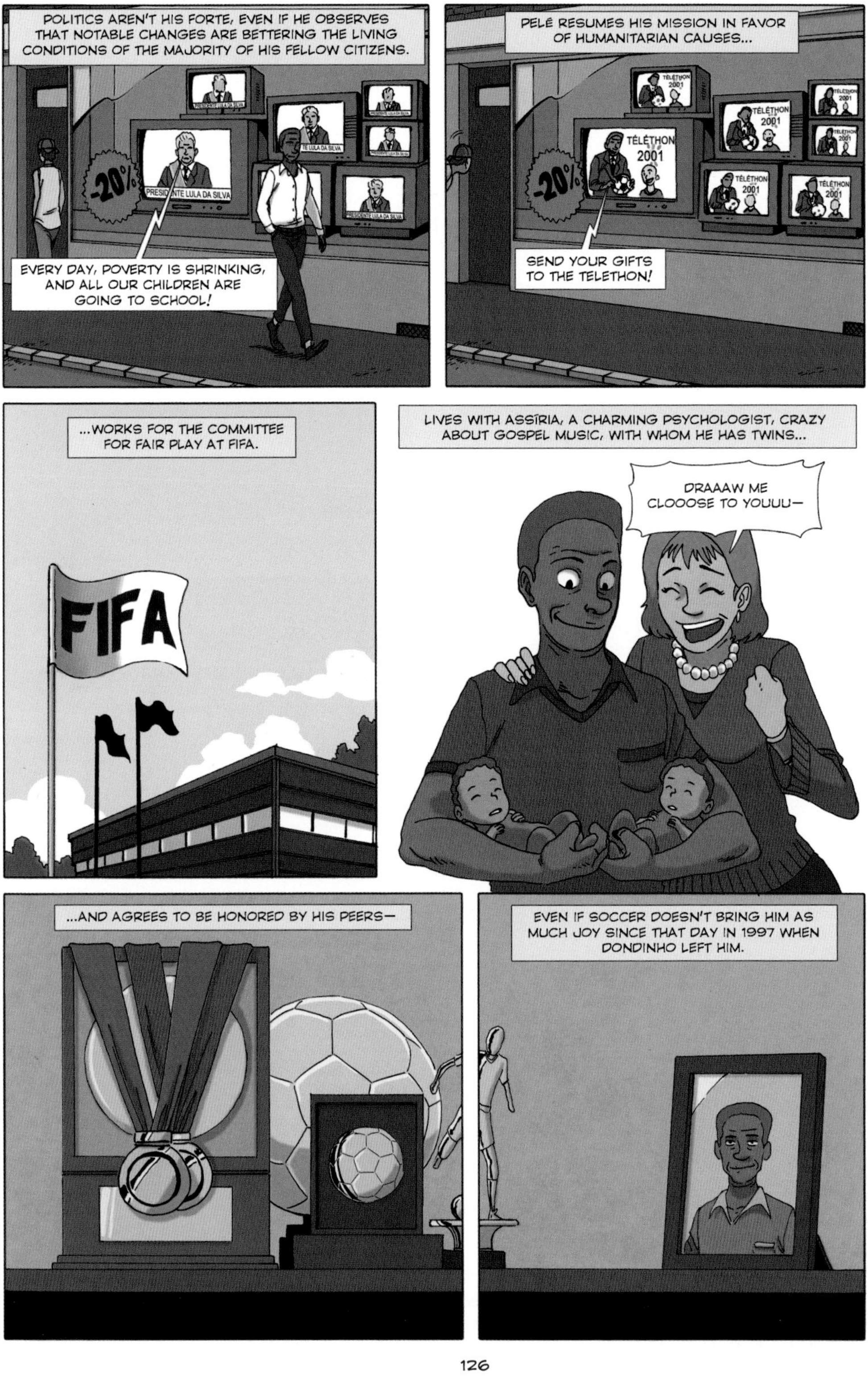
POLITICS AREN'T HIS FORTE, EVEN IF HE OBSERVES THAT NOTABLE CHANGES ARE BETTERING THE LIVING CONDITIONS OF THE MAJORITY OF HIS FELLOW CITIZENS.
PRESIDENTE LULA DA SILVA
-20%
EVERY DAY, POVERTY IS SHRINKING, AND ALL OUR CHILDREN ARE GOING TO SCHOOL!
PELÉ RESUMES HIS MISSION IN FAVOR OF HUMANITARIAN CAUSES...
TÉLÉTHON 2001
-20%
SEND YOUR GIFTS TO THE TELETHON!
...WORKS FOR THE COMMITTEE FOR FAIR PLAY AT FIFA.
FIFA
LIVES WITH ASSÍRIA, A CHARMING PSYCHOLOGIST, CRAZY ABOUT GOSPEL MUSIC, WITH WHOM HE HAS TWINS...
DRAAAW ME CLOOOSE TO YOUUU—
...AND AGREES TO BE HONORED BY HIS PEERS—
EVEN IF SOCCER DOESN'T BRING HIM AS MUCH JOY SINCE THAT DAY IN 1997 WHEN DONDINHO LEFT HIM.

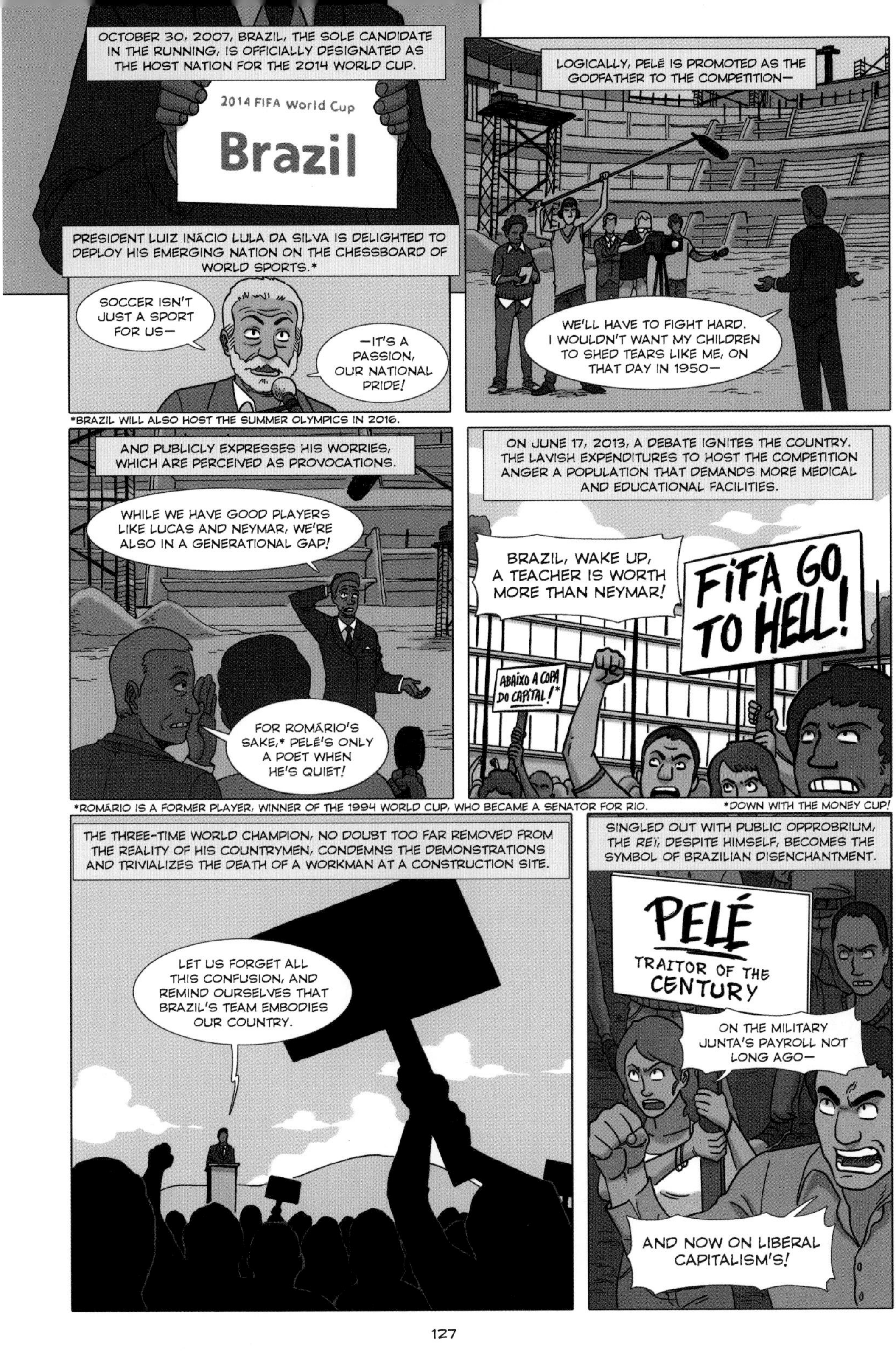
OCTOBER 30, 2007, BRAZIL, THE SOLE CANDIDATE IN THE RUNNING, IS OFFICIALLY DESIGNATED AS THE HOST NATION FOR THE 2014 WORLD CUP.
2014 FIFA World Cup
Brazil
PRESIDENT LUIZ INÁCIO LULA DA SILVA IS DELIGHTED TO DEPLOY HIS EMERGING NATION ON THE CHESSBOARD OF WORLD SPORTS.*
SOCCER ISN'T JUST A SPORT FOR US—
—IT'S A PASSION, OUR NATIONAL PRIDE!
*BRAZIL WILL ALSO HOST THE SUMMER OLYMPICS IN 2016.
LOGICALLY, PELÉ IS PROMOTED AS THE GODFATHER TO THE COMPETITION—
WE'LL HAVE TO FIGHT HARD. I WOULDN'T WANT MY CHILDREN TO SHED TEARS LIKE ME, ON THAT DAY IN 1950—
AND PUBLICLY EXPRESSES HIS WORRIES, WHICH ARE PERCEIVED AS PROVOCATIONS.
WHILE WE HAVE GOOD PLAYERS LIKE LUCAS AND NEYMAR, WE'RE ALSO IN A GENERATIONAL GAP!
FOR ROMÁRIO'S SAKE,* PELÉ'S ONLY A POET WHEN HE'S QUIET!
*ROMÁRIO IS A FORMER PLAYER, WINNER OF THE 1994 WORLD CUP, WHO BECAME A SENATOR FOR RIO.
ON JUNE 17, 2013, A DEBATE IGNITES THE COUNTRY. THE LAVISH EXPENDITURES TO HOST THE COMPETITION ANGER A POPULATION THAT DEMANDS MORE MEDICAL AND EDUCATIONAL FACILITIES.
BRAZIL, WAKE UP, A TEACHER IS WORTH MORE THAN NEYMAR!
FIFA GO TO HELL!
ABAIXO A COPA DO CAPITAL!*
*DOWN WITH THE MONEY CUP!
THE THREE-TIME WORLD CHAMPION, NO DOUBT TOO FAR REMOVED FROM THE REALITY OF HIS COUNTRYMEN, CONDEMNS THE DEMONSTRATIONS AND TRIVIALIZES THE DEATH OF A WORKMAN AT A CONSTRUCTION SITE.
LET US FORGET ALL THIS CONFUSION, AND REMIND OURSELVES THAT BRAZIL'S TEAM EMBODIES OUR COUNTRY.
SINGLED OUT WITH PUBLIC OPPROBRIUM, THE REI, DESPITE HIMSELF, BECOMES THE SYMBOL OF BRAZILIAN DISENCHANTMENT.
PELÉ TRAITOR OF THE CENTURY
ON THE MILITARY JUNTA'S PAYROLL NOT LONG AGO—
AND NOW ON LIBERAL CAPITALISM'S!

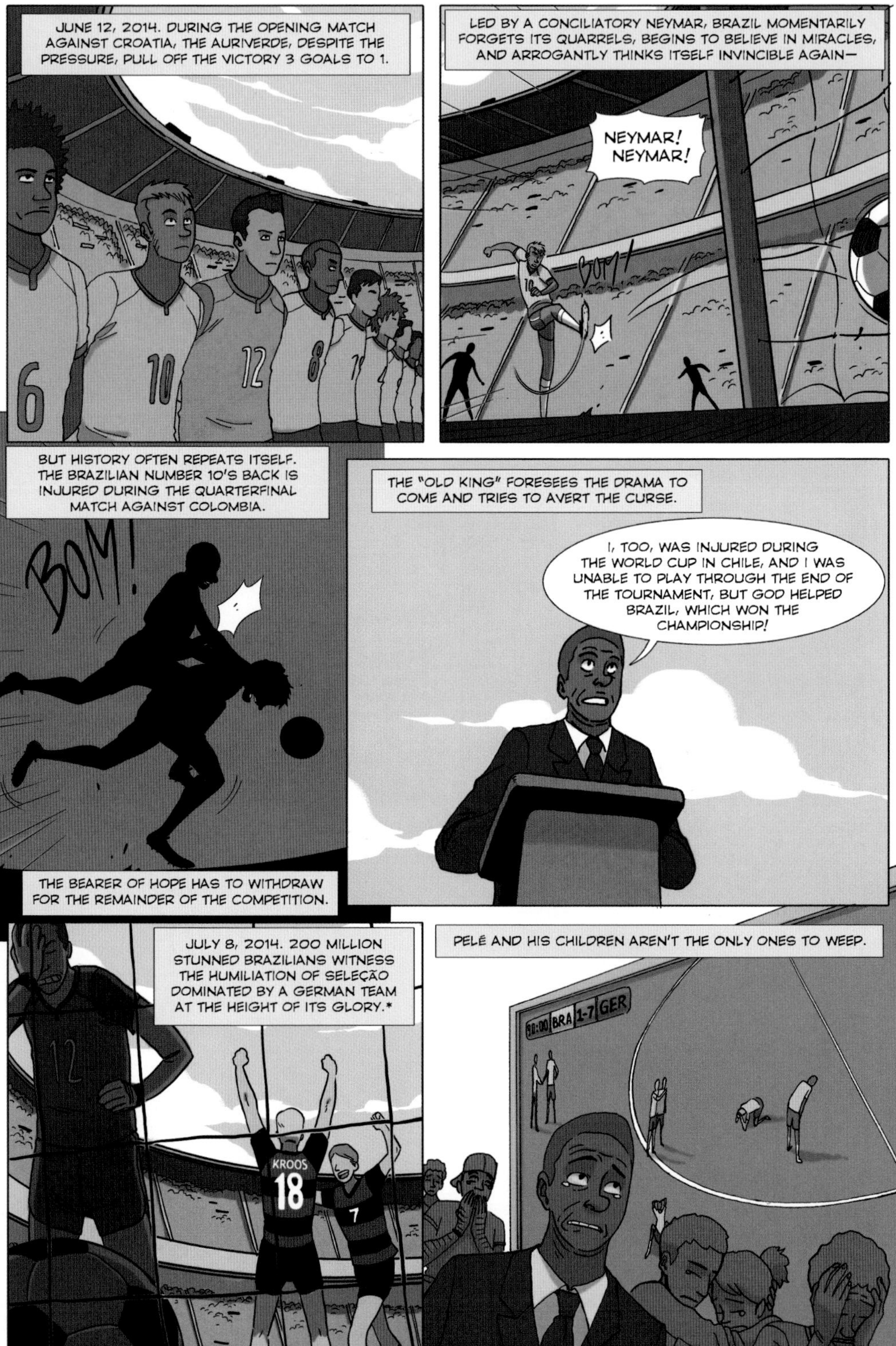
JUNE 12, 2014. DURING THE OPENING MATCH AGAINST CROATIA, THE AURIVERDE, DESPITE THE PRESSURE, PULL OFF THE VICTORY 3 GOALS TO 1.
LED BY A CONCILIATORY NEYMAR, BRAZIL MOMENTARILY FORGETS ITS QUARRELS, BEGINS TO BELIEVE IN MIRACLES, AND ARROGANTLY THINKS ITSELF INVINCIBLE AGAIN—
NEYMAR! NEYMAR!
BOM!
BUT HISTORY OFTEN REPEATS ITSELF. THE BRAZILIAN NUMBER 10'S BACK IS INJURED DURING THE QUARTERFINAL MATCH AGAINST COLOMBIA.
BOM!
THE BEARER OF HOPE HAS TO WITHDRAW FOR THE REMAINDER OF THE COMPETITION.
THE "OLD KING" FORESEES THE DRAMA TO COME AND TRIES TO AVERT THE CURSE.
I, TOO, WAS INJURED DURING THE WORLD CUP IN CHILE, AND I WAS UNABLE TO PLAY THROUGH THE END OF THE TOURNAMENT, BUT GOD HELPED BRAZIL, WHICH WON THE CHAMPIONSHIP!
JULY 8, 2014. 200 MILLION STUNNED BRAZILIANS WITNESS THE HUMILIATION OF SELEÇÃO DOMINATED BY A GERMAN TEAM AT THE HEIGHT OF ITS GLORY.*
KROOS
18
PELÉ AND HIS CHILDREN AREN'T THE ONLY ONES TO WEEP.
90:00 BRA 1-7 GER

*GERMANY WILL BE CROWNED CHAMPION AGAINST ARGENTINA.

Extra Time
Sudden-Death Overtime!

"How do you spell Pelé? G-O-D."
—*Sunday Times*, 1970

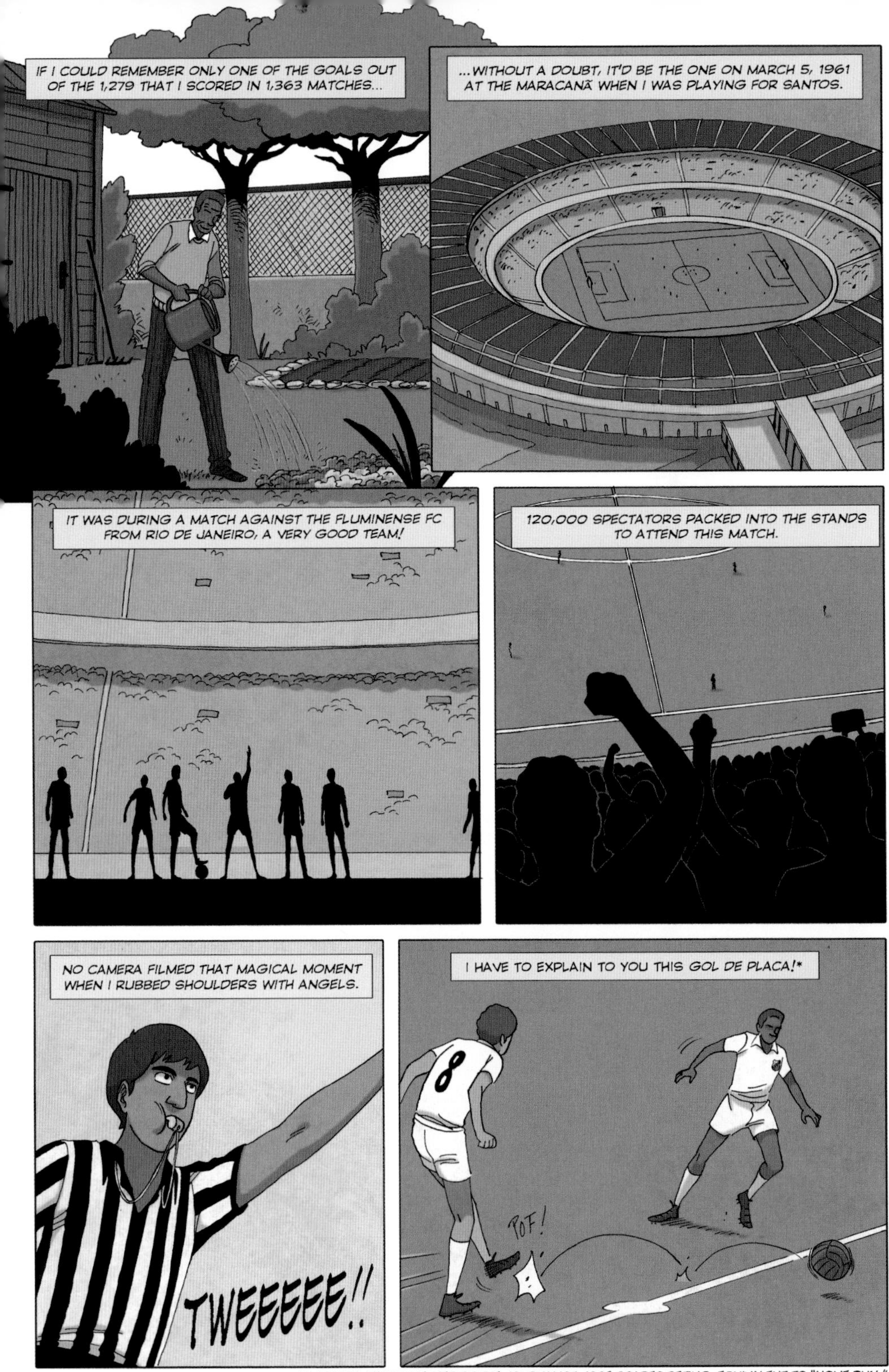
IF I COULD REMEMBER ONLY ONE OF THE GOALS OUT OF THE 1,279 THAT I SCORED IN 1,363 MATCHES...
...WITHOUT A DOUBT, IT'D BE THE ONE ON MARCH 5, 1961 AT THE MARACANÃ WHEN I WAS PLAYING FOR SANTOS.
IT WAS DURING A MATCH AGAINST THE FLUMINENSE FC FROM RIO DE JANEIRO, A VERY GOOD TEAM!
120,000 SPECTATORS PACKED INTO THE STANDS TO ATTEND THIS MATCH.
NO CAMERA FILMED THAT MAGICAL MOMENT WHEN I RUBBED SHOULDERS WITH ANGELS.
TWEEEEE!!
I HAVE TO EXPLAIN TO YOU THIS GOL DE PLACA!*
POF!

*A SPORTS TERM INVENTED BY THE JOURNALIST JOSÉ SOARES BETING, EQUIVALENT TO "HOME RUN."

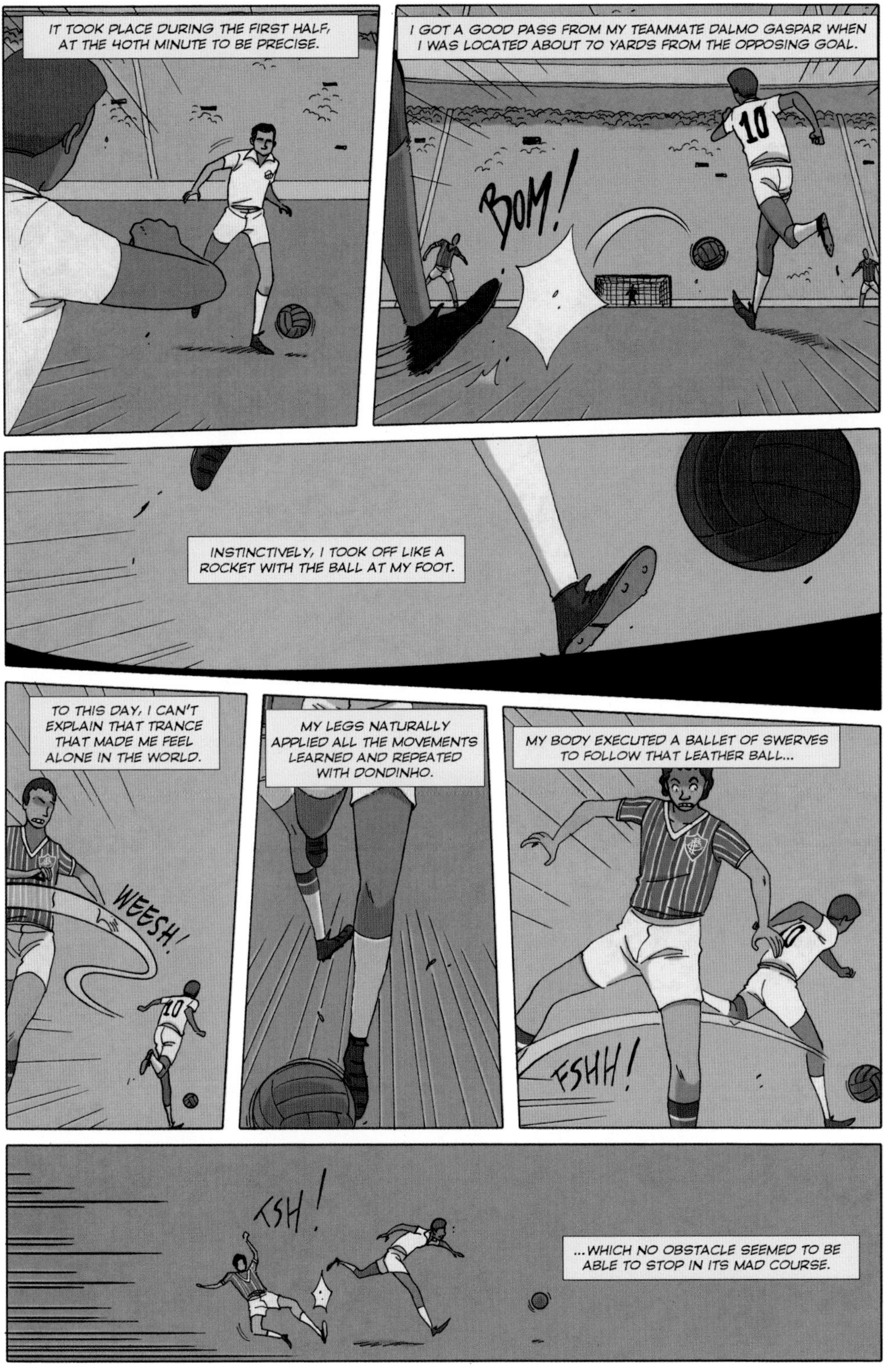
IT TOOK PLACE DURING THE FIRST HALF, AT THE 40TH MINUTE TO BE PRECISE.
I GOT A GOOD PASS FROM MY TEAMMATE DALMO GASPAR WHEN I WAS LOCATED ABOUT 70 YARDS FROM THE OPPOSING GOAL.
BOM!
10
INSTINCTIVELY, I TOOK OFF LIKE A ROCKET WITH THE BALL AT MY FOOT.
TO THIS DAY, I CAN'T EXPLAIN THAT TRANCE THAT MADE ME FEEL ALONE IN THE WORLD.
WEEESH!
10
MY LEGS NATURALLY APPLIED ALL THE MOVEMENTS LEARNED AND REPEATED WITH DONDINHO.
MY BODY EXECUTED A BALLET OF SWERVES TO FOLLOW THAT LEATHER BALL...
FSHH!
TSH!
...WHICH NO OBSTACLE SEEMED TO BE ABLE TO STOP IN ITS MAD COURSE.

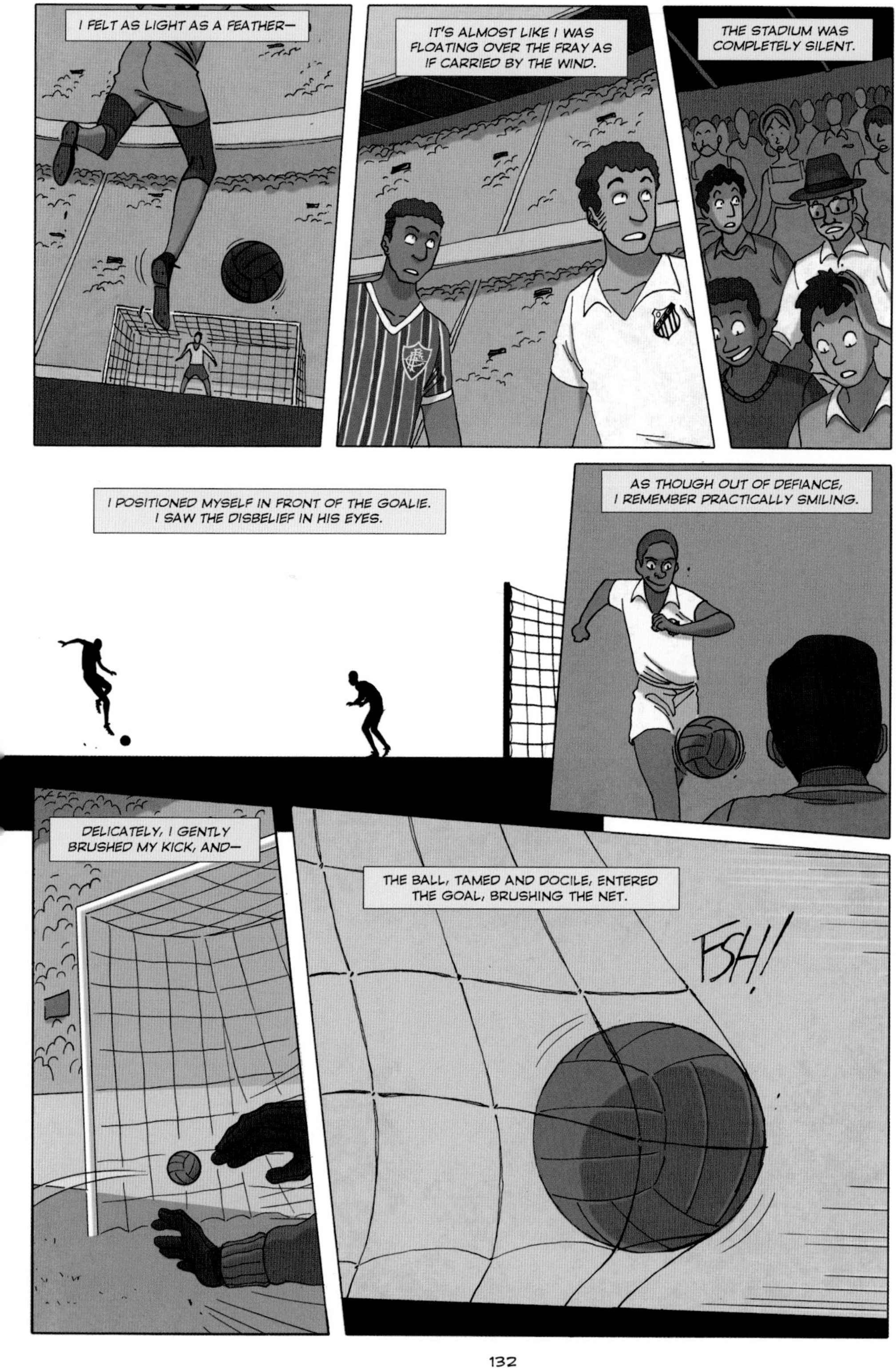
I FELT AS LIGHT AS A FEATHER—
IT'S ALMOST LIKE I WAS FLOATING OVER THE FRAY AS IF CARRIED BY THE WIND.
THE STADIUM WAS COMPLETELY SILENT.
I POSITIONED MYSELF IN FRONT OF THE GOALIE. I SAW THE DISBELIEF IN HIS EYES.
AS THOUGH OUT OF DEFIANCE, I REMEMBER PRACTICALLY SMILING.
DELICATELY, I GENTLY BRUSHED MY KICK, AND—
THE BALL, TAMED AND DOCILE, ENTERED THE GOAL, BRUSHING THE NET.
FSH!

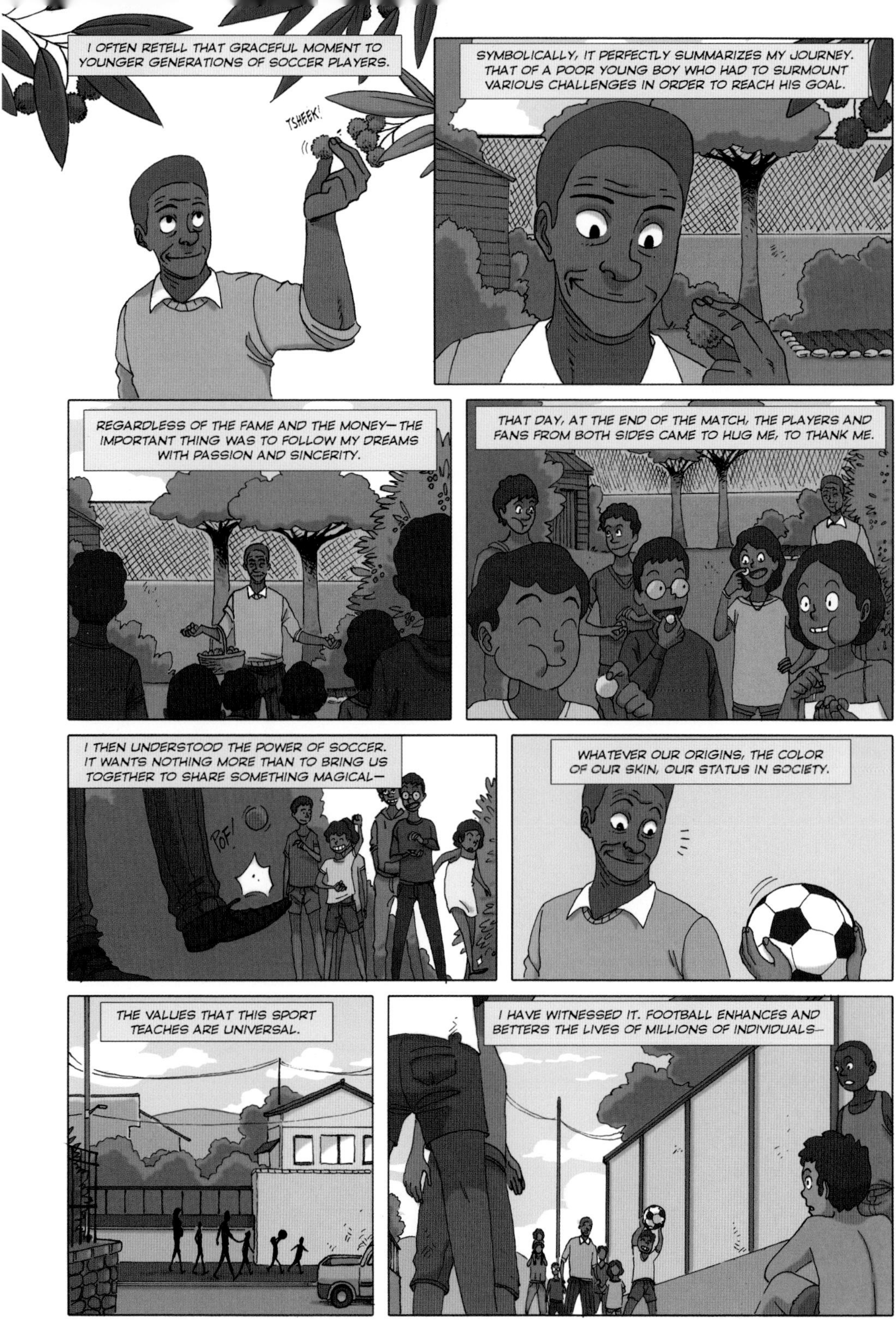
I OFTEN RETELL THAT GRACEFUL MOMENT TO YOUNGER GENERATIONS OF SOCCER PLAYERS.
TSHEEK!
SYMBOLICALLY, IT PERFECTLY SUMMARIZES MY JOURNEY. THAT OF A POOR YOUNG BOY WHO HAD TO SURMOUNT VARIOUS CHALLENGES IN ORDER TO REACH HIS GOAL.
REGARDLESS OF THE FAME AND THE MONEY—THE IMPORTANT THING WAS TO FOLLOW MY DREAMS WITH PASSION AND SINCERITY.
THAT DAY, AT THE END OF THE MATCH, THE PLAYERS AND FANS FROM BOTH SIDES CAME TO HUG ME, TO THANK ME.
I THEN UNDERSTOOD THE POWER OF SOCCER. IT WANTS NOTHING MORE THAN TO BRING US TOGETHER TO SHARE SOMETHING MAGICAL—
POF!
WHATEVER OUR ORIGINS, THE COLOR OF OUR SKIN, OUR STATUS IN SOCIETY.
THE VALUES THAT THIS SPORT TEACHES ARE UNIVERSAL.
I HAVE WITNESSED IT. FOOTBALL ENHANCES AND BETTERS THE LIVES OF MILLIONS OF INDIVIDUALS—

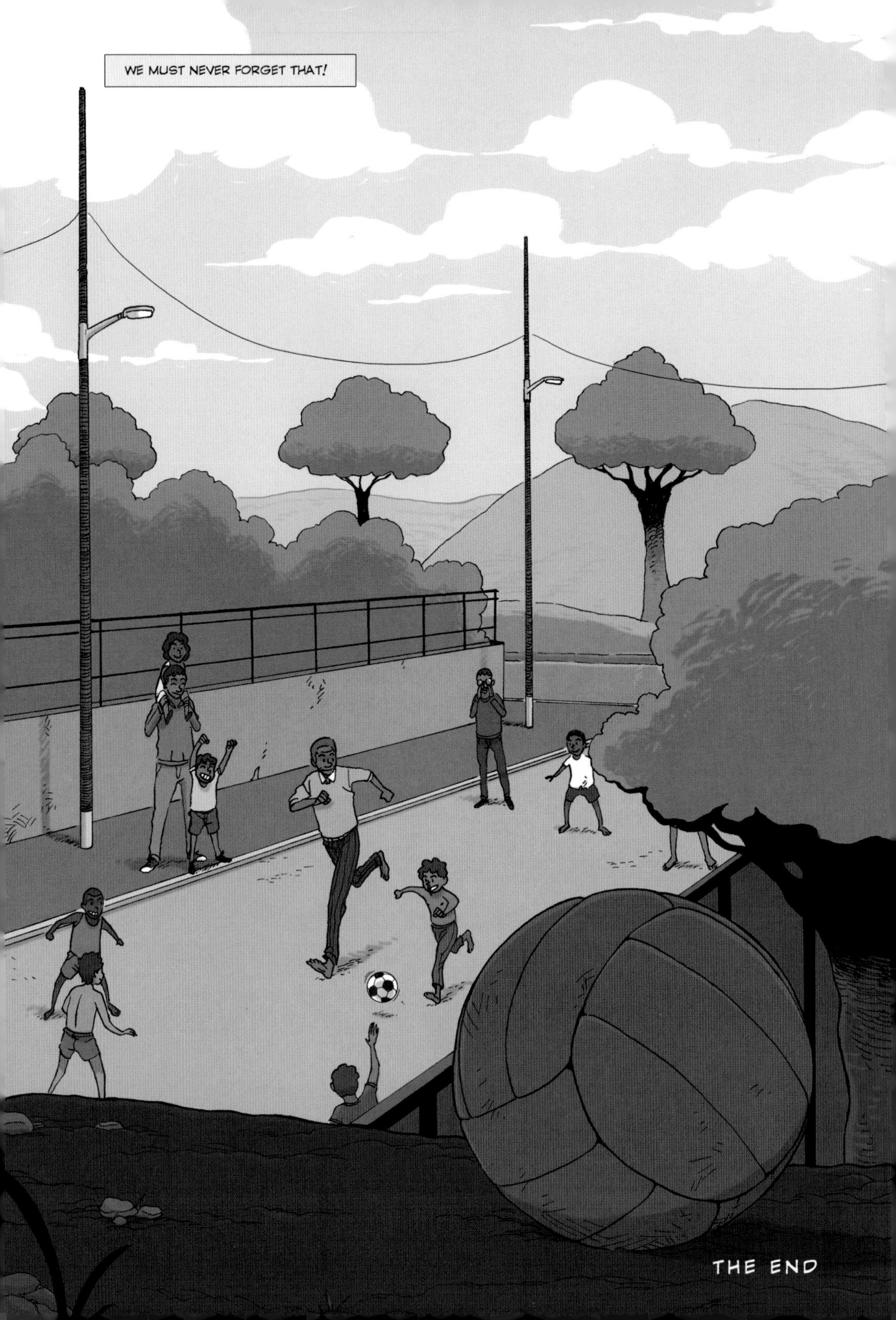
WE MUST NEVER FORGET THAT!
THE END

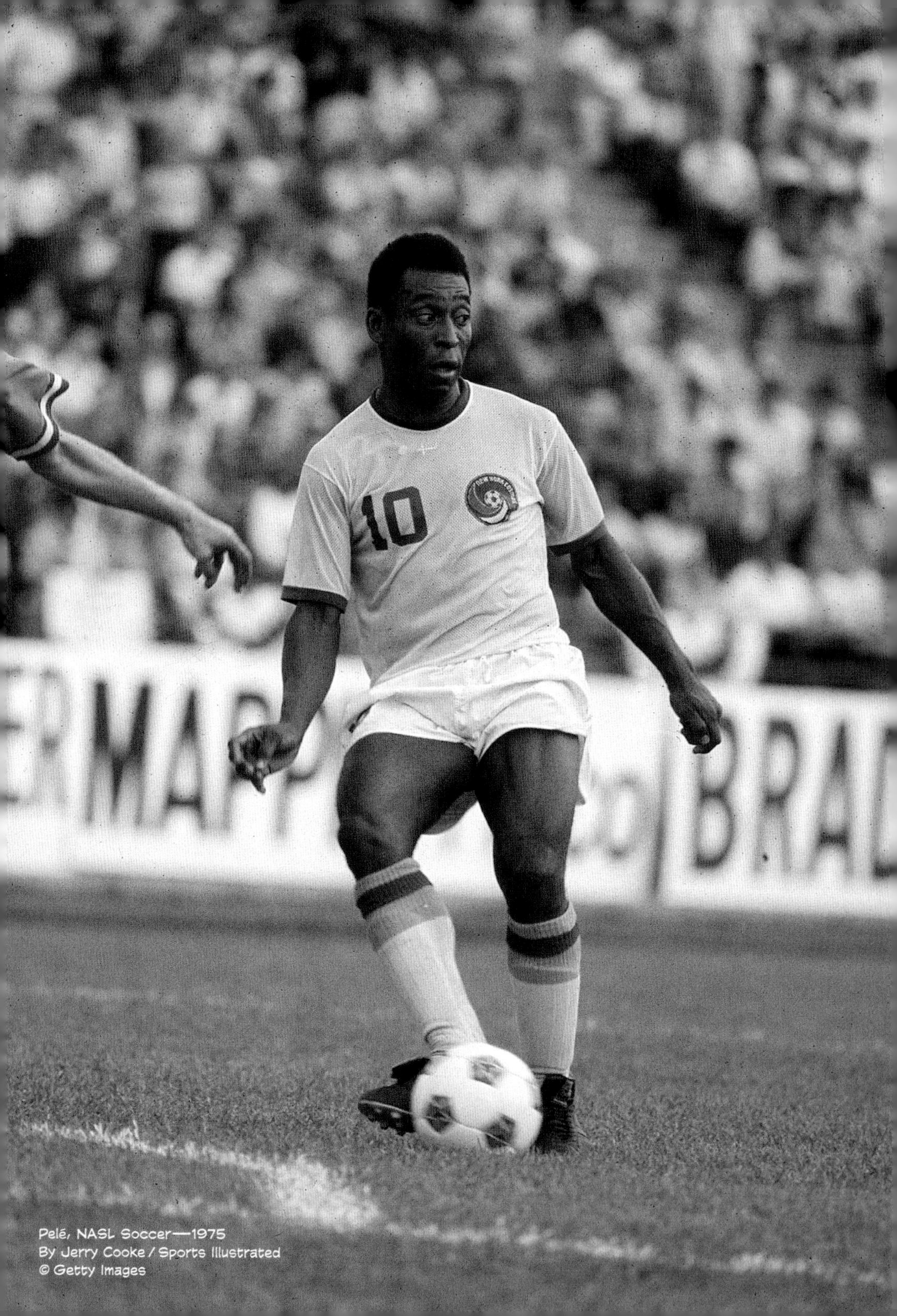
10

Pelé, NASL Soccer—1975
By Jerry Cooke / Sports Illustrated

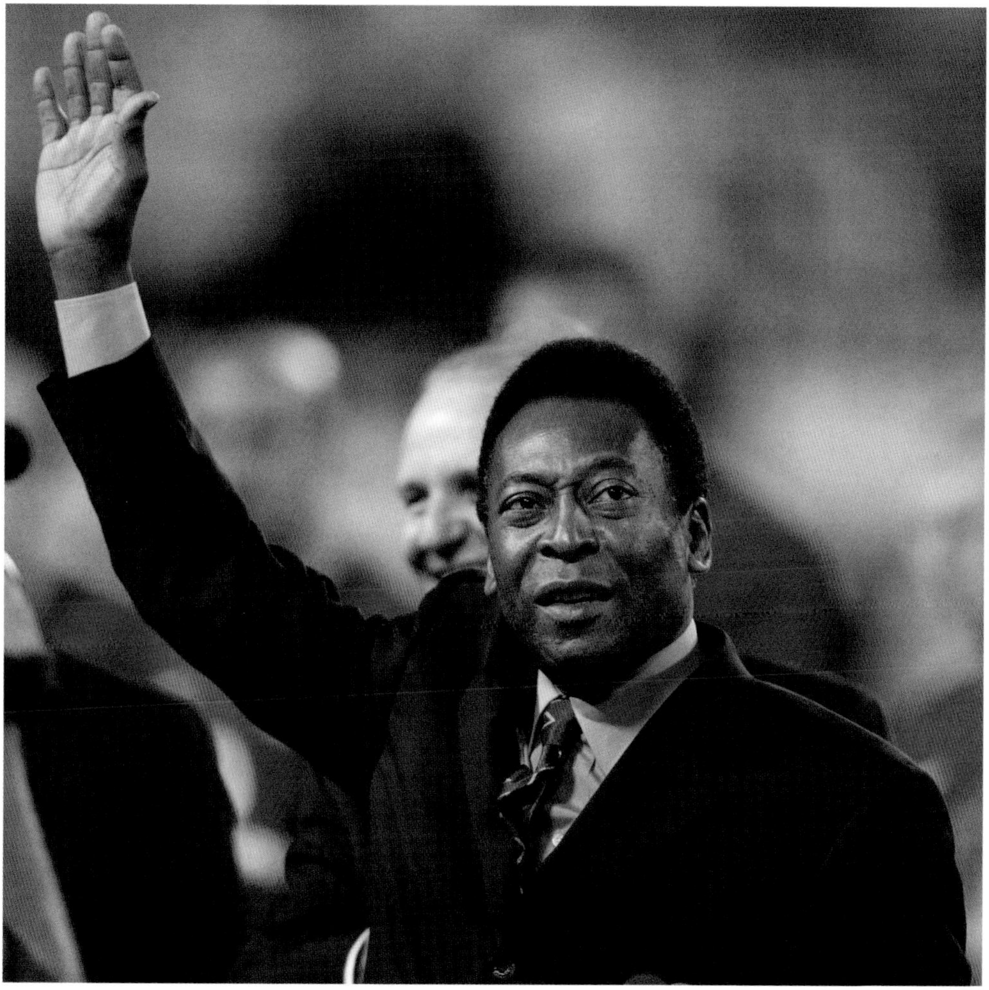

Pelé—2003

"I'm not afraid of dying, because I have three hearts.
I was born in 'Três Corações' [Three Hearts], don't forget!
After my death, I'd like people to remember I was a good person
who always wanted to bring people of all kinds together.
And that they also remember that I was—a good player!"

Edson Arantes do Nascimento, or "Pelé"

First Second

English translation by Joe Johnson
English translation © 2017 by Roaring Brook Press,
a division of Holtzbrink Publishing Holdings Limited Partnership

Published by First Second
First Second is an imprint of Roaring Brook Press, a division
of Holtzbrinck Publishing Holdings Limited Partnership
175 Fifth Avenue, New York, New York 10010
All rights reserved

Library of Congress Control Number: 2016961595

Paperback ISBN: 978-1-62672-755-7
Hardcover ISBN: 978-1-62672-979-7

Our books may be purchased in bulk for promotional, educational, or business use. Please
contact your local bookseller or the Macmillan Corporate and Premium Sales Department
at (800) 221-7945 ext. 5442 or by e-mail at MacmillanSpecialMarkets@macmillan.com.

Originally published in 2016 in French by 21g, a division of Blue Lotus Prod
as *Le Roi Pelé - L'Homme et la Légende* © 2016 by Blue Lotus Prod

First American edition 2017
Book design by Gordon Whiteside

Printed in China by RR Donnelly Asia Printing Solutions Ltd.,
Dongguan City, Guangdong Province
Paperback: 10 9 8 7 6 5 4 3 2 1
Hardcover: 10 9 8 7 6 5 4 3 2 1